JUST FINE IN VIETNAM

Copyright © 2024 by Bo Hardin. All rights reserved.

This book or any portion thereof may not be reproduced or used in any manner whatsoever without the express written permission of the publisher except for the use of brief quotations in a scholarly work or book review. For permissions or further information contact Braughler Books LLC at info@braughlerbooks.com.

The views and opinions expressed in this work are those of the author and do not necessarily reflect the views and opinions of Braughler Books LLC.

Printed in the United States of America

First Printing, 2024

ISBN 978-1-955791-94-6

Library of Congress Control Number: 2024902926

Ordering Information: Special discounts are available on quantity purchases by bookstores, corporations, associations, and others. For details, contact the publisher at sales@braughlerbooks.com or at 937-58-BOOKS.

For questions or comments about this book, please write to info@braughlerbooks.com.

JUST FINE IN VIETNAM

by

BO HARDIN

I would like to dedicate this book to the
fearless soldiers of the 145th Aviation Battalion,
68th Armed Helicopter Company
and 173rd Airborne Brigade, and to the men
and women of Vietnam who did their best
to make us feel at home.

CHAPTER 1

I heard the rattle of the machine gun from the other side of the helicopter ringing in my ears and I knew that Steve, the gunner, was firing in the "Rock and Roll," rapid fire mode. The fact that he wasn't firing in short bursts of four to six rounds, which was the acceptable method, told me that either he had a target or he felt there was reason to blanket the area with a hail of bullets. My side was the friendly side, and I had been given strict orders not to fire via a "negative suppressive fire" command delivered in the operations order prior to take-off. This meant that there were friendly forces on my side, and the other side, Steve's side, was not secure. This kind of event usually came about when we were picking up U.S. or allied soldiers in a hot zone. One side of the landing zone (LZ) was secured, but for one reason or another, the other side was not. We could only surmise that it couldn't be secured because of enemy activity seen in the area, or there wasn't enough time to send in patrols to reconnoiter the terrain and clear it. You felt very naked in these situations, and the aviators, who relied upon you to protect them, found it an equally harrowing experience. The apt vernacular for this kind of dilemma was "your sphincter was tight enough to sever a ten-penny nail."

Anybody that's been to Vietnam and worked in a bullet ridden environment can tell you about that "feeling" experienced when expressions such as "impending doom," "tit in a wringer," or "when the shit hits the fan" are the most descriptive of their predicament. You become very conscious of your stomach because it now has a sensation that is reserved especially for occasions like this. It is not a pain or a spasm; it is something different. What comes to mind in the way of a comparison is that feeling you get in the movies when a swimmer faces the inevitability of getting eaten alive by the heralded shark, Jaws. One could deduce that the "feeling" is triggered by absolute and total helplessness. The after effect is equally disturbing, as far as after effects go. Some people laugh, some actually cry, some throw up, which is not recommended in a helicopter where the wind swirls from the front to the back at unusually high speeds, depositing bits and pieces indiscriminately. Some people just want to jabber garrulously, so much so that shooting them becomes a plausible alternative.

Steve quit firing as we descended to the ground. The helicopter created a ground cushion of sorts and we began to settle slowly to an LZ of earth that had been hastily prepared. Trees had been cut down with machetes and there were some stumps and mounds of earth that prevented some of the choppers from completely landing. This was anathema to helicopter pilots. It meant they were going to have to hold the aircraft steady while equipment-laden troops crawled on board. This would be followed with a take-off which required pulling enough pitch in the blades to get the helicopter up and away from the ground and moving up and over the trees. Our co-pilot, who had been awarded the sobriquet of Mouse because of his miniature size, had already crashed one helicopter under similar circumstances. He began a woeful diatribe, suggesting that we should forego the pick-up and attempt it elsewhere. He was clearly uncomfortable with the situation and continued with a steady stream of objections. It was clear that the pilot was getting a little aggravated with Mouse's rant but dismissed it without a response. He held the aircraft steady as it hovered over the LZ.

Troops were coming out of the wood line headed in our direction. They had already been broken up into groups of seven, as they were trained to do. Loading seven passengers worked well when the aircraft was sitting on land but it really got iffy when you were hovering three to five feet off the ground and in close proximity to other aircraft that were also being loaded in a similar precarious way. Sixty-to-eighty-foot trees loomed a mere 150 yards ahead, which meant the rate of ascent had to be rather dramatic to get it up and over them. Some aviators called this rapid ascent maneuver "screwing it into the sky," and it rated high on the list of not recommended, hard to do, low-recovery, feats that should be avoided except when there's an enemy battalion in the LZ you're leaving.

The troops began loading the helicopter, grabbing onto the skids and pulling themselves up far enough to get a knee in place before taking the last step inside. Their equipment was heavy and they were wet from the swamp below. Mortar baseplates had to be passed up from someone on the ground to another soldier perilously hanging out the side of the helicopter with one foot on the skid and one hand clinging to the seat support. Several helicopters moved eerily left and right, with pilots trying desperately to maintain their altitude and hold the helicopter steady. It wasn't easy. After the last man was loaded, the flight commander acknowledged that all aircraft were ready for liftoff. The nose of the lead helicopter dipped and the blades slowed as the pitch increased. Trailing helicopters waited for the corridor to clear and watched intently as the lead helicopter began to make its ascent. The lead helicopter strained to get off the ground cushion then labored into the air, finally making its way up and over the nearby tree-line. It was somewhat easier for the next helicopter because there was more room to maneuver with the lead helicopter out of the way. Eventually, all helicopters were airborne and I leaned back in my seat, rested my machinegun on my lap and breathed a sigh of relief. But relief can be ephemeral in Vietnam, and this was no exception.

The first bullet came in through the bottom of the helicopter somewhere beneath me. It was closely followed by one through the windshield and one hit a rotor blade which suddenly had the sound of a tire going flat. The pilot did a hard right and moved away from the formation. This may have been done because he thought he was losing control of the helicopter and wanted to get away from the others in the flight formation or it could have been because he had been hit. I heard Mouse yell "Shit." I saw him glance at the pilot long enough to ensure that he was unharmed. To be sure, Mouse yelled "Have you got it?" I heard the pilot say that he did. The soldier immediately in front of me in the belly of the helicopter was holding his leg and moving back and forth at the waist. He moved his leg ever so slightly and looked up to me as if to say "What now?" I saw the blood now, running rapidly across the floor and toward my ammunition box as if it were in a hurry to get there. I turned away from him looking in the triple-canopy trees below for anything that would tell me the location of the enemy who was firing his weapon at us. I heard Steve yell "Can we fire?" The pilot said to standby and contacted the flight leader. I heard the flight leader respond. "We're going to tree-top and suppressive fire for the next 30 seconds. The gun ships are providing flank support. Report any casualties." I pushed my mike button and told the pilot that we had a bleeder in the floor. I pulled the trigger and started feeding the belt of ammunition to my machinegun which began to disperse bullets consisting of a tracer followed by four non-tracers over the tree-tops. I saw the "mustang" gunships roll into position and heard the distinctive sound of the mini-guns blanketing the area with fire. The gun ship's 2.75 rockets made their way lazily into the trees and exploded upon contact when they hit something solid. The last traffic I heard on the radio was the flight leader indicating that Tiger 3 was down.

Another memorial service, and the unit stood in formation to pay homage to four friends, pals, and acquaintances that we had known. It was an all too common yet perfunctory exercise, one that certainly no one looked forward to, and an event that would pray on the minds of many in later years. The chaplain's words were as penetrating and consoling as they could possibly be under the circumstances. It had been a week since their deaths and the initial anguish one experiences from the death of another had subsided. Everyone had lived through the but-by-the-grace-of-God-there-go-I period. The standard length of time to overcome caution had passed and most had returned to the it-will-never-happen-to-me mode.

The chaplain ended the ceremony with the familiar cliché: duty, honor, and country. There was no command to dismiss. Everyone knew it was over and we began to move in a meandering way away from empty caskets, mere simulacrums of those now gone, draped in four of the six flags we kept in the company area specifically for such occasions. If more flags were needed, Smoky in the Battalion S-4 shop, known for his capabilities to provide just about anything on short notice, including ladies of the evening, would be happy to oblige.

My mind wandered on the way back to my tent. War and suffering had been the common thread of America since the day of its inception. We started dying on the battlefields to establish our independence, and since that time we have been dying for everyone else's. It's not that we're looking for an excuse to fight. The changing world continues to provide us with good causes, everything from protecting American interests to overthrowing tyrants who hint at the eventual destruction of the USA. Hell, we'll serve up our young for just about any good cause in the name of world peace and tranquility. One day, I thought, some scientist or brilliant underpaid college professor will isolate the enzyme or ideology that has made us the armipotent world-keepers that we are. Hopefully, the conclusion will not be that all of this was tied to a biological phenomenon. That would be a bad denouement to the daunting play of world havoc and mayhem we had become famous for, and total anathema to all the military commanders who sent waves of ground troops into harm's way. Moreover, there would be a flash mob of world power-brokers chain-condemning the USA for bacchanalian barbarianism and the unnecessary deaths of millions of people. There are a couple of other considerations that could account for our prolific war-like capabilities. One is that we truly are the home of the brave and we're willing to go anywhere for any reason to prove it, or quite possibly our technological superiority in developing new and exciting weapons begets the continuing need for greater amounts of real estate and adversarial people upon which to test them. History speaks to other countries that preceded us along this path, but not nearly so preeminently. The Romans ruled the world until their divine mastery of common sense deflated, culminating with bestiality in public arenas. And France and England had interests everywhere, as did Spain, long before America was even born. And then there was Hitler, who really should have known better than to slaughter thousands as part of his war campaign, because Americans bond like super glue when wanna-be dictators use willy-nilly killing as a stratagem. The theory has always been that the USA is a clean, well-kept place with lots of neat people who live well and do not have to fear dictatorial oppression. This love of democracy creates much antipathy for any person or country that would, through their actions, suggest that they could be a threat to the way of life to which Americans have become accustomed. When all of the elements of a bona fide threat to the American way of life are recognized by its citizenry, you can expect that America and the full force of its military will come pay you a visit.

The primary advantage of youth is the inherent, incipient stupidity that accompanies it. I was 22 with a mature body, armed with a heightened sense of sex and the ability to inflict pain and death; an art learned through a kick-ass training program provided by Uncle Sam. My existence now relied, in great part, on how well I was trained. In time I would learn that military training was like no other in terms of excellence. The methodology was different from civilian training programs, which play out much more like seminars. The military approach comprises lecturing, demonstrating, pupil participation, testing, and critiquing. If you don't successfully pass the test, you get to repeat the entire process. Those are the rules, and they're not altered for anyone. It is an absolute paradigm for learning, and I don't, to this day, see how you can train anyone in any other way.

Everyone eventually made their way to the little PX, which means Post Exchange for those of you that haven't had military experience. The PX is synonymous with department store in stateside settings, but in Vietnam it means anywhere you buy anything that is provided by the PX service. Our little PX was nothing more than a canteen, or beer-tent in Bama language. But to us it was more than a beer tent. This was the place we played cards in the corner, anything from hearts to poker, and a place that we talked about all of our personal problems. The jukebox poured out the kind of music that could only make you homesick. We would listen to The Green, Green Grass of Home and If You're Going to San Francisco, and after a few beers the effects of the music had their way with us. Reactions ranged from sadness to tears or more frequently a lot of masculine hubris to masquerade the truth. If walls could talk, the little PX could relate stories of ended marriages, Dear John letters, the greatest hotrod in the world sitting in the garage back home (most were imagined), war stories that stretched the very fabric of imagination, voluptuous girlfriends that were sitting home dutifully waiting to meet the returning vet in a 5-star hotel, and rich parents that were going to cough up the money for medical or law school. The little PX was the tribal meeting place for all that was holy, and anything else that the day's events or personal situations dictated.

    I found a spot in the corner away from the recently acquired jukebox and sat down. My friend, Craig Hitechew, sat down next to me. He had joined the unit some months ago and was recognized as someone smarter than most. He was a medic but his interests were broad and he quickly established himself as an ambidextrous soul who would not be limited to a sedentary life in the base camp aid station. Included in his repertoire of talents was his ability to speak French. This proved to be invaluable both on the warfront and in nearby villages where many of the older folks spoke French. Craig had been able to talk to a French farmer who told him that when we left, the Viet Cong would return and exact a just revenge on those that supported the Americans. He made a number of suggestions for ensuring the safety of the locals, all of which we followed. It amounted to conducting interviews in tents where no one could hear what was being said and forgoing all niceties such as smiles and handshakes in public.

One night Craig and I were in a bar in Vung Tau where we were taking an in-country R&R of sorts. Craig began speaking French with the woman that owned the bar. We drank all night on the house and were rewarded with rather attractive and supple companions and a place to stay. The crux of Craig's talents rested not in the mere ability to speak the language, but in his humorous anecdotes, his mannerisms, and his compelling personality. He could be as complex or as simple as he desired, connecting intellectually with a general or a Private, making each feel good about the experience.

Craig smiled. "Enough of the dead soldier routine," he said, referring to the association between the adage meaning discarded beer bottles and the real dead soldiers we had just honored. "It's time for some live ones." He laughed. "Is that the correct metaphor? If an empty beer bottle is a dead soldier, is a full bottle a live soldier?

"You're awfully morbid, ole boy," I replied. "Have a little respect for unknown soldiers in a bottle."

"Tis the time and the season," he retorted. "Look, the only reason we are having this discussion is because we are here in this hot tent with hot air being blown around by a hot air fan in Bien Hoa, Vietnam. No one seems to have a patent on dying and few of us believe that it will never happen to us, but it obviously will. You have been here way too long and I believe that you have a death wish and every day you stay in this country, the odds for your demise increase exponentially. We are drinking beer because there is virtually nothing else to do. No one has the zeal, or is so inclined, at least until we have a couple of these live soldiers, to try to get to the ville and chase pussy. And you really don't chase pussy because there is little need to do so. Pussy doesn't run from you in the ville, if you haven't noticed. So, faced with dead buddies here and no immediate plans to pursue stationary pussy in the ville, one has little to do but delve into the facts surrounding the consumption and disposal of beer, er, uh, live soldiers. Besides, I don't bowl and you don't like big screen movies and neither is available. God, I'm really upset about the relative pussy situation. See what you've made me do? I'm beside myself with emotion."

Ah, the rantings of Craig the philosopher, I thought. I knew he could go on like that forever. Craig never tried to be intentionally funny, maybe amusing or enlightening, but not funny. He was just a phase II thinker with a zeal for enjoying the moment. He wasn't always an engaging personality. He could be moody, he could be daunting in a subject he enjoyed, or he could be quiet and reserved. We played this mind game of words, a decoupage of thoughts, ideas and concepts, occasionally stretching the envelope of decorum and sanity.

Craig continued on for a while and the conversation eventually turned to our departed soldiers. Soon the tent was filled with people and the air was turning stale from the smoke as well as with comments that dispelled a variety of emotions relative to how and why our friends had died. In moments such as these it becomes apparent that everyone is not immortal, most experience fear, and everyone is afraid of death. Fear, I thought, is designed to keep heroism in check, and death, besides its permanency, means for a moment that your side is losing.

Simply put, I could never look death in the face. I didn't run from it but I never liked the aura that lingered around it.

It was filled with too many emotions with which I just wasn't comfortable, including fear. My father used to say that fear was a learned behavior, something you weren't born with and that you were better off avoiding its use as a defensive mechanism. It came in handy in tense situations when the adrenalin needed to be kicked into high gear, but other than that it had little use other than to make you a babbling idiot in an overt display of insecurity. Courage is not about overcoming fear, it is what you do in the face of it. Fear undermines courage, and often jerks defeat from the jaws of victory. I have seen large men cower and little men display the testosterone levels of giants in fearful situations, so I learned very quickly not to second guess courage based upon size and stature. I have learned in later years that fear is not confined to the battlefield. Chief Executive Officers, politicians, police and firemen live with it daily and routinely show their mettle in a plethora of situations. Those that are without fear, or know how to manage it, do well. Unlike my father, who never seemed to have it in his repertoire of emotions, I do experience fear. My experience is that it always comes, rather uncharacteristically, after the event that caused it. I rode a helicopter in on one occasion, mystically crashing its way through the trees, breaking branches and limbs for what seemed to be an eternity, finally crashing somewhere below and belching me out reasonably unharmed. After performing all the actions necessary to get everyone out and away from the remnants of that which used to fly, then later being retrieved by a ground unit, I began to shake. My speech was slurred and rapid, and the perspiration you would expect with soaring temperatures disappeared. A seasoned veteran who knows the value of training would summarize my capacity to perform under stress as the results of excellent Army training. Training overcomes fear because you perform as a matter of rote, they would say. And that is true except in the little PX where heroes drink beer and attest to their courageous actions as those of a fearless and intrepid man who put the lives of his friends ahead of his own. It was grit and guts that got him through the moment, not training, or circumstance, or fortuitous coincidence.

Steve Anderson made his way inside the tent followed by James Carson. They grabbed a couple of chairs and pulled them up to our table. Steve was a rather predictable guy. One of North Carolina's finest; he was small, with brown hair and a little weather-beaten appearance who could easily be stereotyped as a farmer. He was hard working and rarely ever complained about anything. He had a better constitution than most, electing not to overdo it with the booze or spend too much time in the ville. I liked him because he was dependable. As a door gunner he was required to help with the aircraft inspection and keep the weapons cleaned. When we flew together, we made it a point of helping each other. When the day was over, if I finished first, I would help him and vice versus. He was really quiet and gave you the idea that he was doing his time in Vietnam but had no interests in staying in the Army.

James Carson was different. He was the life of the party, always humorous, and fun to be with. He was from the Piney Woods of New Jersey. He had been raised well, not wealthy, but well. He had a sense of moral turpitude, traditionally noted in families with strong unions and core values. His slightly built body, though not small, was topped with jet black hair.

James looked around the tent and remarked, "Gosh, I haven't seen this many people here at one time since I can't remember when. I guess it takes a death in the family to get us a day down. Too bad about Dillon."

"Too bad about all of them," said Steve. "They were all short, too. In another month they would have been out of here. One thing for sure, you can never guess what's going to happen tomorrow."

Craig laughed. "That's why I live for today. Existentialism lives. We are the makers of our own destiny. They happened to be at the same spot as a bullet that happened to be fired by a little Charley that was probably tied to a tree to make sure he couldn't run. The bullet struck the pilot in the head and he probably jerked the cyclic stick out of the floor before the co-pilot could gain control of the aircraft. At least that's what everyone is hypothesizing based upon observation reports. The helicopter did a hard bank left and lost altitude and fell into the trees. There was no chance for anybody to do anything. At least it was fast. I'm just glad I wasn't in the back. I know I'd be screaming like a little girl, that is, of course, if I could get my breath. But Hardin here is different. He would have jumped out of the chopper with a knife between his teeth and into the tree or hole where that little bastard was and chopped him to little pieces. Right Sarge?"

I laughed. Craig was looking for a humorous response that I just didn't feel like giving him. Regardless, I acquiesced. "I think I would have tried to fly like a bird, if that was possible, but I don't think they really had enough time to think about it. I hate the cliché, but their number was up. No other way to explain it."

"The unit has a down day," said James. "I don't know if we're flying tomorrow. Ops says there are no major lifts scheduled, but we know that doesn't mean anything. What are you doing for the rest of the day?"

Craig smiled cunningly. "If I can talk Hardin here into it, I thought we might cruise the ville to look for some softer companionship."

I laughed. "You're going to get me into big trouble. If Hoa finds out I've been running the bars, I'll have hell to pay. Hell hath no fury like a woman scorned, or so it goes. I haven't really made up my mind what I want to do. I could work out, Lord knows I need it, or I could go to Bien Hoa."

Craig knew about Hoa but really didn't think much of my relationship with her. Hoa was a girl I had met in my early days in country. She worked at the Hope Bar, which was the hangout for most of the unit. She had been the girlfriend of a soldier by the name of Comanchu who was assigned to another helicopter assault unit known as "The Rattlesnakes." The romance was purportedly "serious" and she wound up pregnant. Comanchu shipped out before the baby was born. When I visited her in the hospital after learning of the baby's birth, she told me the baby had died. I learned later that the baby didn't die but had been sent to live with her family in a village far away from Bien Hoa. She was not particularly good looking but she had a gentle disposition and an innate kindness that made you want to be protective of her. She was a young, soft-spoken girl for whom I felt sorrow but not passion. She was too kind and gentle for the world of prostitutes and bar flies she lived in, and I felt a compelling need to watch over her. She would not prostitute herself even though to do so would have meant a fortune by Vietnamese standards. The average national income was about $300.00 a year. Between tips and drinks, for which the girls got a kickback, a prostitute could make as much in a month. Hoa was always short of money because she sent just about everything she made to her family who had nothing. When the Viet Cong were stealing their rice and threatening to force her brother into service as a Viet Cong, her family sent her to Bien Hoa to get out of the way and "help out." A Vietnamese military cohort of mine arranged for her to live in a Vietnamese military housing area for which she was grateful. The rent was $12.00 a month, which I paid. I would drop by her place to see her when I came in from the field. I would bring her canned goods from the mess hall and items from the PX for which she was grateful. She kept what she needed and sold the rest. In time, we grew closer and even intimate, but I never attempted to elevate the relationship to that of girlfriend-boyfriend. There weren't any promises made by either of us, and she knew that in time, I would go away just like Comanchu. I gave her the will to go on and a degree of security by arranging a place for her to live. She gave me comfort and a place to rest. We watched out for each other. I knew in time that our lives would change dramatically. No war lasts forever, and ultimately, the victor makes the rules.

"I'll buy the first round at the Hope Bar," said James.

"Why not?" I said resignedly, remembering for a moment that I had promised myself not to be as impulsive as I had in the past. Besides, if we went to the Hope Bar, Hoa would be there so there would be no need for questions about my evening's antics, nor would I hear any of the soft, motherly reprimands that were delivered more out of a sense of worry than anger.

We agreed to meet at the company headquarters in thirty minutes. There was a truck that went back and forth to the villa where the pilots were quartered and we could catch it there. The trip to the city was interrupted by an inspection of the truck at the main gate entry point. Identification cards had to be checked as well as the vehicle authorization. This procedure was somewhat unusual for outbound vehicles. It meant that for some unknown reason the MPs had increased the security level. Sometimes everybody knew, sometimes they didn't.

The old Army five-quarter, as it was named, rumbled on across tattered and bumpy roads. The scene was familiar. There was a cart outside the main gate filled with meats and vegetables and large loaves of French bread. The owner, who everyone called Papasan, a name used for just about anybody over forty, would make you a hoagie, deemed "Super Slope" by the GIs. The cost was 25 piasters, or about 20 cents given the exchange rate at that time. Craig, the medic, would warn against buying food from Papasan; it could be old and spoiled and cause a plethora of medical problems. We heeded his advice except when we were starving and on those all too frequent occasions when beer and cheap whiskey made us believe that we were absolutely invulnerable to the ill effects of food.

Tetracycline was the much sought after antibiotic du jour. It was used to ward off the evils of sex in the villages and for light injuries of soldiers in the field. A soldier intending to have sex would take one pill before he engaged in such activities and one afterwards believing that such a dose would protect him from disease, hence it became known as the "no sweat" pill. It probably did little to protect anyone, but it did serve to legitimize the act when the power of perceived love and the effects of liquor overcame good common sense. However, I do believe it was useful in the field. Field medics would often treat a cut or a rash with tetracycline to prevent infections. It was difficult to keep anything clean and infections were common. Perhaps tetracycline combined with a concerted effort to protect the wound kept people in the field that would have otherwise become casualties and evacuees.

Within 200 yards of the gate was an Indian clothing shop. They are a ubiquitous part of any shopping area anywhere in the world. I would imagine that the Indians came to Vietnam after the arrival of American forces. The competition would not have been keen. Vietnamese tailors and clothing shops were rare and the thread and material was not as substantial or fashionable as that of Indian clothiers. Cashmere sport coats were $35.00 at the Indian store. You bought them to take home with you. Anyone wearing a cashmere sport jacket in Bien Hoa would be as obvious as a wart on a prom queen.

We passed the Hope Bar and the driver continued a little further down the road, all the while looking for MPs before slowing down long enough for us to jump from the bed of the five-quarter. Transporting soldiers in military vehicles to bars and places of ill-repute was against Army rules and you could get non-judicial punishment in the form of an Article 15 if you were caught. But rules are made to be broken and most of the time the MPs looked the other way.

After jumping from the truck, we made our way back up the road to the Hope Bar. The Mamasan, a term generally applied for a woman over forty, who usually adorned the entrance, was there begging for money and I dropped five or ten dong into her outstretched hands. She smiled at me like she usually did through teeth almost completely black from years of using Betelnut, a wild growing drug that would give you a low-grade high. Was this like giving alcohol to an alcoholic? I didn't think so, and it wouldn't have made any difference.

The glamour of the Hope Bar was expressed not in its ambiance or décor, but in the people who were there. Its main floor contained 10 or 12 small round tables and a rudely constructed bar was situated along one wall primarily to prepare drinks that the girls carried to tables. The girls that worked there wore American or European style clothes, much in contrast to the Ao Dai, the clothing typically worn by Vietnamese women. They walked awkwardly in high heels. In some cases, they seemed to almost stab the floor as they made their way hurriedly from the bar to the tables. The makeup was crude and thick, suggestive of that worn by a young 13-year-old girl who has yet to learn the art of subtlety and the rule that sometimes less is more. The climate was one of hurriedness and hustle even if there were only a few people in the bar. The bar owner's wife, Big Mama as she was called, barked short and succinct orders in a starchy and urgent voice. You could see the pace quicken every time she opened her mouth to objurgate the staff of women as a group, or to scold a single girl for spending too much time with a patron without coaxing him into buying her a drink, commonly referred to as a Saigon Tea. Time was money, especially in the Hope Bar. We were old timers who did not buy drinks for girls. The 60 piasters, usually referred to as 60P, spent on a Saigon Tea would buy you about five minutes of very well-rehearsed conversation that included a standard set of questions. What your name? How long you been Vietnam? You have girlfriend? You stay Bien Hoa? I'm sure these questions were taught in bargirl 101 by Big Mama and reinforced by the girls that had achieved tenure over three or four months. These questions summed up everything a girl needed to know to maximize the potential profits from a continued relationship. Propitious answers meant that she might stay with you even longer than five minutes. The fifth drink might even be free. By that time, she would have told you that she "likes you too much," and "you look too good." If you inadvertently exposed a substantial sum of money, you might even be asked to take her home. But a patron couldn't become outwardly inebriated. The MPs came through about once every four hours looking for those who could become rowdy or not take care of themselves. Those that were drunk got escorted back to post and their pass was confiscated. Those that were drunk and unruly were escorted to a conex container, which amounted to a steel cargo container about six feet square. A grill of about 18 inches was cut into the entry door to provide an air source. You were hosed down with water on the hour to prevent heat exhaustion. Having your unit pick you up from the conex container meant that you weren't going to have a pass for a while. Your pass privileges and freedom of movement were in the hands of the first sergeant. He could elect to commemorate your act of stupidity in the most painful and laborious ways. Matters could be complicated if the MPs had found it necessary to charge you with disorderly conduct or assaulting a military police officer. That could mean non-judicial punishment and could include the loss of rank, money, or both.

I didn't see Hoa as we sat down. She could be running errands, or picking up food for the girls. Big Mama pointed an assigning finger at Carson as he fell rather clumsily into his chair, and a girl came scurrying over to take his order. "Whiskey and coke," uttered Carson in a barely audible voice. The girl scurried to get him a drink. She returned as quickly as she had left, I'm sure to impress Big Mama. The girl was new and was out to make an impression. Carson took the words out of her mouth as she sat the drink down. "No Saigon Tea," he said. "No cheap talk or hollow promises. I'm a number fucking ten GI." The girl lingered for just a moment, trying to run the words through her mind, comparing them to their meaning based on what she'd learned in Bargirl 101. Convinced by his demeanor more than an understanding of what he'd said, she concluded that he didn't want any company. Big Mama validated her suspicions with a choice grunt and a few sharp words. The tone was clear in any language; get away from him.

Craig was freelancing. Not one for being overly engaging with any of the bargirls and leaving no room for doubt, he walked up to the bar and said "Big Mama, give me a Bamouiba, which means 33 in Vietnamese but also is the name of a beer. Termed "cow piss" by many GIs, Bamouiba was much like Scotch. You either developed a taste for it or drank it out of desperation.

Completely out of character, Steve was making goo-goo eyes at the new girl who was pleased that he found her attractive and probably believed at that moment that she had found her niche. Steve was youthful looking and the new girl seized the moment to ask one of the few questions she had learned in English, specifically how old he was. When she asked, Steve replied, "647 years old." The look of the deer caught in the headlights now showed clearly on her face. Quick math for a newly hired Vietnamese bargirl just doesn't work well in these situations. In time she would be able to retort, "Oh, you must be related to Methuselah," but that wasn't going to happen today.

"Steve, you can be a hard man to deal with," I said. "Give the girl a chance. Be supportive. She's in training."

Steve continued looking at the girl with a suggestive gaze, much like Clark Gable without the moustache, good looks and panache. "I think I don't love you enough."

The girl responded with a recently learned Bargirl 101 sentence that sounded faintly similar. "I think I love you too much." The lack of intonations made the acclamation sound as flat and insouciant as directions to the bathroom.

Steve wasn't finished. "But the rain in Spain falls mainly on the plain. What you name?"

All the rain in Spain nonsense went zinging by her but she understood the second part. "My name is Fifi, she said." And with that she was gone, probably to regurgitate to Big Mama or one of the girls some of what Steve had said in hopes of getting a translation.

Craig returned with his Bamouiba. "Fifi is her name. Gosh, she could be French or Belgian, or even Italian perhaps. Like So-phi-a, So-phi-phi. Get my drift. Don't lose me now. But I'm betting, or at least getting vibes, that the overly used match of a French father and Vietnamese mother is not what we have here. What we have here is a stage name. Fifi. I like it. It has a certain flair of originality to it, does it not? And what might be Fifi's fee, it can't be free, but we will have to see what it must be. God, I hate being poetic. But Fifi is just a trinket, mere remuneration for the trials and tribulations that face us, is she not? Or is she something bigger in the universal scheme of things? As a matter of fact, I do believe she could be Steve's new squeeze for he has already introduced himself as a man of great years and one who denies a love that overcomes him now. Isn't it clear for all to see?"

I could have said, well spoken ye, but it just seemed a little too childish. I would not begin to play this game with Craig. Besides, I was too busy trying to pick the mosquito from my drink that Big Mama had sat before me in the midst of Craig's ode to Steve and Fifi.

Steve said that he needed a drink. Big Mama poured him a coke, and Fifi, still showing signs of shell-shock from being badly trick-screwed, made her way to the table with it.

Fifi sat the coke down and said, "You number hucking eight, GI. Vietnamese do have 'F' problems and although Fifi misspoke, the meaning was clear.

Steve laughed and said, "Senloi," which is "sorry" in Vietnamese. Fifi turned and left the table expressionless.

Number hucking eight is not nearly as bad as number hucking ten. Being called number ten is tantamount to saying that anything and everything about you is disgusting. Number eight, I would imagine, gives you a little room for reprieve.

James pointed at Hoa to acknowledge her arrival as she entered the door with rice and other food for the girls. She walked around the tables without fanfare and to the bar where she sat down the food before coming to the table where we sat.

She placed her hands on my shoulders. "Bo, you buy me Saigon Tea?" She laughed, knowing that it was a question to which she would not receive a meaningful answer.

"Sure," I said. "Make it two for you and one for the road."

"You're not working today?"

"Very good," I replied, referring to her proper use of the contraction "you're" and the verb "working." Contractions and verb conjugations were something we had been working on for some time. Combining "you" and "are" into "you're" had been difficult for Hoa. The Vietnamese language, as GIs knew it, just wasn't structured like that. If you wanted to say "Are you going to Ham Tan" in Vietnamese, you said "Ban di Ham Tan," literally, "You go Ham Tan." Not that there isn't a proper or more grammatically correct way to say it, but that was the way it was taught in the Vietnamese Language School at Fort Bliss, Texas, which I attended for 12 long weeks between tours in Vietnam. Obviously, the Vietnamese were similarly educated in the use of English.

Hoa had a genuine interest in being able to express herself in a way that assured she could be understood. She had a lot to say about a lot of things and nothing was more perplexing to her than this inability to converse easily and effectively. On more than one occasion she had said, "I cannot tell you how I feel or what I want you to know." This bothered me because I had felt the same way but in quite different circumstances. There were times I could not converse with allies such as Koreans and Thais, and it drove me crazy when I had to look for a translator to make my point or obtain information.

Usually, there was always someone in a military setting that could translate sufficiently to keep the operation underway. But the military talked about troops, the tactical movement of men and machinery, and mutual support. We did not discuss feelings and emotions such as anger and urgency; they were understood. The words used to describe the heart of battle and those used to describe the heart of man vary greatly in their construction and delivery. Alas, the end result for both can be extraordinarily destructive. Hoa labored to find a way to speak her heart. She was always reading, writing and studying. Her nights were spent engaged in trying lucubration, often by candlelight.

"You no get drunk, OK?" she said with a laugh.

Oh well, I thought. That last faux pas would be another class. As long as she didn't become disheartened with learning this very difficult language.

James pondered his drink. "Too bad they don't have darts in here. In New Jersey some bars have dart boards. It's becoming the craze."

I laughed. "If they had darts in here, they would be used as weapons. At night when this place is loaded, darts would be flying around here like we had been invaded by the Montagnards. Do Montagnards use blowguns?"

"I doubt it," said James. "I don't like the basic operations of blowguns. You got to remember to blow rather than suck."

Steve wasn't amused by the conversation and went to join Fifi, most likely to heal the subtle flesh wounds he had inflicted. I watched him smile largely as he approached her. She would do well in due time. Her hair was a little longer than most girls wore it and the hips were a little wider than average. She had the kind of breasts that caught your eye, especially in the silk blouse with red and effervescent green tones. She would face the indubitable realities of the profession she had chosen soon enough. In time she would make decisions about whether she was going to be just a bargirl or something much more sinister.

It was really not our place to judge what anyone did in their country. When you are young you don't know what difficulties these people, or any people for that matter have faced, and what they feel they must do to cope with a particular situation. Many of the girls came from poor disadvantaged families, yet some did not. It was not unusual to meet college students and children of parents that had once been wealthy, by Vietnamese standards. Many family fortunes had been lost via political strife or at the direction of the government, often in the name of supporting the war against the north. In Vietnam, like most oriental countries, influential friends, particularly those in positions of power, were important, and keeping them well supplied with donations was even more important. If you wanted something done, you paid for it; if you wanted something done quickly, you paid more for it.

Craig was getting restless. He said "Do you want to finish this drink and do a walkabout?

Craig had recently picked up the term "walkabout" from the Australian allies who were camped on Baria Mountain near Vung Tau on the coast. I had been there on several missions and on one occasion remained overnight. The Aussies entertainment included a game that started with everyone in a pit about six feet deep and eight feet wide. When the whistle blew, everyone started throwing each other out. The last person standing in the pit after everyone else had been thrown out was the King of the pit, so to speak. By design, there was much beer and whiskey consumed prior to entering the pit which made for a jolly good time and a lot of bruises. We entered the pit but allowed ourselves to be quickly discharged. Nothing could be worse than a couple of yankee blokes fighting to stay in a pit with a bunch of drunk Aussies. Trust me on this one.

"I think a walkabout would be in order," I said. "Steve should dislodge himself shortly and James here is game for just about anything. What say you, James."

James nodded in the affirmative and began to drink his whiskey and coke a little faster.

It amazed me that we were leaving so soon. Generally speaking, we would stay here at the Hope Bar until later on in the evening, eventually walk back and visit Papasan's super slope Hoagie stand outside of the main gate to pick up our "hepahoagie," a word coined by Craig meaning hoagie loaded with hepatitis bacteria.

We lingered for another ten minutes or so before departing the Hope Bar and walking in the direction of the city square. There were no parting salutations other than me saying goodbye to Hoa. I noticed that there never were hail and farewell greetings in Vietnam similar to those experienced in America. People just got up and left. There was some body language amounting to a nod or a wave but the niceties shared in America were not duplicated here. Of course, this shortcoming might have been perceived rather than real. We were Americans who didn't have command of the language and couldn't be expected to say anything beyond Tan Biet, which was goodbye.

The walk from the Hope Bar to the city square and beyond was earmarked with smells of nuoc mam (Vietnamese fish oil) that's as hard to adjust to as cheap Scotch and Sloe Cherry Gin, as well as young pimps trying to sell their wares. "You want number one cherry girl" was the garden variety opening line. The response was "I hope you're not talking about your mother." On one occasion we were approached by a young fellow that said "Hey GI, I show you something you never see before." Craig replied, "What you got, leprosy?" The language was crude, equaled only by the environment, and the ambiance was suited to young men not yet accustomed to anything better. An occasional rat, the size of a cat, scurried to pick up a dropped morsel of food, and the road gutters revealed several dead ones that hadn't been as successful in this endeavor, some of which would wind up hanging in the market place and ultimately on someone's table.

The city square was no more than a convergence of the main roads that intersected in the city. Most vehicles or foot traffic had to pass through it, particularly those going to or from the military installation. Charley (the Viet Cong) had their intelligence types watching the square to determine what new units were arriving and any other data they could collect from reading bumper markings indicating the unit to which vehicles were assigned, types of cargo being moved and vehicular troop movements. Of course, the list goes on and includes frequency of use by vehicles of a certain type, and the times of movement. Anything could be intelligence information, and Charley had to have adequate intelligence to maneuver combat elements in a land where he was outgunned and outmanned.

Sometimes, it appeared that the intelligence effort was much too blatant. Men in Vietnamese traditional dress could be seen standing idly at the square's perimeter and watching intently enough to qualify as an intelligence collector. I would imagine that our intelligence group, as well as the Vietnamese intelligence group, were aware of this and were monitoring their activities. The theory behind letting them operate in the open may have been similar to the concept adopted for snipers that shot at, but rarely hit helicopters arriving or departing airstrips. If they can't hit anything, don't kill them; they're likely to be replaced with snipers that can. As a matter of fact, an airstrip

I visited at some remote location had a sign that stated precisely that.

Today was no different. As we passed through the square, there were two men standing on the east side of the square doing much of nothing yet it was clear they were intently watching people and vehicles passing through. As we passed by one of them, James muttered a barely audible question that sounded more like a statement of fact. "You VC?" he said. There was no answer from the slightly built older man. He turned away as if to protect his face and acted as though he hadn't heard the question.

We continued walking up the hill toward the Universal Bar which was noted more for its food and less for its ambiance. Rat Ralphy would come to your table and eat dropped French-fries for no additional fee. This was the only entertainment at the Universal Bar. Once you got accustomed to Ralphy, it wasn't really all that bad. The food was actually pretty good. I found the Shrimp Fried Rice to my liking. It was fried shrimp made with eggs and spices, and herbs I could never have identified, topped with a red sauce. It was particularly palatable and there had been a time when I ate three servings at a cost of about thirty cents a plate.

Craig spoke as he walked. "Do you really like this place?"

"Sure," I replied. I've been here over two years and I got nothing better to do. It's kind of grown on me. The city meets my needs, the people are really nice when you make an effort to understand them and speak a little of their language. I guess this place is what I call home."

Craig laughed. "You're hurting Hardin. I can't imagine getting to the point that I could call this home. I've got too much back in the land of the big PX to ever think that I could be at peace with staying here one second longer than the Army requires. God strike me dead if that happens. You've walked the chalk-line too many times. You could write a book on near misses. They don't call you magnet ass for nothing. Don't you ever feel like disaster is right around the corner? Hell man, do you ever think about going home? Can you picture yourself in a nice car with a girl at your side headed for the beach or some other fun place? Don't you miss the feel of a large round-eyed woman? Do you remember what long legs look like? Let me jog your memory; they start at the feet and go all the way to heaven."

I smiled at his vivid descriptions. "I'm a lifer," I said. "This war is going to be over some day and I want to be here when it happens. I've got a couple of other in-country assignments lined up after this tour is completed. My father was a WWII vet and spent a career in the Navy. He always talked about having to leave his friends behind and hated the fact that he left when he did. He went to Okinawa and even spent some time in Vung Tau. They did not go to war for 12-month stints. They were there, virtually, until it was almost over. As a doctor, he took a reassignment to the Philadelphia Naval Hospital when the war was coming to a close to tend to returning wounded veterans. In later years he saw that as a mistake. He said he should have stayed where the action was until it was over. I don't want to make the same mistake. I have a lot of friends here in Bien Hoa, and our mission, though tricky, doesn't put me in the throes of combat day in and day out. I know there's a bullet out there somewhere with my name on it, but I want to ride this out."

Craig sidestepped a Solex (small motorbike) that came a little too close. "You've done your part several times over. Maybe it's somebody else's turn."

"I don't think so," I said. "I'd just like to be in a position someday to say I was there during the good times and the bad, and rode it out." Some guy down in Finance has been here about five years. He's gone from E-4 to E-7 in that timeframe so there's a good side to all of this. You could never do that in the states. Besides, riding that helicopter into a nest of those bastards gives me a thrill. The pilots have really been well trained. I don't worry so much about them as I do helicopter maintenance."

James laughed, "I still don't have the greatest faith in that Jesus nut that holds on the rotor head. I am forever looking up there to see that it's still in place. A good 50 cal shot in the right place will bring that baby down and us with it."

"Have you ever seen one come off?" I asked.

"No," James replied. "And I don't want to."

Craig looked bemused. "Hey, I fly with you guys based on your assurances that that bird will fly anywhere under any circumstances, and nothing short of a rocket will bring it down. I don't want to get cold feet now so let's change the subject."

"Well let's see," pondered James out loud. "In the last six months, one helicopter had a grenade dropped in the gas tank; that took care of that one. One hit a power cable; that was pilot error. One got shot out of the sky and several actually went down from maintenance problems. But we were able to get most of those folks out without too much difficulty. We inflict more damage than we suffer. We've probably killed a couple of hundred Charleys, I don't know how many weapons caches, not to mention elephants and a few water buffaloes. The water buffaloes were collateral damage. Who would want to shoot what could be supper at the Universal Bar? Hernandez took one right up the Sphincter. He elected to wear his armor vest rather than sit on it. We've lost a few other crewmembers but not recently, except for the last four we officially said goodbye to today."

Craig said, "Yeah and there's the other related stuff like Hardin's hemorrhoids that have been sliced and diced. You really need to have those things removed. And there's brass and barrel burns. You guys insist on grabbing hot stuff without the asbestos gloves, and of course, both Steve and Hardin have that gross stuff all over their hands that looks like nuclear chicken pox from time to time, probably from gun cleaning solvents and tainted vaginal fluids or a combination thereof."

The flow of conversation was interrupted by two GIs running by us at breakneck speed followed closely behind by two white mice, the term used for local police. Vietnamese men tend to run flat footed, especially when they are wearing boots. The GIs began to widen the gap between themselves and the police. The trailing policeman began to blow his whistle hoping that other policemen would come to their aid.

"Well, I wonder what that was all about" I said.

"Didn't pay a tab somewhere, I would imagine," James quipped.

Craig philosophized. "There's a way to put an end to that nonsense. The government should just pay the town a gazillion dollars a month. All the whores, bar owners, and restaurants should just divide the money based on previous income experience and then we could come down here and eat, drink and be merry without having to cough up piasters and haggle prices. The Army could use the money that usually goes into the service clubs for this purpose, and the GIs could supplement the obvious shortage in the fund with 25.00 each month for a town pass."

"Too many problems with that," I said, laughing at his idea.

"What happens when the town goes off-limits. You can't get rain checks for days missed. Too much accounting. The town would be off limits until the accounts were straightened out. We'd spend the rest of our lives waiting for official adjustments. Besides, a lot of people don't come down here that often."

"Then they must be queer." James jested. He began to shuffle his feet. "Tap dance if you're not queer."

Craig complied with James's rhetoric and began to briefly shuffle his feet. He looked at me with mock horror and said "I always knew there was something funny about you."

"Ah, the truth is out, I can't dance," I said.

The Universal Bar was a few steps away. I was first to enter and made my way through the candlelit room to a table in the corner. The darkness was by design. I didn't want to see the filth and they really didn't want to show it to me. Not that I expected the ambiance of the Waldorf Astoria. Indeed, there was no four-star rating on the front door. The fact it had a front door made it superior to most places which had no door at all. I was amazed to find tablecloths. Rather innovative, I thought.

I hadn't seen tablecloths in a long time. We didn't have them in the mess hall except on special occasions, specifically Thanksgiving and Christmas. Many of us did not care what day of the week it was. In fact, most didn't know what day of the month it was. The tablecloths and meager decorations were a clue that it was a holiday. Sometime before I had been in a three-way argument with two other lifers who had been in Vietnam more than a year about what month and day it was. All three of us were wrong about the day. Only two got the month right. We had to go to the orderly room to find out for sure, and the morning report clerk had to find the morning report he had already filed to confirm his suspicions.

Papasan came to the table and gave us the familiar "what you want" look. Craig addressed him in a French accented nasal tone. "We'll start with a side salad followed by Vichyssoise and Potato Au Gratin Soup, then Chateaubriand, and lastly Cherries Jubilee. Oh, and the wine, a fine Château Cos-d'Estournel would suffice."

Much to our surprise, Papasan, now smiling through stained and missing teeth, broke into his best French. The accent was not contrived and his voice was as pure as the words were clear. He virtually became someone else as he spoke back to Craig in a language that only Craig and he could understand. Quite remarkably, Craig had awakened a side of him that lay buried in the dust of yesteryear when the French ruled. Evidently, the dignity and respect from that era of his life had been overcome by the labyrinth of confusion and humiliation wrought by the Americans, prevailing Vietnamese government, Viet Cong and North Vietnamese."

After a conversation that lasted some five minutes, Craig looked at us and said, "Papasan says we're a little late for the finer foods, but he can offer us shrimp or chicken fried rice and pomme frites."

"That would be fine, of course," I said.

Papasan bowed in the direction of Craig as if to say "Thanks for the honor" and when he walked away, it was with a lively step and a purposeful air.

James had a look of awe on his face. He had heard and observed something that just didn't happen in a small town in New Jersey. "Where in the hell did you learn to talk like that, anyhow?" he said.

Craig replied, "Just part of the curriculum at good ole San Jose State. I do believe we made Papasan's day. And by the way, he has a name; it is Trung. Also, I think everyone should speak a second language. Truong speaks three and possibly more. Bo here is pretty good with Vietnamese and I speak enough French to get us by. Steve speaks "Noth Carlina" so perhaps the lot of us can start our own USO. It could do wonders for US-Vietnamese relations."

I laughed. "Yes, monsieur," I conceded. "Your French does help with the friendlies. You have a real talent. I'm all for improving relations but there's a few evil forces at work in this country that wouldn't agree with our well-intended efforts. Now if you could just use your French to get us a free meal."

"Ain't gonna happen," said Craig. "I think Trung is on a shoe-string budget. He said that he once owned a nice restaurant on the square. He leased the building from a Frenchman. After the Viet Minh overthrew the French, they seized the restaurant and he lost everything. He had a car and a nice home. Now he lives with his entire family, which includes sisters and brothers, in a shack on the other side of the Vietnamese compound where Hoa resides. It takes everything he can make to support his family and keep his head above water. He pays taxes to the government for the windfall profits he is making off Americans and slips another ten percent to the cowboys and Viet Cong to stay off his back."

I knew that Trung's assessment was probably accurate. The VC ruled the streets at night. In supplement to being combatants, they were the resident extortion artists for city businesses. They also extorted money from Hamlet Chiefs in the outlying towns and villages. It was either pay up or see your daughters raped and your sons pressed into service with the Viet Cong. Cowboys aped the tactics of their mafia cousins. They were mostly young men, some as young as eight, who would jump a lone GI in an alley, pummeling him with rocks and bricks to take his money. They extorted shop owners by threatening to destroy their business or steal their goods if they didn't pay up. The Cowboys were not well organized, and on many occasions shop owners would form a special alliance with the police to ensure their property was protected. Sometimes it worked, sometimes it didn't. The advantage in this kind of alliance was that the towns were small and the police knew who the cowboys were. Furthermore, the police did not have to meet the U.S. rights-warning criteria established by the Miranda Act. Their unconventional methods were indeed effective, and the recidivism rate for repeat offenders was low.

"There are a million stories in the naked city," added James, stealing a line from the TV series, Dragnet. "Speaking of naked, check out the ta-tas on the waitress."

"I wouldn't mess with that," I said. "That's probably Trung's first born. Besides, Craig has already established some good will and grounds for a long-term relationship with Trung. It would be a bittersweet night for everyone concerned if you tried to talk Miss Universal Restaurant out of her clothes. Something tells me she wouldn't be here waiting tables if she was inclined to make her fortunes in horizontal recreation."

James was often amused at Craig's exaggerated attempt at mimicking his quaint southern accent and tried pitifully to retaliate with some bad French that sounded like "Comantalleyvu." Then Craig said something in perfect French that made Trung and other members of the French-speaking staff chortle.

Steve caught up with us at the restaurant. "Where the hell did you guys go," he said.

"Well, you looked like you had your hands full," I responded.

"Well shucks," he laughed. Could be something to that Fifi. I'm impressed."

"She'll grow on you," I laughed.

"Hopefully not," said Craig.

"Be nice, Craig," I said. "Make room for young love,"

In my years of military service, I had discovered something about southern accents. Some sound suave and sophisticated, some don't. The suave southern accents come from educated or well-bred folks who could be lawyers, business men and the like, who do not have to stumble for words. Everything just seems to flow, especially for the people from Charleston, South Carolina and New Orleans, Louisiana, who seem to have the verbal finesse of the British, but speak with a southern accent. If the southern suave have occasion to curse in the course of a conversation, the curse word comes across as acceptable syntax used to enunciate or express the point they are making. Ostensibly, their place of birth below the Mason Dixon Line does not include them in the less prominent class of garden variety rednecks. They are proud of their heritage and southern upbringing and are excellent debaters. Conversely, there are certifiable rednecks of similar origin found at the other end of the austral spectrum which are of a different and unique species. Their speech is easily identified as southern but it lacks the charm and grace of the suave and sophisticated southerner. When they curse, it is meant to be foul and degrading and preeminently intended to get a point across quickly and succinctly. Litterally speaking, the emotion of the speaker is equal to the word's severity and depths of depravity. As an example of a milder form, "My goodness" for the southern suave, equates to "Holy shit" for the southern redneck. As an example of a harsher form, "I find that totally unacceptable" for the southern suave, equates to "The fuck you say" for the southern redneck. Rednecks are also proud of their heritage and southern upbringing and are excellent debaters until they exhaust their word supply or just get mad enough to "kick your ass." Steve was somewhere in between. He wasn't an avid curser nor was he highly emotional. He liked being part of our little group and I doubt he would have felt at home with a group whose membership criteria was lots of profane language and an occasional wad of chewing tobacco. He was merely an admirable and dependable friend of austral origin.

Craig was picking through his fried rice looking for "unwelcome varmints" with his chop sticks. "So, what are you going to do about Sergeant Jennings?" he said.

"I don't know," I replied.

"Why don't you just kick his butt?"

"Not my style," I said.

Jennings was the First Platoon Sergeant who had been with the unit all of about three months. Aside from being an alcoholic, he had taken it upon himself to act as a virtual deity for everyone assigned to the unit, regardless of whether he supervised them or not. He had been to the first sergeant on a number of occasions to advise him of the names of married guys who were going to the ville and having "sexual interludes" with (to quote the Uniform Code of Military Justice) "strange women other than their wives." To make matters worse, he would verbally accost soldiers returning from the ville regarding their whereabouts and actions. There were times he would conduct late night or early morning inspections of his platoon's aircraft and roust people from their beds to clean up or repair petty items that often were not the crewmember's fault. Maintenance personnel would often check downed or idle aircraft to check specific items of interest designated by the maintenance officer. It wasn't unusual for them to leave a rag on the floor or track mud into the cabin when conducting these inspections. Jennings would find the rag or mud and drag the crew chief and door gunner out to the flight-line to make the necessary corrections. In his short tenure, he had managed to aggravate far too many people. We all hoped that he would not be the ruin of some well-intentioned soldier before he destroyed himself.

I had several conversations with him trying to find a nice way to tell him to back off. His preposterous and intractable attitude made reasoning with him impossible. He had become untrusting of my motives and quite cynical towards me. He never missed an opportunity to belittle me in front of my superiors and word had gotten back to me that he would seize upon the first opportunity to see me degraded and maligned. His problem with me was twofold: I fraternized with junior enlisted men to the extent that I went to the ville with them and drank with them, and I had a female friend with whom I was intimate even though I was, at that time, married. He was right on both counts. I was married but that marriage was legitimately coming to an end, and I did drink with the men I worked with. There was a time for work and a time for play, and rarely did anyone working for me confuse the two.

Jennings' vendetta had become sufficiently notorious to keep the flight officers out of the ville for fear of being accused of some perceived or actual wrongdoing. This was something they could not afford. Their careers were based on periodic efficiency reports. Under normal circumstances, people of all ranks turned a blind eye to the happenings in Bien Hoa, but when you have someone like Jennings lurking in the shadows hell-bent on exposing those who technically could be deemed violators of military regulations, you just have to take yourself off the playing field. The officers had compensated for this conundrum by building a bar and steam bath in their compound. No longer did they visit the bar and shopping area of the ville. If you saw them, it was in a vehicle en route to their compound on the east side of the ville. If they needed to purchase something on the economy, they sent a hoochmaid or Vietnamese driver to procure it.

Actually, I had been less than honest when I said that kicking Jennings' butt was not my style. It had been my style for too many years. In the two years I had been in Vietnam, I had matured. When I wasn't flying or in the field, my first year was spent in youthful vigor running the bars, fighting for kicks, and engaging in puerile antics that could have easily ruined a military career. Somehow, I survived that era and somewhere along the way I settled down. I imagined that a few friends and superiors saw something salvageable in my character and personality, in some of my rare lucid moments, and helped pave the way to positions of greater responsibility and a chance to redeem myself. I will be forever grateful.

Craig continued. "Well, somebody has to do something. This bastard has got to be put in his place."

"He'll get his in due time," I replied.

"I heard the old man was trying to get him transferred," said Steve.

"Me too," said James. "The company clerk related something to that effect to Cookie in the mess hall. Cookie hates the guy's guts. He comes in the mess hall at four in the morning and wants to get fed. Cookie doesn't open the line until five so Jennings just walks into the kitchen and helps himself. Cookie is pissed, but you know Cookie; he won't say anything to the mess officer."

"Perhaps Jennings has an Achilles heel," I said. "We know the guy drinks during what we would call normal duty hours but this is Vietnam and there aren't really any normal duty hours. We work day and night. Flights go out around the clock and when we're in the field, Jennings is back at base camp. I'm a flying platoon sergeant because we're short of people. I don't think Jennings has flown one mission."

"Not that I know of," said Craig.

"Me neither," said James.

"Here's something else to ponder," I said. Jennings goes to the ville by himself purportedly looking for sinners and heathens that he can tattle on. He goes, from what I understand, quite frequently. But what does he really do in the ville?"

"Perhaps we should find out," said James.

"I'm game for this," said Craig. "Let's do what we did when we tailed Richards to the whorehouse to get his cherry broke. We'll get half a dozen guys with the old PRC 10 radios stationed along the way to keep tabs on his every move. If he enters a whorehouse, we'll take pictures of him going in and coming out."

"Hell, if he goes to Big Mama's, you can take pictures of him while he's in the whorehouse," quipped James.

James was right. The crude beds in Big Mama's house of ill repute were a mere three to four feet apart. Curtains amounted to transparent material with the consistency of mosquito nets. Candles placed on bed stands gave you enough light to see everything happening on either side of you. Perhaps it was that way by design. Mood enhancing images probably got you in and out, excuse the pun, a little faster than normal and freed up a bed for the next customer.

The conversation about Jennings eventually faltered. He

just wasn't that much fun to talk about. He was an asshole, and in Vietnam where your life becomes everybody's business, you have to be a cautious and exacting asshole to survive. I knew that Jennings would fall prey to his own demise, sooner or later.

We eventually left the Universal Restaurant and headed into the night. There was something special about Bien Hoa after dark. For a town that had many of the offerings of Las Vegas, it had its own special brilliance without the glare of neon lights and reverberating sounds of slot machines. Soldiers and prostitutes strolled about in the middle of the street much the same as they would on Bourbon Street in New Orleans. We walked the most southern part of the city where bars lined the street and vendors sold just about anything that would attract a buyer. Each bar provided a different view of frivolity and each was, in its own special way, enticing. Little attention was paid to the rats or smell of raw sewer. It was something you grew accustomed to within the first few weeks in Vietnam and the olfactory senses adjusted accordingly. It was the sport of the evening, just walking and looking in amazement at all there was to see. We had done it many times and it never grew old. Every night was different. If you stayed out of trouble and at arm's reach from situations that could cause you problems, you were alright. If you didn't, you could spend the night in a Military Police Conex container and perspire away 10 pounds and all the Bamouiba you drank the night before. I heard the ville likened to Nardin Park near the intersection of Grand Rivers and Livernois in Detroit. It was best not to walk through either one alone. If we were going to the ville on foot, we always went en masse to ensure each other's safety.

We were a pretty docile looking bunch walking down the middle of the road. Still boys at heart, looking at the world through rose-colored glasses, I thought. I had felt the same when I was much younger digging through old abandoned houses with my friends in obscure locations well off the beaten path. The hills of Tennessee were full of such places and my friends and I often combed them in search of buried treasure. We relied on our numbers to ensure our safety. Little had changed since then. We were always searching for something. We were easily satisfied; a little sex, a little booze, a lot of laughter and an ego-boosting war story or two was all it took. Men are indeed simple creatures.

We trudged along, looking at the sights for some time before deciding to return to the Hope Bar. We made our way back along the route we had traveled through the square, noting along the way that Charley must be off duty for the night. If he was there, we didn't see him. Maybe he had dressed in camouflaged fatigues or changed attire to blend into the darkness that began to cloak the night. James joked that even Charley must have a curfew and quite possibly he needed a town pass to stay out after dark. We laughed without comment.

Fifi and Hoa were still there and the bar had become a little livelier. Eight or nine GIs wearing 25th Infantry Division patches were there, and war stories about the infamous "Wolfhounds," a unit in the 25th Infantry Division that had been chopped up rather badly in Hobo Woods, were being recounted in a loud and obstreperous way. One had the hots for Hoa and she was laying it on thick. A light touch to the neck, a smile that was full of promises, a display of a normally well-hidden breast, and an exaggerated walk that emphasized her butt were all part of the many strands of silk that comprised the web of seduction. At closing time, she would disappear into thin air leaving a distraught and horny soldier in her wake. She was very good at what she did, and she did it in a calculating and unabashed way that did not include any consideration for my feelings or any need for my approval. I knew that her objective was to extract and abscond with every piaster she could squeeze out of a customer. We both knew that I was not a paying customer, and mutually agreed that I was not to interfere. My job, if you want to call it that, was to perpetually stand in the wings at show time. Beyond that, she needed me and I needed her, each for our own reasons that had little to do with money. Indeed, she was an artist and I adored her work and admired her zeal.

Fifi welcomed Steve like an old lost friend. I guessed everything had been forgiven. It was either that or she had a class on reaffirming client relationships while we were gone. She had changed her clothes and her long hair made her look rather enticing as it swung freely down her back, oscillating to and fro across the widest part of her anatomy. She brought him the drink of his choice, which could have been sarsaparilla or milk depending on his mood and simple desires. He smiled and they reconvened the boy-meets-barely-English-speaking girl in a foreign country diatribe. From his demeanor I could tell that he was hoping the language of lust would compensate for the inability to carry out a meaningful conversation with all the innuendos, metaphorical syntax and silly rhetoric that people use to convey one thing and mean or suggest another. I was surprised when he showed this much interest. He was usually content to stay in the shadows and avoid any connection with women. It was his style. He didn't tell jokes but would laugh at them. It just wasn't his style. He was content as a member of the DooWa group. As long as we had known him and as many things as we had done together, it always seemed that he had just tagged along to be with the group. It was not like him to be forthcoming with a lot of facts about his home life back in "the world" and if you wanted his thoughts on something, you had to dig it out of him. He was noncommittal in every sense of the word.

I saw Fifi dart for the bar with piasters or script in her hand which probably meant that Steve had bought her a Saigon Tea. This, I thought could be a gesture of apology or it could be an attempt to get closer to this young maiden. Looks like it's time to add a chapter to Steve's memoirs, I thought.

What Steve didn't realize that one of the Wolfhounds also had ideas about concreting a relationship with Fifi. Craig and I watched as the Wolfhound squirmed in his seat and provided an assortment of body language that could mean a variety of things. One was that he was pretty damned drunk. Another was that he had certain designs on Fifi and Steve had become a bona fide firewall for getting closer to her. This whole event had bad overtones that could only become worse. The terrible truth about soldiers who get in bar fights is that they are trained to kill, some more proficiently than others, and whoever is left in the prone position when the final blow is thrown usually doesn't look like he's going to be ready to go to the senior prom for quite a while. There would be some complicated dental work, not to mention the time it takes for mother nature to repair gaping facial tears, contusions and rearranged testicles. Not only were these guys in great shape, but they had been trained to react decisively and with great force. Not that Steve wasn't up to it. Quite to the contrary, he was what you would call "scrappy" and he could hold his own. But there were many of them and a few of us. The math would not work in our favor if this misadventure turned into a brawl. Intelligence is always superior to macho imagination, but booze and lust seems to abate one's ability to remember that.

Steve had already sensed that the Wolfhound was upset or possibly looking to rumble and did his best to avoid the stares as well as the imperceptible and hardly audible comments that he was making to friends who shared his table. He walked away from Fifi and moved to the bar where he sipped on his drink and ignored everything that was going on behind him. I heard James say "Oh, shit. We don't need this."

Wolfhound followed Steve to the bar. His stocky frame was a forbidding sight and I could see that Steve was physically outmatched. The walk was an ambulating statement of power and bad intentions and I knew that save a miracle, things were going to get testy. Steve knew that the Wolfhound was drunk. Although we couldn't hear the verbal exchange that was taking place between them, we could see Steve dodging a stream of alcohol laden breath that could double as a discharged but unlit flamethrower. The conversation continued with little eye contact between the two. The Wolfhound's rage eventually turned to looks of concern and sympathy. Steve continued to look down rather submissively and in a sad and dejected way. The Wolfhound said something we couldn't hear from where we stood and walked toward the back door where the water closet was located. Both he and Steve disappeared into the corridor that led to the water closet. In about 30 seconds both reappeared. The Wolfhound yelled at Fifi to "give that man a drink on me."

Then it hit me what had just happened. About a month before when we had returned from a support mission in Ia Drang Valley, someone in our tent had been the recipient of several bottles of choice whiskey; Johnny Walker, Crown Royal and several other bottles I'd prefer to forget. Completely out of character, Steve drank himself into a state just short of alcohol poisoning. About ten of us were seated in a loose circle passing bottles around and relating camouflaged truths about girls back home, the things we had done, and what the future held when we returned home. Steve had in his possession a pair of crotchless panties that had been sent to someone in the platoon who had rotated back to the states and left them behind. Out of nowhere Steve appeared and strutted right through the seated group wearing the crotchless panties. He had pulled the tubular hardware back between his legs, which gave the impression that there was nothing there but testicles. They were clear to see, clearly too large to hide, but the penis was tucked neatly between his cheeks behind him. We roared at his antics and taunted him for weeks afterwards. I was sure that he had told Wolfhound that he was no threat, in reality a eunuch, and that he got his dick shot off. I imagined that Wolfhound demanded to see for himself if Steve was telling the truth but wouldn't have spent a lot of time inspecting Steve's genitals in his drunken state for fear of being adjudged a homosexual. My suspicions were confirmed when I saw the sly smile appear on Steve's face as he turned back to the bar and drop his head in mock shame. I was getting a bad case of the childish giggles but Wolfhound made the whole charade even funnier when he returned to the tables where his friends lingered in anticipation and refused to say anything about what he thought he had not seen. I guess there's always a little chivalry somewhere and you find it in the weirdest places. Steve, I thought, you are one slick devil.

By this time Craig mentally grasped this creative bit of subterfuge, but James was still in a fog. Craig and I turned our backs to hide our faces from the rest of the patrons and begin to laugh uncontrollably. My sides were splitting while I was trying to tell Craig to suppress the laughter, lest we let the cat out of the bag.

Suddenly James, who was still waiting for the fight to start, says, "What the hell's so funny? We got to protect his ass, man. I'm ready to rumble." That made it even funnier. We laughed harder than ever. The tears were flowing down my face.

Craig, in an attempt to tell him what was going on, said

"He's got no dick."

James replied, "Hell, he's got a dick. We've seen his dick."

Fortunately, the music from the Hope Bar's Kenwood tuner and cheap speakers was enough to drown out his exclamations and we eventually quit laughing long enough to make a reasonable explanation. Fifi, Hoa, and the rest of the girls had no idea what was so funny, but they weren't accustomed to paying much attention to people laughing, particularly when they could not understand everything that was said which caused the laughter.

"It's time to go," I said, and we did. Outside in the street Steve recanted the story he told Wolfhound. As he related it, we laughed, and James, who finally got it, had to stable himself against a building.

"When Wolfhound and I were talking at the bar, I told him that Fifi was only being nice to me because she felt sorry for me and that we were more like brother and sister. Then he said he was going to whip my ass because I was making a move on something he was going to spend the night with. I told him that I was not a threat because I got my dick shot off. I told him that we were going in on a gun run firing at a nest of VC in support of the Wolfhounds in Hobo Woods and an explosion under the aircraft tore my dick off but left my balls. He said that I was lying and he wanted to see it. I said not here but I'll show you in the water closet where nobody else can see. He said OK. On the way back to the bathroom, I shifted the lizard back between my legs and up the crack of my ass. He actually closed his eyes while I pulled down my pants. I had the scar at the top of where my penis would normally be where they dug some shrapnel out about 6 months ago. When he looked, it was only briefly and he said "My God" and turned around and walked out and back onto the bar. When I returned to the bar, Fifi brought me the drink he bought for me. That was the first time that I knew for sure that he had bought the stratagem.

Man, was he drunk. Really, really drunk. He probably won't remember any of this tomorrow.

"And thank goodness he doesn't know where you live," I retorted.

"Did Fifi know what was going on," he asked.

"I doubt it," said Craig, "unless Wolfhound decides to lay it all out for his buddies. I think his take on this is that he has a need to keep this quiet lest the facts be confused or a deep-seated fear he might have of actually getting his own dick shot off. Not surprising, I guess. Hey, you got a free drink out of it."

"Make that half a drink," said Steve. "I left half of it because I didn't want to stick around. I thought you guys would never leave. I was ready to walk by myself. No, make that run. All that cackling you guys were doing at the bar didn't help things either. I believe the red-headed guy he was with, who was also drunk, was chewing at the bit to get it on and he could have cared less about the circumstances or Wolfhound's sudden change of heart. Man, what I have to do to get along in this world!"

James couldn't let the opportunity pass without getting in a few digs of his own. "Guess you gotta be built just right to pull that off. Long dick, or substantial cheeks, or both. Did you ever wonder if that thing was going to slip out? Hey, you can't have sex with yourself, can you? You could save a lot of money with that kind of mechanical arrangement. You could give your butt a name and fall in love with it. I'll come to the wedding."

Craig joined in. "Better bring Titi (meaning little or small in Vietnamese) LaPew in for a checkup tomorrow, Steve."

Steve took everything in stride and laughed with us. We continued on toward Bien Hoa Airbase chiding Steve and laughing at the situation. Steve had given us a creative moment of levity and we were taken with his wit and ingenuity. Perhaps Fifi had made him a little more daring than usual.

CHAPTER 2

The morning sun had not yet shown its rays above the horizon. The operations briefing had delayed the pilots a little longer than usual. We had been notified at about three in the morning that the stand-down was over and we would have an early morning mission. Needless to say, those of us that had gone to the ville the night before were totally unprepared. Although we had returned to the barracks before curfew, we remained awake in my room, drinking what was left of a bottle of Johnny Walker I had received the week before from pen pals in Pennsylvania. We continued to laugh about Steve's incident at the Hope Bar, which had now been coined with several newly contrived terms including strip screw, stripterfuge, and tricktease.

I might have had thirty minutes sleep when I was nudged awake by a runner from operations. I got dressed quickly, grabbed my weapon and made it to the flight line. In my condition, wrought more by the lack of sleep than the Johnnie Walker, the soft wind in my face was more an annoyance than the soothing effusion of air that I had grown to appreciate on hot and clammy mornings. It was said that an hour's sleep is worse than none at all and I couldn't help but agree.

Steve and I got the weapons in place and I performed an inspection of the helicopter to make doubly sure that all mechanical moving parts including the "almighty Jesus nut," were flight worthy. All the safety wire that that was threaded through the holes above the hundred or so exposed nuts had been replaced by the maintenance crew during the last periodic inspection, fluid levels were exactly where they were supposed to be and I felt confident that we would fly without any mechanical difficulties. The pilots had moved to areas where they were conducting individual platoon briefings, awkwardly holding flashlights to illuminate maps. For that reason, I knew this was a mission that was put together hastily, and given the early hour, assumed that we would be making a night insertion or pickup.

I didn't like any operation that was conducted in the dark. Dark is for sex, not flying helicopters or using equipment that is better and more safely operated when you can see. The nemeses for helicopters are power lines, trees, mountains that leap up out of nowhere, and other helicopters that just don't see you until it's too late. The last word you want to hear the pilot say on the intercom during night flights is "oops." Vees of three and trail formations are hairy enough during daylight hours when pilots can actually see the rotor blades on surrounding aircraft. On numerous occasions, pilots swear and vociferate great displeasure over all-to-frequent near misses, particularly when the aircraft ahead of you flares to slow down during an approach to a landing zone. It has a domino effect; the first aircraft to flare causes the others behind it to do the same and makes for some very anxious moments. Some pilots "peel off" to get out of the highly unstable array of thrashing blades. Those that should have and didn't aren't here to critique what went wrong.

Lum Edgars was the flight leader that day. I liked his no-nonsense approach to leadership. He was a short and stocky captain who was to the point when he needed to be and rather amiable when the mission was behind us. He wasn't demeaning or condescending with the troops and the word was that he had once been an enlisted man. I appreciated folks like him because you could be truthful and respectful at the same time. Enlisted folks have the tendency to color coat and enhance responses to officers who only want to hear the best, and find anything else, including the truth, "unacceptable." Lum wasn't like that. He wanted to hear the problems and viewed his job as one of a solution finder. He would be there when the other officers had gone. If there was a question about an operation, he would go to operations to get an answer. If a helicopter crew chief felt that he needed a periodic inspection performed because it was almost due and wouldn't get through the next day's flight without running over the time it was to be performed, Lum would go down to see the maintenance officer and manage to get it done. If a gunner or crew chief felt there was a problem with the weapons systems, he would have avionics check wiring and weapons systems. Lum would often butt heads with those that outranked him, but like all good soldiers, he was recognized as a professional and the arguments he had were based upon an unmistakable enthusiasm for getting the job done right and taking care of everybody's needs. In time he became the Operations Officer and put the same effort into the intricacies of coordinating flights and support functions as he did with taking care of men and equipment as a platoon leader.

Steve had the weapons mounted on the aircraft and the two of us lugged the regulated amounts to the aircraft. There could be 2000 rounds; not 2001 or 1999. In an earlier incident when the company was stationed in Vung Tau, a previous unit commander, Lieutenant Colonel Honeywell, had certain idiosyncrasies that caused much grief with both the pilots and crewmembers. One was the amount of ammunition in an ammo box. His edict was that there would be no more or no less than 2000 rounds. This could become complicated, especially if you left Vung Tau, rearmed rapidly at a field location and then returned to Vung Tau. As hard as you tried, it was difficult to assure that when you landed, you had no more than 2000 rounds. After one flight was completed, which included rearming at another location, Honeywell counted the rounds in each door box. More rounds were discovered in one door box than he could tolerate, which resulted in the aircraft commander being disciplined. The unit scuttlebutt was that the aircraft commander was put on arrest of quarters and required to write a 5000-word thesis on the history of the 68th Assault Helicopter Company. Now that may just be nonsense, but other incidents paralleling those of the Caine Mutiny made me tend to believe that it was true. Regardless, from that day forward, rounds were counted on the return trip home, and more often than not, rounds could be seen being thrown from helicopters in flight. When the flight touched down, everyone had 2000 rounds in their ammo box.

Honeywell had the body of a complete tiger painted on the nose of his helicopter to distinguish his aircraft from the rest, which bore only the head of the tiger. I happened to be there when the artist was painting the tiger and Honeywell was admiring his work and I foolishly made the comment that "Charley would certainly know who to shoot at now." I was prone to say stupid things without thinking. Open mouth and insert foot- It's the curse of impetuous youth. Honeywell's response was "They'll never get me, Hardin." About two weeks later he was medically evacuated or "medivaced" out of the country when two rounds pierced his chin bubble and penetrated his leg. He recovered in due time. The company recovered as well, after celebrating his departure for two or three days. I can't condemn or condone his actions because I haven't walked a mile in his shoes.

Although he was gone, we did not forget the moratorium on excessive ammunition, and joked about it when it was time to get the ammo on board the aircraft.

Steve laughed as he put the last ammo box in the aircraft. "Feels like 2001," he said.

"Trying to make a statement?" I asked. "I'll rat you out."

"No," he said with a smile. "It's more a statement of relief, than anything else. I hated living in fear when Honeywell was here, walking around counting bullets and sneaking out to watch night guards walking their posts. That whole thing was absolutely absurd. What a power trip he was on. And this is a good unit. I've been in some bad units, but this is a good one. Everybody seems to work together, except Jennings, of course. And he'll get his due, if he doesn't change his ways. My mother use to say "if you do what you've done, you'll get what you've got." I think his problem may run a little deeper than what people can see, but I really don't care."

The pilots eventually arrived and began their preflight inspection. It was not a thorough inspection. The co-pilot warrant officer climbed on top to check the "Jesus" nut and checked a couple of fluid levels and told the aircraft commander that we were good to go. Steve and I buckled in and gave the clear right and left signals and we were soon lifting off the runway. The first few seconds into the air are always interesting. In that brief moment you can see the things that are familiar to you. The barracks, the mess hall, the latrine and the road to Bien Hoa are unmistakable. When we fly over the east end of the post, you can see the old and yet cleared French mine field that sits just inside the post perimeter, the Hope Bar is visible and the circle where the Viet Cong intelligence agent spends his day all come into view. It is a small piece of real estate but it is the sum total of our world that is available to us when we are not on missions. It is as much a part of us as we are a part of it. I couldn't imagine being anywhere else, but often wondered what I was doing there.

The town was asleep. Nothing was moving as we flew over it. I saw a few dogs trotting alongside the road near the entrance to the post but nothing else moved. Yet I knew that what I saw was limited to the area immediately around the post. Charlie was out there terrorizing villagers and setting up ambushes all over the country. North Vietnamese regulars were making their way into the southern region (III Corp) and providing support to the greatest extent possible to the Viet Cong. Young men were being recruited or forced into service for the other side. Somewhere in this country an American soldier would probably die fighting against tyranny and oppression of a people known to be gentle and kind.

When the flickering lights of Bien Hoa airbase and the city disappeared, I knew that we were being watched carefully by a team of soldiers bent on our destruction that would be radioing ahead to others who would track our movement and make an estimate of our intentions. Our intelligence was not the greatest, but Charley had an advantage in some respects. He always knew where we were.

Soon the lights of Bien Hoa disappeared and we were gaining altitude where we would be able to see lights but not be able to make out the outlines of houses and villages. The lights in Vietnam were low voltage, driven by generators that did not give a steady output of energy. For that reason, you weren't always exactly sure of what was beneath you, or if you were anywhere close to villages. The rivers and streams always provided a clue. They were visible in the reflection of the moonlight and the rural areas of Vietnam were typically constructed near water sources. But the rivers and streams were Charley's super highways. He used them to move men and equipment from location to location based upon intelligence, much of which might well be provided by the lookout in Bien Hoa's hub or the guys who watched our aircraft leave the airstrip early in that morning. The internal waterways were even more important to Charley. Using coastal areas to sail sampans laden with equipment had proven risky and the navy patrol boats were quick to board and seize anything that moved in that manner. Conversely, patrol boats could not get into streams and internal waterways. Aside from a few checkpoints where young South Vietnamese soldiers often slept rather than vigilantly manned their posts, Charley had free unchecked movement. When intelligence information revealed the use of specific waterways, operations would be conducted to shut it down, but restrictions were short lived and within a month or two Charley would be up and running again. You can't have people everywhere all of the time. Again- advantage Charley.

With every flight, I devoted time to remembering our direction of flight and any identifiable landmarks. Many aircraft had gone down in the years past and the crews were faced with making the long trek out to a friendly outpost where they could be reunited with friendly forces. Of course, there were many that fell into enemy hands and were captured or disposed of. I did not relish the idea of being captured, particularly in the south. Experience was that few made it from South Vietnam to the Hanoi Hilton in North Vietnam. I never for a moment thought I would be one of the few. In earlier years, it was the practice of just about everyone to carry a concealed weapon, one that was not issued by the Army, for a plethora of reason. Weapons were not allowed to be carried into the city. Since Charley did not have the same restrictions, we leveled the playing field by carrying our own. Weapons issued to flight members consisted of .45 caliber handguns for the pilots, which were worn in shoulder holsters, and M-14s for the crewmembers. A pretty valid assumption was that if you were in a crash, or forced away from your helicopter due to a fire or having it fall into the hands of the enemy, you would most likely be without a weapon. A concealed weapon was the schoolbook solution to the problem but one the Army did not condone. For years, laws or regulations against concealed weapons were ignored, but the arrival of the aforementioned commander from hell changed all that. He insisted that all unauthorized weapons be turned in immediately upon his verbal proclamation. People were scrambling to and fro to sell, trade, or otherwise dispose of handguns. One crewmember buried his handgun near the PSP runway and got caught in the process. About that time, one of my additional responsibilities at Vung Tau was that of tent chief. I was the ranking man and was responsible for making sure people cleaned their area and acted civilly to others who lived in the tent. Although I was not enamored with the insignificant glory of this responsibility, I had serious problems with one oaf from Arkansas who bullied everybody and woke people up during all hours of the night. This was a real problem because of our schedules. When we weren't on a company-sized mission, individual aircraft were making flights at all times of the day and night. It's bad enough having to sleep in 110 degree heat during the day without having some idiot waking you up and looking through your personal effects for food. I reported some of his puerile antics to the first sergeant for whatever punishment he deemed necessary. When the perpetrator of these offenses reported to the first sergeant, he revealed the fact that I had a weapon in contravention with the commander's policy. I had already sold the weapon to a news correspondent who was glad to pay the $140.00 asking price. That was a lot of money, particularly when I had paid twenty bucks for it. Of course, I got called on the carpet and found myself standing in front of the commander from hell who asked simple questions to which I provided simple answers. I told the unvarnished truth. He excused me and I left after executing a snappy salute and an about face and was never called again regarding the matter. The oaf pulled 30 grueling days of extra duty. I summed up my good fortune to the possibility that the commander from hell had already handed out so much disciplinary action that he would soon be running out of troops, or he found as much hatred and disgust as I did with the idiot I sent to the first sergeant. As much as I hated to admit it, I knew the commander's order to turn in handguns was justified. Accidents happen, and if someone was shot and killed accidentally, he would be the one with the gruesome task of writing the letter to the loved ones of the deceased. I wouldn't have had any room for complaints had he imposed non-judicial punishment against me. This was one of the many times in my military career that I would sneak by unscathed. In retrospect, I believe that the Big Ranger in the sky had a hand in each.

I watched the winding river beneath me and knew from its horseshoe shape that we were in the Duc Hue/Duc Hoa area. Charley owned this waterway. There were stories that a tacit agreement existed between Charley and MACV units in the area. Charley would take one can of coke out of every case that came through his checkpoint on the river and MACV would do something in kind. How true that was could not be confirmed. Personally, I would not drink the cokes.

The whop-whop rhythm of the rotor blades had put Steve to sleep. His dark visor protected his eyes, but the downward angle of his head that placed his chin on the top of his chest protector was unmistakably that of someone asleep. The danger of sleeping like this, and everyone did, was that the aircraft would hit a bump in the road, so to speak, and the crewmember would wake up thinking that he had landed. The first order of business when an aircraft landed was to get out of the aircraft and open the door of the pilot seated ahead of you. A story abounded that one crewmember had awoken in this manner, quickly unsnapped his safety belt and stepped out into a thousand feet of open space. Admittedly, it could get confusing. Once upon a time, probably through the end of 1965, crewmembers were secured by an extended safety belt which permitted them to lean out the open door and direct machinegun fire on a target beneath or near vertical to the aircraft. The machineguns were hung on bungee cords and could be moved independently. In late 1965, bungee cords were replaced by steel machinegun mounts and safety belts were shortened. This may have come about as a safety measure. Crewmembers, who had either been hit by ground fire or for some reason lost control of their weapon, had fired their machineguns inside the aircraft. The machinegun mounts restricted lateral movement making it impossible to fire a round inside the aircraft.

The pilots were unusually quiet today and I assumed there had been an order for radio silence and minimal chatter over the intercom. Of course, the early hour might have had something to do with it too. Such an early take off was rare unless we were flying a long distance to make a pickup far away from our home station. In such an instance we would refuel shortly before or after the troop insertion or pickup.

I noted that we had a full complement of gunships that were flying in the usual flank positions. The old B model Hueys were telltale when they were loaded. The nose was always a little higher, indicating that the angle of the blade had to be changed in order to carry the load. The flight held its position and we could eventually see the light coming over the horizon. You get a view from the air that you don't get from the ground. It was dark where we were and light on the horizon. Mother Nature had placed a majestic division in the heavens for us to enjoy. We started our dissent and I knew that admiring Mother Nature's wonder would have to wait. We were going back down into the night to take care of the business of war. I heard the flight leader say that we were three minutes out from the LZ. I picked up the machinegun kit bag that contained an extra barrel and asbestos glove and used it to poke Steve in the leg. He looked over at me and gave me a thumbs up to acknowledge he was awake. Thank goodness, I thought. After a long night of merriment, he didn't wake up and jump out the door.

The effusion of darkness appeared as fast as the light of the horizon had disappeared. We were at an altitude of about five hundred feet when what appeared to be the LZ came into focus. I saw smoke coming from the north end of an open stretch of terrain and I guessed that the smoke would mark the north end of the LZ. The strip was clear and for a moment I thought there was nothing there. When we were on short final, I begin to see troops moving out of the trees. I could tell at a glance that the uniforms weren't the normal uniforms of the military and the equipment was definitely different. These were mercenaries and they didn't play by the book. Au contraire, they didn't have a book.

I heard Lum, the flight leader, come over the air. "Get them on board and get out of this LZ. We've got about three minutes to clear the area."

Our pilot glanced at the co-pilot. "You think that's just enthusiasm or are we in trouble."

The co-pilot retorted. "No, I think we've got 3 minutes. It's not Lum's style to get excited."

As we landed the pilot turned to face Steve and me and said "Let's get them on board quickly." "Roger that," I said as I unbuckled my safety belt to move from my seat and assist those running toward the aircraft with equipment.

The first two or three people to reach the aircraft were yelling to others to join them instead of going to another aircraft. Obviously, there was some confusion about which aircraft people were going to load. They had not properly rehearsed the loading and divided themselves into groups of six or seven, depending on the weight of the equipment they were carrying. A minute after we had touched down, we had three people on board and one wanted to get off to fetch someone. That's way too slow for a pickup. By this time, we should have had everyone on board except the outlying security forces, which at this point should be vacating their positions and doing a one-hundred-yard dash for the aircraft.

I could tell the pilot was upset. He yelled "Just get me six or seven people on board." I removed my helmet and stepped away from the aircraft where I was able to grab three more people and escort them onto the aircraft. Now it became a waiting game. Another minute went by and I still saw a dozen or so people that had not loaded. We were just about three minutes into the pickup when I saw more people coming out of the wood line. I assumed they were security personnel that were finally withdrawing. The pilot was yelling from his window and I gathered he was saying to get on board.

The first volley of enemy fire came from the west side of the LZ. As I put my helmet on, I heard the flight leader say, "We're lifting off in ten seconds."

There is a mad dash for the helicopters now by those who just seconds before stood idle as if there was no hurry. One more person ran for our aircraft and literally dove into the pile of people already sitting in the floor. Another tried the same tactic but I grabbed him and sent him back to the helicopter behind us.

There was more enemy fire now and the people on board were sporadically returning fire. I jumped back into my seat to ensure that I would not be inadvertently shot by someone already on board. I heard the flight leader say. "Pick them up. We're getting out of here."

The lead ship lifted upward and began his assent. Each aircraft followed in succession. We were taking fire and the mercenaries were firing back. There were still mercenaries running for cover in the wood line on the east side of the LZ.

The flight leader was presented with a bad situation. We could not provide suppressive fire in the direction of the west wood line because we could not distinguish friendly forces from enemy forces. We were still receiving fire and no one could account for the location of the mercenary commander. Crewmembers were stopping loaded mercenaries from firing but most of the mercenaries did not speak English and we could not get any quick information relative to the size of the force still left on the ground.

I heard the flight leader inquiring as to the location of the mercenary commander. He advised the gunships to remain on site and try to make sense out of what they could see on the ground. A poll of the pickup aircraft, or slicks as they are commonly referred to, revealed that we were twenty or so pax (people) short of a full load. All aircraft had at least four pax, some as many as seven.

One of the mercenary leaders was located on one of the aircraft and after a short discussion a decision was made to strafe the west side of the LZ with rockets and miniguns. The gunships rolled into position and began lighting up the west side. The flight began a westerly movement which enabled me to see the LZ from the left rear of my aircraft. I could see muzzle flashes of weapons on both sides of the LZ. An occasional tracer was fired from the east side to the west side and would often hit something solid and veer lazily into oblivion. In my last glimpse of the area, I could see enemy personnel moving from the west wood line in the direction of the east wood line. This meant that the bad guys were advancing on the good guys. Essentially, it was over for the mercenaries who remained in the LZ. If the gunships could inflict casualties in the enemy ranks, it might give the mercenaries time to reposition themselves in an area where they could be extracted. Depending on where we would be dropping off the group we just picked up, there might be enough fuel time left to return and extract some or all of those left behind. It all depended on Charley's personnel strength and what he was willing to lose. Our experience was that Charley savored victory, no matter how small or costly, and his continued success, like ours, was tied to body counts that the American news system would tout for him. What he probably didn't know was that this victory, if that was what it was to be, would not be reported. These were mercenaries that were paid a base salary for intelligence data, with bonuses for significant body counts. If there was any value here, it would be derived from the concessions received from governments when captured personnel from their countries were exploited for political purposes. That didn't happen much in the south of

Vietnam. It was too difficult for Charley to house prisoners and conduct political operations in an area where his detection was more probable than not and continued operations hinged on continuous movement of forces and headquarters elements.

One of the mercenaries sitting at my feet tugged on my leg. "Not to worry, he said in a thick British accent. "They're Cambodes," the term used for Cambodian soldiers.

"What do you mean," I said.

"The chaps left behind, they're Cambodians. We've been trying to get rid of them for some time. No good in the woods. They make too much noise. Sound like water buffalo in the jungles. The chief put them on security to get them blasted. We don't need them."

"Thanks," I replied.

I relayed this conversation to the pilot who said that evidently the British chap was speaking accurately. The mercenary leader that had been located on another aircraft indicated that he did not want to make another attempt to extract anyone. According to the mercenary leader, the use of the gunships was fine, which would give them a chance to break contact, but there should not be any attempts to extract them. He added that basic operations plans contained escape and evasion procedures for personnel left behind and that would be sufficient. Any protracted operations to extract them might lead to American casualties and equipment losses. Since they were operating incognito, such losses could not be attributed to their actions in the field. Such an event would lead to the acknowledgement of adjunct force operations and could attract negative world press reviews. Ultimately, it could undermine continued operations.

Dang, I thought. I wouldn't want to be a member of that organization. You get caught behind- you get left behind.

Somehow, I didn't remember that motto in any of the Soldiers of Fortune magazines I read. But then again, I wouldn't be lollygagging around when the helicopters landed. I would have been the first guy on board. If one round was fired, I'd be the first guy on board that left a very discernable green and brown trail behind him. It's not just that I've grown accustomed to uninterrupted breathing, I have a passionate aversion to having my fingernails plucked out, chopsticks penetrating any of my body parts, and sleeping in something the size of a pet carrier. My price for being a mercenary just jumped to a million dollars a day and a rapid response Army and Air Force on standby in the event I needed a change in environments.

We picked up a northerly heading for about five minutes then changed headings for another five minutes. We did a slow arcing turn over a 5-kilometer area then headed back to the west, finally arriving at a dirt airstrip with a small building at the north end. We sat the flight down without incident, dropped off the mercenaries and were back in the air within a minute. On our way out we passed a small Air America aircraft headed in the direction of the airstrip.

I noted that the mercenaries didn't seem to be excited about security when they landed. There was no direction given, that I could tell, to get listening or observation posts into the wood line to establish perimeter security. Obviously, they must have felt secure in their surroundings. If the Air America aircraft was headed to the airstrip we just left, they must have felt that it was safe to land.

I keyed my mike to talk to the pilot. "What was that all about?" I asked.

"What was what all about," he replied.

"That mission we just flew," I responded.

"What mission," he said.

"The mission we just didn't fly," I said.

"You got it," he replied.

Steve smiled that North Carolina guess-you-asked-the-stupid-question smile. It wasn't a stupid question. It just turned out to be an unauthorized question for which I received an authorized yet unsanctioned response. I was un-officially un-confused.

It was daylight now. The sun had risen and shone brightly from the east. I saw a friend sitting in the door of the gunship that flew 100 meters away from me. I waved and he waved back. We were flying at about 1500 feet. We were a very small target for anyone with anything smaller than a .50 caliber weapon. The methodical and rhythmic noise of the rotor blades became a sleep-inducing metronome. Steve's dark visor was already down and his chin rested on his chest plate. I reached up and pulled mine down as well. I did not go to sleep, but I did go inactive.

I revived myself when we were on short final to the Bien Hoa airstrip. The aircraft landed safely and pilots and crewmembers were out of the aircraft while the blades turned slowly to a halt. The maintenance crew was making the rounds to each aircraft asking if anything was wrong. I checked the fluid levels and looked for bullet holes before I gave the maintenance crew a thumbs up when it was my turn to respond. The fuel truck was making the rounds and Steve was taking the weapons to the cleaning area where they would be cleaned then returned to the aircraft. They would remain there for the day with the ammunition in place in the event that there was another mission that required a quick response.

Craig walked up to the aircraft. "Everything OK?" he asked.

"Sure," I said. "Why wouldn't it be?"

"Well, I guess your mission went well, asshole."

"I laughed. "What mission?"

"The one you just came back from."

"Officially, we didn't just come back from anything."

"Well, it's a good thing nobody got hurt because we couldn't treat them, officially.

I laughed. "But I don't want to be treated officially. I want to be treated tenderly."

"You got the wrong guy for that," he said. "You need to see Nurse Hoa."

"I need sleep, and lots of it," I said. "Besides, you are a bad influence, according to my mother."

His eyes widened in mock horror. "You told your mother about us. This could be serious."

"Not about you specifically, but anybody I stayed up late with when I was a kid got labeled as a bad influence, so if I told her your name and what happened, she would say you were a bad influence, so you must be a bad influence."

Craig smiled. "I don't tell my mother about the ville or carousing, drinking, screwing, etc., etc., etc. There are psychiatric labels for narcissistic people who have special relationships with their mothers, you know. Maybe we need to set you up with an appointment with the special doctor."

"And who might that special doctor be?" I asked.

"Well, I just happen to be the special doctor. My office hours are six to nine at the Hope Bar. I'll be working tonight as a matter of fact."

"Huh uh, no, no, never, never," I said. "If that's an invite, I pass. The sandman and the tooth fairy are ahead of the special doctor. I need a wisdom tooth pulled and about two days of extreme respite."

"Hardin," said Craig, "It's hard to be sarcastic when you're more sarcasticer. Sooner or later, it's inevitable. I'll have your name sewn on a body bag."

I chuckled as Craig made his way to the next aircraft. He was a hell of a guy, always concerned about doing the job he was sent there to do, full of humor, with an elastic and active imagination.

Steve and I took care of the helicopter and eventually made our way back to the barracks area. I opened my door to the six by eight containment I called home, a.k.a. Room 1, Building 0. I dropped my gear, stumbled over a box of books and fell headlong onto the bed and into a deep sleep.

I awoke at about 10 pm. There was some stirring of people in the barracks. My neighbor on the other side of the wall had just returned from a night mission. He had been flying "lightning bug" missions for some time now. This consisted of a helicopter flying over suspected enemy areas at an altitude of five or six hundred feet with a landing light on. This presented just too great a target for Charley to pass on. When Charley opened fire, displaying muzzle flashes that gave away his location, the pilot would turn the landing light off and quickly vacate the area. An Air Force fixed wing gunship, often referred to as Puff the Magic Dragon, would be flying well above the helicopter with the capabilities to pummel the area with a variety of different munitions. When the helicopter was out of the way, the gunship would douse the area with a fatal barrage of bullets and other things that go bang, causing great death and destruction. Since enemy forces consisted of so many ad hoc groups of Viet Cong who were not intertwined with continuous communications and daily Intelligence Summaries, deemed INTSUMs by American forces, word just didn't get around between groups of bad guys that you shouldn't fire at helicopters that were flying around shining landing lights at areas below them. Besides, shooting upwards at a moving target is much more difficult than shooting downward from an aircraft at a fixed target. Advantage- Americans.

Feeling the need for a cup of coffee, I went down to the mess hall to listen to Cookie grumble about his problems du jour and see if I could coax him out of an impromptu meal. When I arrived at the mess hall Cookie was mopping floors.

"Glad to see you're keeping the Ritz Hotel Restaurant in shape," I said.

"It's always in shape," he replied.

"Got any box lunches?" I asked.

"You just come off a flight?" he grumbled.

"Yes I did, earlier in the day, but I really didn't because it wasn't official," I said with a smile.

"So, you did, or you didn't?" he retorted.

Cookie and I had been having this same conversation at nights for at least a year. He guarded the food as if he had paid for it. Box lunches were prepared for crewmembers who were working odd hours. He would poormouth me for a short but interminable period then finally give me something better than the stale sandwiches and dried up fruit, usually a banana, that was contained in the boxes.

Cookie was indeed Staff Sergeant Jose Emanuel, but everyone called him Cookie. He was a Puerto Rican transplant that had been in the Army for ten years. He had been in country for more than a year, deciding to stay beyond the normal tour of duty after discovering that his wife had found someone else to her liking. She had sent him a Dear John letter that detailed the sordid events of the marital misdemeanor. He had no children and was quick to agree to a divorce. He had received the sign-here-and-you're-free documents comprising a no-fault divorce, then signed and returned them after acknowledgement from his mother that his wife had delivered all of his personal property to her address in New York City.

Cookie was not the axiomatic, loquacious New Yorker. He could be, but most of the time he was quiet unless he was disturbed or having a fit over poor food preparation or cleanliness. My experience was that talking was a sport for garden variety Yankees and they could spend hours in petty conversation. Southern folk have a tendency to get to the point quickly. Conversely, Yankees will spend an hour getting there. Cookie didn't belabor anything. He was a man of precisely enough words. If you came in during the middle of the night, he would make you beg for your food then sit there next to you and watch you eat it without comment. You were forced to make conversation unless having someone sit quietly in the next seat and watch you eat didn't bother you. He had no friends that I knew of. Craig found a way to humor him from time to time, but that was Craig's style. James thought he was weird and Steve didn't care. I personally liked Cookie. It was a tough job he had and he did it well.

None of the cook's helpers who worked for him, which included several Vietnamese women, got a break. After being in numerous mess halls, I surmised that part of his basic course for cooks training included a section on how to run a mess hall with a restive and cantankerous personality. Cookie was a testy and misanthropic ruler in the kitchen with personality shades of Marquis de Sade and Genghis Kahn. Orders were snapped, and someone caught doing something wrong was hovered over and berated incessantly in such a way that the same mistake was never made twice. I asked him once why he was so hard on the troops. He said "Cleanliness."

He was right about that. Vietnam was not like America. Bacteria accumulated in ways and places like we had never seen. Hygiene was not at the top of the training schedule either. In fact, the 68th Assault Helicopter Company didn't have a training schedule. If we would have had one, it would have read- Monday through Sunday, Week 1: War; Monday thorough Sunday, Week 2: War, and so on. Any kind of training, including mess hall hygiene, was a personal responsibility.

Cookie had an immaculate mess hall and meant to keep it that way. If someone staggered in with greasy hands, they weren't getting fed until they cleaned up. Army deliveries of food supplies were maintained outside the mess hall in a storage building where they were removed from boxes before being brought into the mess hall. Cans and packaging material were cleaned and inspected and old delivery boxes were burned.

I laughed anew at his antics. "It's this way," I said. "What we did today we didn't do and if I have to tell you, some spooks may come in here and kill you."

"Oh," he said. "You were on that mercenary flight this morning. Yep, never heard a thing about it. What you want, spaghetti and meatballs or meatloaf?"

"I kind of had my heart set on some T-bone."

"Then you'll love the meatloaf."

I watched Cookie scramble to the kitchen and within seconds return with a tray of food. The meatloaf wasn't bad and the bread was great.

"Not bad," I said. "Especially the bread."

"Well now that I've trained a baker, we should be having a few things on the menu we haven't had before."

"Well, that's good to know," I said.

"The last baker I had was a Vietnamese girl from Saigon," he continued. "She fell in love with one of my helpers and they got married. I knew something was fishy cause they were always going back to that cooler together. You think that's clean, them back there fucking in the cooler? Hell no, it ain't. When they told me they were getting married, I told them that if they wanted to fuck each other's brains out they could use the mess truck, but wash up before they come back into the mess hall. I could smell both of them after that for two months or more until they left. Forget about it."

"Maybe you could smell them because you knew what they were doing," I said. It couldn't have been that, could it?"

"Nah…yeah, well maybe," he said thoughtfully. "Speaking of filth, Jennings was in here last night talking all kinds of extraneous crap about getting a transfer and how everybody was out to get him. What's his problem anyhow? He's always so tense about everything. I think the guy's having a nervous breakdown or something. Boy, he's got a case of the hips for you. Did you cross his path or something?"

"Nope," I said. I haven't had much to say to him since he got here. On one occasion he tried to jerk some of my guys around and I told him he was out of his jurisdiction and to back off, but beyond that we have successfully avoided each other." I think he's got problems, maybe at home or with a promotion, or something like that, perhaps. His anger is obvious, and it's also obvious that it's eating him up inside. Every time I see the first sergeant, he tells me that Jennings has been to him crying about something. I don't even pay any attention to the guy."

"He's really pissing off the troops," said Cookie. "I've overheard several conversations by the people that work for him and they are not happy with his attitude and the way he jerks them around. Somebody needs to get hold of this situation before it gets out of hand."

"Well," I said. "Until he crosses the line of decorum or breaks a regulation, there's nothing anyone can do."

I had finished my meal and knew I needed to drop by the operations building on the way back to the barracks. Officially, we were still on down time for at least another day, despite the unofficial flight that we didn't go on this morning. I would get an update from operations to see if things had changed.

"Cookie, what do you want me to do with this tray?" I asked.

"Nothing," he replied. "I'll take care of it."

I left the mess hall and walked slowly toward the operations building. Two black soldiers were standing near the entrance to the orderly room dapping. Dapping had become the new craze. To me it was like playing patty cakes and I couldn't really see the use of such a hand game to establish any form of ethnic pride. But I wasn't black, and didn't know the intricacies of its origin or meaning. Whatever works for you, I thought.

When I reached the operations building, I entered the door to find Arseneaux, the night operations clerk, on his knees in a straight back chair. He was thrusting his pelvis forward and backward. He didn't seem to be concerned with my presence and continued his exercise, if that's what it was.

"What, pray tell, are you doing?" I asked.

"It's an exercise," he said, huffing in a way that made me think he'd been doing it for some time. "It's supposed to build up the muscles that you need for sex and strengthen your core muscles at the same time. Mutual benefit. It'll make you stronger and give you endurance."

"And where did you hear about this?" I asked.

"From an article my brother sent me. He clipped it out of a magazine. It's called sexercise."

I just had to bite. "Does it work?"

"I don't know yet. This is the first night I've tried it."

"Well perhaps you could stop long enough to give me tomorrow's flight schedule," I said.

"Sure Sarge. I don't think there's anything on it for your platoon. Somebody's got to fly a III Corp chaplain around tomorrow to some field units, but aside from that there's nothing."

"Good," I said.

I looked over the flight schedule and saw nothing that concerned me, said thanks and left Arseneaux to his sexercise. On my way out he said he'd let me know if it improved his sex life. I told him that he needn't bother. I was sure that it would.

I took the scenic route back to my barracks, passing by the new latrine and paying a perfunctory visit. It was indeed a sight to behold, a great improvement over the community three-holers we had endured for some time. The new latrine had showers, real commodes and doors and walls between them to provide privacy not heretofore enjoyed. When the bathrooms were first constructed, everyone wrote on the walls. This can be attributed more to the uniqueness of the bathrooms in Vietnam and having the opportunity to scribe some catty little tidbit of lust and disgust just like you would in the "real world." The hieroglyphics and graffiti were not the same as those you'd see in America. The comments written on the walls were funny to some degree, a little offensive to people whose names were mentioned, but otherwise fairly innocuous. The first sergeant couldn't condone the destruction of government property and put up a sign that read: If you continue to write on the walls, the doors will be removed. Some bright soldier wrote underneath the first sergeant's warning: If we write on the doors, will you remove the walls.

I saw the Repair and Utilities (R&U) specialist, John England, taking a shower. We would all be happy about that. He was notorious for his body odor and wore it with pride. John was a person who would look unkempt and ragged with a makeover and a $500.00 tuxedo. The first night the latrine was constructed, he was threatened with bodily harm if he didn't take a shower. When England went to the shower after most had retired, James got his camera and perched atop a wash bowl to snap a picture of England over the partition that separated the wash bowl area from the showers. The bowl broke under his weight and James, his camera, and everything else went crashing to the floor. England was none the wiser and no one knew about this except James and me. I elected to keep my mouth shut. The war story was worth the bowl it cost the Army and we did get a picture of England that was anonymously posted in the company area.

The big artillery pieces were firing over our compound, and with the trajectory of the rounds coming over our heads, the noise of the weapons came with them. It was something to which you had to become accustomed. When the first sergeant was newly assigned and spent his first night in the barracks, the guns were particularly active. All of a sudden, he was standing at the foot of my bed with helmet and M-14 in hand, yelling "Run for your life, we're getting hit." My initial reaction was to jump up and grab my pants until I realized it was just the big artillery pieces from III Corp or the 173rd Airborne Brigade. In just a few moments the rookie first sergeant had flushed out half the barracks yelling insanely to take cover. It took me a while to convince him that it was alright to leave the confines of the sandbagged reinforced bunker built especially for enemy rocket attacks. After a few nights and a handful of No Doze, he eventually settled in and learned how to sleep through the noise like the rest of us.

There are a lot of psychological and physical trials and tribulations for new arrivals in Vietnam. What you eat and how you eat; what you wear and what you can't; when you sleep and how you sleep; how to deal with bugs, insects, snakes and flying cockroaches larger than Palmetto bugs; rotten crotch and jungle rot; and cleanliness and hopelessness, to name but a few. Some folks are "homesick to death" as expressed by a friend from Tennessee, and drive themselves crazy darkening in calendar dates as each day passes. They seem to have the longest tour. One of the gunners watched his watch closely, and at 12 a.m. or p.m. he would darken in the first or remaining half of the calendar date.

I approached the west door of the barracks where my room was located and heard the running footsteps of someone coming toward me. I stepped back to avoid being hit by the door. The figure ran past me clutching a helmet and flak vest. I recognized him as Sergeant Jennings from his red hair and burr cut. He was making those unmistakable whining noises that people make when they are really scared. He sped around the south side of the bunker and through its door into the darkness within. I ambled into my room thinking this event was not that extreme considering the tempo of the day, but had second thoughts once inside. I picked up my Army issue flashlight and walked to the door of the bunker. I hesitated briefly before entering the bunker as anyone would when there is a perceived need for caution.

"Jennings," I said. "Are you alright?"

When I got no response from within, I said again, "Jennings, are you in there?" Still nothing.

I shined the light immediately at the base of the door and let my feet catch up with the beam. Still a little cautious about going in until I knew Jennings' state of mind, I said again, "Jennings, are you in there?"

Finally, I got a reply. "Yes," he said in a strained voice.

I moved further into the bunker and could see him sitting in the corner clutching his knees to his chest with his head bent forward. I noted, gratefully, that he had no weapon.

"What are you doing in here," I asked?" "Are you OK?"

I got no answer and decided to just sit it out until he was ready to talk. This was a grown man who appeared to have all his mental faculties about him, and other than the fact he was a Class A asshole and purportedly a drunk, you would think that he would be much like the rest of us. I noted that his breathing came a little faster than usual which would indicate he was either out of breath from the sprint to the bunker, or he was under some kind of physical or mental stress. We sat motionless for some time except for his gentle rocking back and forth.

"I just can't take it," he said.

"Take what?"

"This whole place."

"What specifically do you mean?"

"I mean this whole place. Nobody seems to care about the people dying and lives being shattered, and the lives of wives and children being disrupted back in the states. Nobody seems to care about anything but blowing somebody's head off and getting laid, and drinking. This is a world gone mad. There is no sense of normalcy or morality here. There is nothing regimental about the way we get things accomplished. You don't know when and where those damn Charley rockets are going to fall. Hell, Charley could be coming over the wire right now. We've got Air Force patrols guarding the perimeter, and kids barely out of basic training are walking guard posts around helicopters to keep Charley from dropping grenades in the fuel tanks. Don't you see, it's just a matter of time before some or all of us get wasted. Those goddamn helicopters are flying coffins. Over in the bone yard there's a dozen or so that blew up or got blown away by enemy munitions or ground fire. There seems to be a complacent attitude about everything by everyone. I know the Bien Hoa airstrip and the old James Honour Compound were virtually destroyed before I got here. The Long Bien Ammo dump went up in smoke and Charley routinely kills ARVN troops all over the place. They just knocked out a VC checkpoint between here and Bien Het and someone almost became a prisoner of war not long ago in Bien Hoa. It is just a matter of time before something happens here or somewhere and I'm sure I'm going to be in the middle of it."

I let that sink in for a while and elected to let him amplify any more of the problems that seemed to be driving him mad. It was clear that Jennings had some deep-seated fears about being in Vietnam. I'm sure the head doctors had a detailed diagnosis for this kind of paranoia. I knew I didn't, and I also knew that regardless of what I thought I could do, this was something beyond a simple fix by a non-layman.

"You come out here often," I asked.

"Yes, almost every night. Most of the mortar attacks usually come between eleven at night and one in the morning. I don't want to get caught in the clear like so many others and get my head blown off on the way to the bunkers."

That comment caught me off guard. We had a few guys get banged up but rarely anything as serious as losing a head. Must have been a figure of speech, I thought.

I could see that he was crying now. The flashlight cast a shadow on a single solitary tear that rolled down his left cheek. He made no effort to wipe it away. He was still rocking back and forth and I detected a tic in his left cheek. Not good at all, I thought. This chap needs some help. I knew that in his present state he shouldn't be in a leadership position, and especially here where weapons abounded for very lethal reasons. I didn't smell alcohol on his breath but I could imagine that if he drank to excess, it was to abate the consciousness of this perceived, self-imposed dilemma from which he suffered.

I needed to find a way to ameliorate this situation and possibly calm him down, but I really wasn't sure how to do it. I had seen people crack before, but it was usually ephemeral, amounting to extreme anger or sorrow that played itself out in a matter of minutes. I didn't want to mention the drinking. That could set him off anew with other abnormal narratives.

Craig would know how to handle this. If I didn't get to him tonight, I'd do it in the morning. He could get him in to see Doc Quackenbush and unless the situation had changed by that time, they would probably call for the guys in the little white coats, as the expression goes. I didn't know if the Bien Hoa Army Hospital was set up to handle this kind of malady. Hell, they might have to send him back to the states. Then everybody's problems would be solved.

"Jennings," I said. "You can't do anything tonight about this problem. Try to get a good night's sleep and deal with it in the morning."

"What's to deal with," he responded. I got nine months to go. Might as well be a hundred."

Oops, I thought, there's that defeatist thingy again.

"Hey, I'll meet you for breakfast tomorrow," I said. "We'll talk about it some more.

"Nothing to talk about," he said.

"Well, I've got things to do tomorrow. Regardless, I'll see you then. I left Jennings in the dark and headed for my room. If Jennings was to follow, I didn't want him to know I was going to sic the doc on him. I waited around for another ten minutes or so and went to Craig's barracks. I related the story to Craig who was half asleep. He said he'd "jump on it tomorrow as soon as he saw Quackenbush."

I went back to my quarters and recapped the Jennings event. Being homesick wasn't all that unusual. I remembered when I first got in country and was living in a six-man tent. We had two guys that were criers. It was always at night. When everyone had gone to sleep, you could hear the soft but telltale sobs of one or the other crying softly. It was fairly well disguised but you knew what you heard. It usually lasted about ten minutes. I could never imagine what it was about or what caused it. Perhaps a girlfriend, or just missing the folks back home. It's hard to say, really. You don't condemn someone for the very human act of crying. Quite to the contrary, you can only be sympathetic and possibly a little jealous that there is someone so dear and so important that it precipitates that kind of reaction. Conversely, I can never remember being that profoundly sad. Quite distressingly, in most of my relationships, there had always been a preference to forget rather than remember, and little reason to cry.

I slept lightly that night. For some unexplained, out-of-character reason I was concerned about Jennings. I could not understand his misery, but it explained his attitude. The man was scared to death. I wondered whether he had spent the entire night in the bunker but I wasn't going to go poke my head inside to confirm my suspicions. He was way too fragile and I had an image of him holed up with a weapon ready to take a shot at anybody entering the door.

The next morning, I went to the mess hall. Emanuel wasn't there, but the on-duty cooks had prepared the basic fundamental breakfast. Breakfast was something that never changed. Supper could be a surprise, but breakfast was always eggs, a meat, toast and milk, coffee, and orange juice. Sometimes there would be farina, oatmeal or grits, but not always. I didn't see Jennings there, but I did see the first sergeant. I told him I'd drop by the orderly room later to talk about something. He grunted to acknowledge my comment. I went to the infirmary to talk to Craig who was conducting sick call. When he saw me he said, "Oh yeah, now I remember." I told him we'd talk later and proceeded toward the orderly room where I would speak with the first sergeant.

Top, as the first sergeant is called, meaning he is the ranking enlisted man in the company, leaned back in his chair when I strolled in to his office.

"What you got, Hardin," he asked.

I related the events of the night before, stating only the facts without passing judgment. Top didn't seem to be too terribly excited about Jennings' plight.

"Hell," he said. "I was just like that when I got here. For the first week I thought I was going to lose my mind. Hell, there ain't nothing unnatural about that. He'll get over it."

"I don't think so, Top," I said. "He's been here three months. He's driving the troops who work for him crazy and he's apparently an alcoholic. I get nothing but complaints about this guy."

"Well, I'll look into it," he said in a rather dismissive tone.

"Sure," I said in an equally dismissive tone.

"No shit. I will, Hardin."

"Fine," I said, and left the office.

I was wondering if Top's lack of concern about Jennings meant that he had found a brother in LaLa land as I walked away. I had done everything I could and that was the end of that as far as I was concerned. I would talk to Craig and see if Doc Quackenbush was going to do anything. Beyond that, we'd just to wait for Jennings to go bananas and run through the barracks area shooting holes in the sides of tents and buildings. Precedence had already been established for this kind of madness. We had picked up a transfer from the Wolfhounds of the 25th Infantry Division who came to us as a door gunner. He got drugged up one night and used his M-14 to shoot up the area. We never saw him again after that. Most likely he was either transferred to the US for trial, or spent time awaiting a court martial in the Bien Hoa Military Stockade. I was convinced that Jennings had reached the point of no return and some type of action should be taken to ensure that he couldn't hurt anyone, including himself.

I proceeded to the airstrip and stopped to check the work that our avionics team was doing to one of the slicks in my platoon. I had been there about ten minutes trying to help them do continuity checks on a weapons system when Craig approached.

"Glad I caught you," he said. "We've got a bit of a conundrum it seems. I told Doc Quackenbush about Jennings and he wants to see him right away. I went to see Top who says there is nothing to worry about. Top called Doc- he wouldn't talk to me. According to Doc, Top already got wind of this situation a couple of weeks ago and called Jennings in for counseling. The chief complaint, that Top was aware of, was Jennings' drinking and his abuse, for lack of a better term, of the troops when he was under the influence. Top used to be an alcoholic and told Jennings he could lick this thing if he put his heart and soul in it, and that he would help him through this precarious time of his life. So Top wants to play ranking Samaritan and get a warm and fuzzy feeling about saving a brother alkie. My guess is that Jennings has been without alcohol for some time now and is going through withdrawal, specifically the DTs. In his condition, he should be under the watchful eyes of psychiatric counselors trained to handle people so afflicted. Doc agrees and was prepared to tell Top to pound sand. He sent me in search of Jennings who- guess what? - is nowhere to be found."

 Just as I began to discuss the Jennings issue with Craig, a helicopter flew by us at a mere six feet off the ground toward an empty revetment some 100 feet away where I thought it would land and shut down. In the next second there was an explosion of sorts and between wincing from the initial crash and running to the other side of the parked helicopter where we stood, we could see that the aircraft that was attempting to park had struck a parked helicopter in the next revetment. Helicopter parts were flying everywhere and we initially took cover behind the aircraft we now stood behind. When I raised my head above the contour of the tail boom, I could see a rotor blade almost floating through the air in the direction of a barracks that sat about 75 yards away from the wrecked helicopter. After determining that there was no immediate fire or other danger to prevent us from assisting the victims of this tragedy, Craig and

I ran across the flight line to the downed helicopter. The rotor blades were gone and the helicopter stabilizer bar had broken loose and penetrated the top of the helicopter right at the back of the cockpit. Craig rushed to the pilot's side of the helicopter and opened the door. I peered inside the cockpit and saw the headless body of the pilot where the end of the stabilizer bar had decapitated him. Blood was shooting in a pulsating way from his neck and I watched what was left of his face slowly unfold downward from his neck to his chest. Finding this repulsive, I moved back instinctively and started looking for survivors. I ran to the other side of the helicopter and saw the crew chief bent over at the waist as if he was going to vomit. By this time the remaining pilot had exited the aircraft and walked beyond the revetment. I saw him throw his helmet down in angst or anger and rest his head in his hands. In a matter of minutes an accident and recovery team arrived. I watched in awe as Craig wrenched the hands of the dead pilot from the controls and took the lead in pulling him from the helicopter.

As I surveyed the area, I saw the undamaged helmet of the dead pilot, with visor intact, lying in front of the helicopter. The force of the stabilizer bar coming through the cockpit had exploded his head and thrown the helmet through the windshield. A crowd of at least 100 people had gathered, and from my vantage point near the helicopter I was suddenly staring into the shocked and sullen faces of pilots, crewmembers, and support personnel, many of whom realized for the very first time that this kind of tragedy can and does happen. You can die in Vietnam and it doesn't have to be in combat. Wanting to remember this moment forever and never wanting to forget those faces, I pulled a small 35-millimeter half frame camera from my pocket and began taking pictures.

As we found out afterwards, the pilot that died that day was new in country and was taken for a check ride by a seasoned pilot. Perhaps a small wind or a lapse in judgment caused him to strike the helicopter in the next revetment. I do not remember the pilot's names or the gore of the event, but the faces in the photographs are etched in my mind forever. And there are 100 people out there somewhere that remember it just as well as I. One of those hundred was Jennings whose face I saw in the back of the crowd.

The rest of the day was spent repairing helicopters that were hit with flying debris and cleaning up the accident site. Little thought was given to Jennings or any of the other duties that were typically handled as a matter of course. Later that day at the little PX we would commemorate and commiserate earlier events, and listen to Tom Jones sing The Green, Green Grass of Home.

CHAPTER 3

The little PX was filled when I finally arrived there after closing the platoon shack where all the gear was stored. Steve had checked out all the weapons with the armorer who replaced a few springs and inserted new spare barrels into the machinegun kit bags. We had just picked up two new soldiers from the states who had processed through Camp Alpha in Saigon and finally made their way to their first assignment. They were the rookies of the group and a lot of 19-year-old "old-timers" were filling them in with war stories and the dos and don'ts of the trade. James had taken the lead with the new guys, officially referred to as fucking new guys or FNGs. He was telling them about the events of yesterday. The facts were not exaggerated like they would be in a typical war story. It was what it was. It was a tragic story that was told with no mention of heroes. Every good war story has heroes. Aside from beginning with "Man, you are not going to believe this shit," they usually were elongated and packed with scintillating details that alluded to the heroics of the story teller. James was the head raconteur in this regard. He had the knack and the glib to portray these harrowing moments of combat, with minor degrees of camouflage, into a story that you could see vividly in the mind's eye. He always gave credit where it was due, and for that reason and the fact that he told them so well, people would ask him to recount events which qualified as war stories.

The FNGs were getting an ear full. It was clear from the looks on their awe-struck faces that they were somewhere between mesmerized and astonished with the incredible details. Fear would overcome them at some point. Their first day on the job, when they would find themselves strapped into a seat behind a machinegun in a helicopter that was lifting away from the comfort and security of Mother Earth, would be a day of butterflies, uncertainties and regrets. Their first near-disaster experience could be a momentary event that would last perhaps for seconds, but would remain in their hearts and souls for a life time. That event, and others like it, would test their mettle. It would speak to their intrepid nature, or devour their courage. Moreover, it would mean they could forever say that they had experienced the worst of times, and everything beyond that could only be better.

The FNGs would not be going on any missions any time soon. They would be put through a relatively new training program that would give them a chance to get over their fears and learn how to control their butterflies. They would spend a few days in the Maintenance shop working with the maintenance people fixing helicopters, then on to their assigned platoon where they would drag ammo and clean and inspect helicopters. As part of the platoon training program, they would be taught how to use a machinegun then taken up on some hairy rides where they would shoot at barrels and other prescribed targets. The pilots would do aerial dives, amounting to some gravity defying descents while the FNG fired at a target, and a few auto rotations to really get the blood flowing. At the end of the second or third day, if the FNG was not throwing up profusely, he would be ordained "good to go." While all of that training is paramount to success as a crew chief or door gunner, it does not include the real-life effects of someone shooting at you, or learning how to react to explosions in and around the aircraft, or having to kick someone off an aircraft, or administering first aid to someone bleeding to death at your feet, or a plethora of other things that are routinely experienced. These are all duties that are part of a process that can only be learned through experience. Obviously, the most important duty is to take care of the pilots. If you falter, they could die. If they die, you are dead.

A few minutes after I arrived at the little PX, Craig arrived. He lingered at the table where James had the full, undivided attention of the FNGs, listened for a few moments and then came to my table. Craig had undergone the gunner training and was well versed in the art of aerial combat techniques. He had done well as a gunner and didn't shy away from flying a mission, regardless of the impending complexities. He had seen his share of bad-guy, good-guy conflicts and if he had any fear, it didn't show. He was doing it for the thrill and the experience. In addition to being a seasoned door gunner, he was a talented medic and it was nice to know you had someone like him available when and if people were injured or needed medical care.

He made his way to the table and sat down. "FNGs huh?" he said.

"Yep," I replied. "Just arrived this morning."

"I haven't received their records yet," he said.

"They'll probably make the rounds tomorrow," I replied.

"Know anything about them?"

"Nope," I said. "Just that they're going to be very confused and bewildered for a few days."

"Tell me, Craig," I said. "How do you look down the throat of someone while the blood is squirting to beat the band without getting both queasy and deranged?"

"I look but I do not see. I touch but I do not feel. You just do it," he said.

"Better you than me," I said. "The blood and guts thing is just something I don't like to contend with. I guess you've got to be clinical about it. I wonder if I have a bona fide aversion to it or if I'm not more swayed by the catchphrase "but by the grace of God, there go I."

Craig smiled. "Death is without sensation but dying is quite another story. The act itself is demoralizing and overwhelmingly devastating," he said. "It is not fun to watch and even less fun to endure." And no one knows for sure what's on the other side of life. Therein lies the greatest fear. What say you? Is there anything hereafter?"

"I just don't know," I said. I was raised in the Baptist faith. I memorized and recited verses from the bible so I could go to summer camp every year in Elizabethton, Tennessee. I always had questions and certainly a lot of doubts. I never quite swallowed all the parables and stories told in the bible because to do so takes the same kind of faith it takes to believe in the Easter Bunny or Santa Claus. When my parents knew it was time for me to know better, I was told that the Easter Bunny and Santa Claus weren't real, but the parting of the Jordan River, Jesus ascending into the heavens, and feeding thousands with a few loaves and fishes were. If you can believe the biblical stories, you should be able to believe that the Easter Bunny can mass produce chicken eggs and Santa Claus can get a hell of a lot of toys in his sleigh, and certainly reindeer can fly as long as they can see where they're going thanks to Rudolph's red nose. Christianity is kind of like an insurance policy, isn't it? If you believe and there is a God, then you go to heaven. If you don't believe and there is a hell, then you go to hell."

Craig showed me the cross around his neck and said "I think that I believe in the evolution of Christian ethics, which are the basis for laws that preserve civilizations. A good illustration of this is the differences in the countries that have separation of church and state versus countries that don't. Americans and European democracies and their governments are free of religious oversight and direction. Conversely, Asian and Eastern countries aren't. The Middle East is a little more radical than Asia in this regard- women must cover their faces and walk behind a man in many places much the same as the bible dictates, they are stoned to death for crimes of the heart and people are ruthlessly murdered for crimes against religion. I think the Americans and Europeans have progressed and evolved more civilly than that. We put equality first, and have taken the Ten Commandments and expanded them to meet changing times and subtle swings in mores. The fact that we, as a heterogeneous group, have excelled socially, industrially, and technologically attests to the success we have had from separation of church and state. And I don't think it is blasphemy to say what history bears out."

"Is there a God," I asked? "Perhaps. Is there a heaven? I don't know. I just know what I know and believe most of what I see. I had faith in the tooth fairy, too. What a letdown that was. She was my only source of income for many years."

Craig took a sip of his beer and mulled over what I said. I really wasn't looking for a response and didn't care if I got one.

"It's a head game, I think," he said. "People believe what they want to believe and all of us believe a little differently. If you can have faith in a concept or idea, you can have faith in a religion or religious ideas. If you have faith that the sun will come up tomorrow, you can have faith in your religion and its teachings. If your church has been the continuous source of great rewards and good feelings, you will believe in religion. The church and religion are environmental and sensuous experiences that grow with you from childhood to adulthood. Those that progress in their faiths and beliefs do so at a rate of their choosing. God will always be real to those who believe he is real. God will never be real to those that cannot demonstrate the capacity to have faith or believe only what they can see."

"Is that a ding?" I asked.

"No, of course not," he replied. "It's only an opinion that may or may not hold water. I'm just playing the role of an opponent on a debating team."

"So, what is your stance or belief on the subject?"

"I'm not sure. I just heard what you said and looked at the flipside of the issue as it pertains to faith and beliefs."

"Surely, you must have some ideas or principles that you've considered," I said.

"Well, to begin with I don't believe that we make that trip into the heavens. I believe we are comforted with the idea that we will. I'm inclined to think that heaven is a long-standing parochial reward established by the religious sect du jour for believing. In that era there was little to look forward to unless you were royalty or part of the elite or illuminati. What was proposed was a life hereafter in a glorious heavenly arena with streets of gold and food aplenty. The opportunity to become a believer that there was such a place became the opium of the working class. I think you have to remember too that life was short and people died daily of disease and accidents. What was the average age? Maybe 33 or less. So why not believe in Shangri-La when you knew that it could or would be just around the corner?"

"A better question is how could anyone believe otherwise," I said.

Craig smiled. "Entre nous, they do because they believe what they want to believe. In the grand scheme of things, I think it plays into life and the interaction of men. There must always be points and counterpoints. There must always be different concepts and definitions of beauty, hate, happiness, and what's good, bad, and ugly. We cannot all think that only one woman is beautiful or one car is the best one, or one style of house is superior. Civilizations are built on the principle of supply and demand and the subtle juxtaposition of differences that exist between products, ideas, desires, ways of life and a host of other tangibles and intangibles that appease and impact homo sapiens. As a case in point, we are here in Vietnam because a lot of bad guys are whipping up on a lot of good guys in the name of communism, amounting to a perceived difference in a way of life and government. Our religions, specifically those practiced in America, suggest that freedom and democracy is rooted in the right to self-govern and that no country should invade another country to impose their will and way of government. That, in and of itself, is the impact of religion on government. We are using the Ten Commandments and the scriptures to formulate policy that is the basis for assisting another country in the defense of its borders. The twist is that we would not be engaged in this war if there wasn't a vested interest in its outcome and the extraordinary impact it would have on our way of life and religious beliefs on a long-term basis. Obviously, the subtitle for this war is "The Crusade to end Communism."

"Makes sense to me," I said. "When you think about it, the same was true in Korea and World War II and a variety of other places. The supposition, I guess, is that religion not only preserves civilization, but protects it and defends it as well. But protects and defends are probably subtitles of preservation. Yea verily, verily, this also suggests that we will be fighting religious-based wars ad infinitum."

"To use your words, yea vĕrily, and SELAH," said Craig.

"But something may loom on the horizon that will lessen the desire for everyone to kill each other," I added. "Foreign trade of industrialized goods and services may bring the believers and the non-believers together. Just as capitalism overcame certain no-noes of American based religions, such as the blue laws and prohibition of topless bars based upon superannuated indecent exposure laws, so to could that happen in China and Russia and other places. Time is of the essence in that regard, and time does not stand still."

Craig replied. "Yeah, but do increases in industrialized capabilities mean increases in the ability to wage war?"

"Only if a country is totally self-sufficient," I commented. "If Russia needs US aiming systems to make artillery pieces, and we need their steel to make our artillery tubes, then waging war becomes a complicated issue. That may be a little abridged in its simplicity, but indeed no man is an island and no country can stand alone."

"One thing for sure," said Craig. Relationships between countries where religious differences are excessively broad are as perplexing and fragile as jello nailed to a tree."

I laughed. "Now in summation, what did we solve?"

"I don't know," said Craig.

"Nor I," I said.

"Change the subject. What happened with Jennings?" I asked.

"Can't find him. He's nowhere to be seen."

"I saw him," I said. He was at the back of the crowd when the helicopter crashed today."

"That was probably not a great morale booster," said Craig.

"Could have put him over the top, don't you think?"

"I don't know, but it's likely that it could," said Craig. "Regardless of when he shows up, Doc wants him in his office. By the way, the night is young. I think I've heard all of the chatter I want to hear about this chopper crash. I need something to wash a few gory images out of my mind. Might go down to the ville for a respite from all of this Army stuff. You game?"

I looked at my Army issue, Elgin, OD green field watch, which always seemed to work as long as you wound it. It was 1930 hours. Without much hesitation I concluded that a change of environment might do me some good.

"Sure, why not, I said. "I'll check operations and see if anything has changed, pick up my pass at the orderly room and meet you at the infirmary in 15 minutes.

Nothing had changed on the schedule in Operations and Arseneaux hadn't come on duty yet so I wasn't blessed or privileged to watch him doing his sexercises. That was a relief.

I dropped by the orderly room and pulled my pass from its slot. The pass board was there to ensure the company could get in touch with you if they needed you quickly. If your pass wasn't there, it meant that it had been pulled for a reason, usually because you had been identified as a person not worthy of a pass because of some trouble you had caused or non-judicial punishment in the form of an article 15. You could also have venereal disease and the doctor may have quarantined you for a month, or the first sergeant had decided he wanted to know that you were close by for some reason. There was hell to pay if your pass wasn't there in the morning. That meant you were either still in the ville or forgot to return it to the slot. If you forgot to return it and the first sergeant had to send the company clerk to your quarters to see if you were present for duty, the pass went from the slot to the first sergeant's locked drawer for a week. If it was a second offense, it could be a lot longer. Nobody was exempt from these rules.

I met Craig at the infirmary. James was there too and decided to come with us after discussing our trek to the ville with Craig. Craig had arranged transportation with a medic who was going to the officers' billets in the city.

When we got near the Hope Bar and the driver knew it was safe, we slithered out of the vehicle and made our way to the entrance. Mamasan the beggar was there and I had a few dongs in my pocket, which I placed in her outstretched hands. Her teeth looked even blacker today from the beetle nut and I kidded with her about them, pointing to my teeth and giving her a thumbs up. She laughed and spoke in a slurred voice with words that I could not understand, which could be the result of too much beetle nut. I wondered if her teeth weren't being held together by the beetle nut. The gums had to be a mess, I thought. Perhaps one day her jaw would fall off but she would probably die before that happened. At least she would depart happy.

A few members of our unit were seated inside and as I approached their table, I could overhear them discussing the day's helicopter accident. One of them recognized Craig and began a conversation about his role in extracting the pilot. Neither Hoa or Fifi was there. Big Mama waved to acknowledge my arrival and Papasan was busy shelving Bamoui bas and storing ice behind the counter.

Ice was stored in 50-pound blocks because there were no coolers in the Hope Bar or anywhere else in Bien Hoa. Ice was procured from ice houses, where obviously there must have been coolers, and delivered by bicycle. Ice blocks always came with rice husks embedded in them. It was not unusual to take a sip of a drink then spit the husks out. It was just another peculiarity to which you grew accustomed. A logical approach to understanding the perils of drinking something with foreign objects in it was that the alcohol would kill whatever bugs, germs or bacteria lay within. I guess it was a valid approach because I'm still here.

James meandered over to the table I had chosen and began talking about the helicopter accident. We discussed it while Craig was making an effort to dislodge himself from any further conversation with several gunners who were intent on getting the ugliest of details. I sensed that he didn't want to discuss this any further and really wanted to wash it out of his mind. For him this was an unfortunate and ugly event that should have never happened. He had felt that it was his duty to pull this lifeless form from the helicopter and pry the hands from the control stick that were locked in a death grip. I didn't have to deal with that, but he did.

War and all that it entails is as preposterous as it is unavoidable, I thought. The cemeteries are full of its victims. Headstones and little white crosses reverently commemorate the annihilations of people because of beasts like Hitler. Others symbolize the defeat of ideologies like communism and fascism, and the demise of arrogant and evil governments that would impose hegemony over peoples and other governments using violent, depraved, and uncivilized methods. This war, like all others, attested to the will of a free people and their fervent desire for global freedom.

The death of a soldier in a combat zone, albeit heroic or otherwise, is still a casualty of war. It had been about eight hours since the death of the pilot, and somewhere back in the "real world" a chaplain or members of a survivor's assistance group was getting a call advising them that they would have to go to the home of the deceased and notify parents or a spouse that their loved one was not returning. The pain and grief for all concerned has to be unimaginable. I would rather be in Vietnam.

James commented that most of the conversation in the bar was about the accident. It is on the front burner today, I mused, but this is Vietnam and before the week was out, there could be another incident that would dwarf this one. Maybe that was one of the principal reasons I had been here as long as I had. The lows were few, the highs were many. Everything moved at mach speed and there was no such thing as mediocrity. We were all young, invincible, and unrealistically ignorant about how vulnerable we really were. Ah, youth. It is as marvelous and wondrous as it is fortuitously short.

Craig eventually made his way to the table and sat down without comment. Big Mama brought him a Bamouiba on the house. Dang, I thought, word does travel fast. Even Big Mama was aware of Craig's heroics and in her own quiet emotionless way acknowledged that she could pay tribute to his efforts. She didn't wait for a thanks. She simply put the beer on the table, said "no money, I give you," and left. We were not accustomed to this kind of treatment from Big Mama. She was usually all business, saying nothing beyond short prickly directives that kept the employees hopping.

"Well, what do you know," I joked. "Just when I thought she was Ho Chi Minh's daughter."

Craig muttered a rhetorical question, "Well just how did I manage to obtain celebrity status in her eyes?"

"Guess there's got to be a man of the hour and this is your hour," I said.

"James added, "Take advantage of the moment. These things don't happen often. No one has ever bought me a drink."

"Excusez moi, mon scoundrel," I interjected. "I have bought you several drinks. You get poor before pay day, remember?"

James replied, "Just a temporary shortfall in cash flow. I'll have my accountant call your accountant and straighten this mess out. I thought you wanted stock options. It's all a big mistake, an accounting error, I'm sure. Let's see, I've got you listed here in accounts payable. Not to worry."

James added rather lightheartedly, "We should take advantage of Craig's celebrity status. This is not an opportunity that comes along all too often."

"Not a good idea," I said. "Perhaps we should change the subject."

I could tell by Craig's demeanor that he was somewhat gloomy and growing rather tied of this whole affair based on what appeared to be a burgeoning insouciant attitude. He was just talked out and the continuous reliving of the day's events was just getting to be too much. Craig had a personality that was playfully entertaining and mischievous. In his mind, what he had done was hardly heroic; it was just something for which few had the stomach.

Craig went quiet for a while and buried himself in thought and a few long drinks from the bottle of Bamouiba. He eyed one of the girls curiously and watched her walk from the bar to the table. Then he turned his attention to people gliding around the black-toothed Mamasan at the front entrance as they entered the bar. I knew that this arcane, people-watching process was something with which only I, and perhaps James, would be familiar. It was a process that was the first step in Craig making a recovery from the mental stress under which he had labored. Craig and I, and sometimes James and Steve, were people observers and we would often find a fixed position and engage in creative wordplay regarding perceived notions about individuals based upon their attire, demeanor, and perceptible emotions.

"Look at the dark-haired GI that just walked through the door," said Craig. "He's a yankee."

"How so," I replied.

"The way he walks. He struts." Craig pointed out. "He walks with a lot of that New York confidence or hauteur. He thinks he's Mr. Wonderful and he never stops talking. He may try to put the move on one of the barflies but he'll have more fun bantering back and forth with them. He'll be unnecessarily rude and won't seem to have a care in the world. He'll be obnoxiously loud and demeaning to his friends, thinking quite incorrectly that they will think that's cool. He'll literally try to force or shame them into buying him a drink. He'll probably ask for something they don't have, like a Manhattan or Rob Roy.

"I have a bit of a different take," said James. "He's a jock from the Midwest or California. He's muscular enough for that to be true and he's been used to getting accolades for his physical prowess. He's the football, or maybe baseball, team captain. He's got a gold bracelet and high-profile watch which would indicate his need to standout in a crowd when he's not on the ball field and people don't know who he is."

"I take a different, yet similar approach," I said. "He could be from anywhere but likes to think he's part of the jet set or illuminati. In reality, he's probably a little withdrawn and tries to make up for it with an overabundance of panache and zeal. The jewelry is completely out of place, given that we are in Vietnam and the weather is not kind to the skin that lies beneath it, so it probably has a special meaning or was given to him by someone that is significant in his life. The optional take is that he was poor and never had anything and now he's making the big everything-is-relative bucks and truly thinks he is somebody. What would support this theory is if he had bad teeth or some other tell-tale sign that would indicate he was born with a rusty, rather than silver, spoon in his mouth."

"Hardin, you lose on this one," said Craig. The jungle boots are shiny, which means he just got in country. He's still wearing jewelry because he hasn't been here long enough to get the nasty stuff that accumulates under it."

"Then he's probably not a field soldier, although he could have just been reissued the boots because he wore out the old ones," I said. "Note that his sleeves are not just rolled up above the elbow. They are actually creased, as if he had taken an iron to them himself. Does our Mamasan iron a crease in your rolled up sleeves? No-no, never never! Could he be queer?"

"Not queer," James added. "Perhaps he's strange."

"Strange in a provocative way? A strange personality? Strange in what way?" I asked.

"Strange in an outlandish way," said James. "He looks as if he is too comfortable with everything. I expect him to walk over to the table and ask if we are enjoying the drinks. He's almost condescending in nature."

"Nope." said Craig. "His manner and gestures are more masculine than feminine. He likes to be a man among men, not a pansy among men. You're going down the wrong corridor."

"What about the guys at his table? I asked.

"Two are laughing with him and one is ominously sullen," said Craig.

"Then perhaps the sullen character is angry about something or put out with Mr.

Wonderful's antics?" I queried. Maybe that would account for Mr. Wonderful's demonstrable personality. He's actually aware of the fact that Mr. Sullen is indeed sullen, and his inflated personality, if that's what it is, is an effort to mask what would otherwise be an uncomfortable situation.

James laughed. "Nope, definitely not," he said. "Unless," he continued, everyone else at the table is. Maybe Mr. Sullen is a jilted lover, a stressed-out paramour who just caught him with another fag."

James raised his voice enough to be heard at their table some 15 feet away and said, "Hey you," as he pointed at Mr. Wonderful. "Are you from New York?"

"Yeah, Queens," he said in a New York accent. "How about you?"

"James gave him a thumbs up and said, "I'm from Jersey. I thought we were neighbors when I heard you speak."

"How long you been here?" asked James.

"About a week," he replied. I'm being assigned to MACV Team 97."

"Have a good tour," said James.

"You can count on it," said Mr. Wonderful in a cocky kind of way.

"That's one for me," said Craig.

"Yep, you win again," I replied.

"Where's team 97?" I asked.

"I believe they're in Ngui Ba Dinh," said James, "but I'm not sure. He better deposit his jewelry in the company safe before he goes there. I think Team 97 has been working with the Nungs and the Cambodes and some Civil Indigenous Units. He's liable to get killed for his watch. Man, that's an assignment I can live without. The few Americans that are stationed with 97 live in a concealed underground bunker when they're not in the field. Trust me, none of the comforts of home and a war story a day, if you live to tell them."

"He'll probably live," I said. "Do you know why?" I asked rhetorically. "One big reason- he's an asshole. Just think about it. Every asshole that has ever been a member of this unit has walked away unscathed with one exception, and that was Honeywell. And he really doesn't count because he was looking for it. He volunteered to take a bullet when he had that tiger painted on the nose of his aircraft. He wanted a silver star for his chest and one for his epaulet. On the other hand, look at the people who have died that were nice guys. We could sit here all day and rattle the names off, especially the ones that really went overboard to make a contribution. We've lain to rest four people who were flying when they were too short to fly. The moral of the story is- if you're an asshole, you're going to make it home."

"But don't get too gloomy yet," I added. "I've defined assholes and nice guys without mentioning the third and most important group. The last group is the larger group. They are neither assholes nor nice guys. They eventually go home to the real world because they don't push the envelope too far in any direction. They're content with meeting the demands of the job at hand. They take calculated risks when it is necessary, but know how to find a hole when it is too risky. They won't let a buddy down, but they'll concentrate more on keeping him out of harm's way than wondering how they're going to drag him out of a kill zone. They can easily identify the thin red line that exists between courage and caution. They are survivors. Now the question is, which one of us is not going to make it home?"

"To ask which one of us is a candidate certainly factors you into the equation," said James. "Do I detect a hint of uncertainty in your voice? "Is there a crack in Sir Galahad's armor? Is it possible that you're not invincible? Do you have an Achilles heel?"

"If I have a weakness, it's the friends I keep," I joked.

Craig laughed. "For the first 10 months we're here, we're all rearranging the chairs on the deck of the Titanic," he said. "For the last two months we should be standing next to the lifeboats. Aren't you pushing the envelope, as you mentioned? Don't you think that the law of averages has you winding up in a VA Hospital somewhere looking through mummy slits for eyes, or even worse, under one of those little white crosses in a military cemetery? There is an end to this, but is there an end for you?"

"The end is always at the opposite end of the beginning, isn't it" I said. "I'm cruising along somewhere in between. The certainty of life is that you must live it. We engineer our destiny and architect our fate as a part of the process. You don't have to spend all of our time in the fast lane, but I refuse to acquiesce to a mundane and safe existence that is devoid of rewards and excitement. We will always make decisions that we regret and do crazy things that we can't always live down, and this may be one of them. I watched my father work his butt off for years doing work that was really important to him. As a doctor and philosopher, he was admired, respected and adored by just about everyone that crossed his path. His favorite recollections were those of his involvement in WWII. He used to say that if he had it to do again, he would never have left his friends. He would have remained in Okinawa or the Japanese Islands until it was truly over. Now that I'm in a similar situation, I understand what he was talking about. It's not just history you're living. This, in due time, becomes a part of you that is a personal asset and part of your net worth. There must be something at the core of each of us that makes us feel worthwhile, makes us feel like contributors, makes us feel like there is a reason we are here. I just can't get up every morning and go to a job. Besides, I don't want a job; I want a way of life."

"Hardin, my man, you are as predictable as you are incorrigible," said James. I'm going back to the piney woods of New Jersey. I'm going to get myself a case of beer and sit on the front porch of my house and never give this place a second thought. I'm going to find me a woman like no other woman and I'm going to make her promise to never ask me a question about Vietnam, or anybody I shot at, or any of the other wild and crazy things I did here. If she does, I'll leave her for another beer-drinking woman who can handle me walking around in flip flops and cutoffs while I peel off major farts."

"Sounds like the more uppity types of trailer trash you're describing," said Craig.

James replied in a mock, southern hard-nosed accent. "To quote so many Army lifers, I couldn't care less."

"Probably my initial foolish sentiments as well," said Craig. "But I'll get over it."

"Life is all about pleasure," said James.

"Life is about worth," I retorted.

"Life is about being there when the good times roll," James replied.

"Life is about living through the hard times so you'll know and appreciate the good times," I countered.

Our "is-too is-not" conversation was interrupted by Mr. Wonderful who dropped by on his way out to say good bye to James. James was courteous and exchanged a few niceties with Mr. Wonderful and his companions.

"How come you don't sound like a Yankee," I asked James.

"Because I'm from the piney woods of New Jersey," he said. "We're kinda like the Cajuns of Louisiana. I guess we're viewed as rednecks or backwoods people. We try not to go to the big cities, but sometimes we make supply runs and encounter real Yankees."

"You're kidding," I said.

"Yeah, of course I'm kidding," he replied. "We do have our differences but it's more provincial than anything else. We just live outside of the rural areas and are privy to a different lifestyle. We call it a normal lifestyle."

We were interrupted by Steve who rushed through the door somewhat out of breath.

"I figured you guys were here," he said. "You're missing the action. Guess who's perched on top of the Buddhist Temple butt naked yelling all kinds of obscenities? Would you believe Jennings? The guy is drunk as a skunk and out of his mind. He's yelling if they don't stop this war he's going to jump."

"You gotta be kidding," I said.

James laughed. "I just have to see this," he said.

We left the Hope Bar and walked hurriedly down the street to the city square and made the turn east to the temple. A crowd had gathered at the base of the temple where Jennings sat on his heels much like a monkey does on a tree limb. He made quite a spectacle for the 100 or so people that had gathered below. He was perched about 40 feet above the ground looking absolutely preposterous. The military police were already there and were trying to coax him down. Occasionally he would stand and yell something almost incoherent and then move back to the squatting position.

Jennings, you fool, I thought, why am I not surprised? Obviously, the booze had gotten to him and he had lost it. The military police were becoming exhausted with trying to reason with him. When the MP in charge would say anything to him, he would resume a standing position yell back an obscenity that none of us could make out. "Fuck you" came through loud and clear a few times. His voice was garbled with the fuzzy sound that is obvious with people who have had too much to drink.

I wondered if he even knew where he was and what was going on. It could be possible that a freelance photographer would hear of the disturbance and observe this indecorous event. Pictures of Jennings sitting naked on top of a Buddhist Temple would give Jennings and the US a derogatory view that would send tremors through General Westmoreland's Headquarters. Some poor overworked information officer would be jumping through his butt trying to control the media while he jockeyed to get pejorative information that would explain Jennings' rather ugly display. The fact that he was perched naked atop a religious shrine could also portray a religious effrontery to Buddhists worldwide and provide yet another potent issue for anti-war pundits to repine and whine about via national and international media. The lust for alcohol would obviously be the touted forerunner for this event and it would be aptly reported to the press.

The front door to the temple opened and a Buddhist monk came outside to look upward as if he had just received the news of someone on the roof. With a glance upward he acknowledged that someone was there and his face attained that oh-shit-look of abject surprise. He hurried back into the temple and was quickly followed by several other monks who chattered briefly then scurried back into the temple.

From the look on Jennings' face, I gathered that he was vacillating between anger and sorrow. Tears streamed down his ruddy face then fell to lithe but muscular legs. I almost wished at times that he would remain standing. When he squatted his testicles hung lower than his ankles, giving him an out of scale appearance that was hardly photogenic and certainly not suitable for the military's image. His footing wasn't that secure and he labored to resituate his weight to keep from falling.

Craig said, "Damn. Isn't that something?"

I replied, "Is there anything you can do?"

"Not until he falls" he replied. "My expertise is with patching the human body. Hope he doesn't fall. I'd truly hate to give that bastard mouth to mouth. Let's see, do you blow or suck? It escapes me."

The crowd was growing and I knew we would soon be a mix of news people, on-lookers and representatives of the installation commander's office and their retinues. The longer this damning situation prevailed, the more complex it was going to become for everyone concerned.

Much to our amazement, Jennings ended it. He rose from his squatted position to a standing position and looked around as though he was confused. From the look on his face, his thoughts appeared to be "Damn, what am I doing here?" or "Is this a bad dream?" It may well have been the alcohol wearing off, I thought. He turned as if he was trying to find a way down, then took an awkward, unsteady step and fell 40 feet to the ground below. It wasn't a dive and clearly something not done on purpose, nonetheless, he plummeted to the ground below. The body fell like a sack of flower. It didn't bounce and there was no indication that Jennings was even conscious when he hit the ground. He lay perfectly still and made no attempt to move. I could not tell whether he was alive or not.

Craig moved forward rather quickly to survey the damage and do what he could. The monks came outside again briefly and hurried back inside, almost as if there was some religious taboo that prevented them from viewing the body.

By this time, medical personnel had arrived from the Bien Hoa hospital and Craig was joined by other medics who were tending to Jennings. Within seconds, Jennings was placed on a stretcher and removed from the scene. I saw a chaplain, with what appeared to be an interpreter at his side, enter the temple.

James had been quiet since we arrived there and through the crowd to where I stood. "Is he dead?" he asked.

"I don't know," I responded. "I couldn't tell if he landed on his head or not. There didn't seem to be a lot of blood, not that it means anything. Did you see him fall?"

"No," said James. "I saw him at the top but the landing was blocked."

I took exception to his use of the term "landing." "That was a landing?"

He grinned a half-smile. "First word that came to mind."

"Close enough," I said.

Craig came back to where we were standing. I watched him weave through the crowd of the little people he towered over.

"Is he dead?" I asked.

"No," he said. But he will be by the time they get him to the hospital. He landed on concrete, or something close to it. He was barely breathing. The alcohol poisoning combined with what appears to be a collapsed lung will send him to the big happy hunting ground in the sky. I don't think he knew where he was or what was going on when he fell. Totally discombobulated."

"Discombobulated!" I said. "Is that a medical term?"

"Nope," Craig replied. "But I like it better than comatose, hallucinatory, wacko, or coo-coo, which is a very scientific term."

It struck me then that we were standing in a crowd. There were all kinds of edicts out on avoiding areas where people congregated. From time to time, Charley would plant a bomb that he could detonate in large crowds, especially if there were enough GIs within it.

"Hey, we better move out of the area. There are too many people here," I said.

We began walking back toward the Hope Bar when a military police vehicle passed. The sergeant in the passenger side was telling people to get back to the base. We continued by the Hope Bar where Hoa, Fifi and several other girls stood outside waving to passersby.

"You go back?" asked Hoa as I passed.

"Yes, I said. "See you in a few days, or when I can."

In other similar instances Hoa had stood at the door of the

Hope Bar waving to friends and customers who were being recalled to post. She knew that the typical reaction to this kind of event would be for the military to put the town off limits until they got a grip on the situation that led to Jennings fall from the temple. The base would have to ascertain the amount of damage control that would be required and take immediate action to put it asunder.

There was a forlorn look on her face, a look I had seen before. It was a look of momentary sadness that went away as fast as it arrived. It could not destroy her from within and she refused to let it. Her life was an amorphous array of ostentatious events, filled with requirements for surrendering human values and making great personal sacrifices. She had done well at controlling those that she could. Her small but fragile world was restricted to a never-ending concern for security. Hope and happiness were always dwarfed by the need to survive.

We eventually caught a ride from a passing company vehicle that was headed back to the company area. The streets were fairly active with people walking back to the base and I found it odd watching everyone walking en masse in that direction. No one was stopping at Papasans at the mobile horse-drawn deli to buy super slopes, and girls of the evening who would have otherwise been looking for clients stood idly by without making the usual noisy solicitations.

The unit area was active. I saw several men drawing C-rations from the mess hall which meant that someone was going on an extended mission that would keep them away from Bien Hoa for a while. I jumped out of the back of the old Army five quarter and headed for operations. Arseneaux was the evening Ops man on duty and he was quick to tell me how marvelous the sexercise was and how he thought it would extend his performance. I mumbled something about how great that was and asked him if anything had changed with the unit schedule. What was supposed to be down time for the last two days had turned into a very active time and I was beginning to wonder if we could ever count on having two or three days when we wouldn't get extraordinary missions.

"Everything has changed," said Arseneaux. "The First Platoon has a MACV mission that will take them away indefinitely, the third platoon has a milk run and two special ops support missions, and you guys are going to Cu Chi in support of the 25th. The gun ships will be on station for the Cu Chi trip. Take off is at 0400 hours tomorrow morning."

Dang, I said to myself. Good ole Hobo Woods. As the expression goes, I'd rather sexually molest a lion in a phone booth than go to Hobo Woods. But we were going tomorrow. If there ever was a time when I thought I wasn't invincible, it was when we were on short final to Hobo Woods. It was a 30-minute trip to Cu Chi so I could easily surmise, and maybe incorrectly, that we were going to be part of an early morning insertion. In the past we had dropped off two-man reconnaissance teams before dawn in the middle of nowhere. You didn't say "Good luck" to these fellows. They had already run out of luck when they got picked to do the recons. You'd say something less poignant like "See you on the flipside" meaning we'll be back to pick you up.

Hobo Woods was Charley country. He had tunnels and well concealed observation and listening posts in every nook and cranny of the jungle. Reconning this area was not a proverbial walk in the park. Even when the area was prepped with B52 bombing runs, which left in their wake 60-foot craters, we would see movement in the area and receive ground fire. Crashing a helicopter in Hobo woods was anathema for pilots and their crews. If you survived the crash and weren't able to be extracted quickly, it was a sure bet that Charley would be closing in to kill survivors and pick the helicopter clean of weapons and equipment.

I had mentally rehearsed the actions to be taken in the event the helicopter went down. After making sure you were in one piece, you verified the health and wellbeing of the rest of the crew, got your weapon and as much ammunition as you could safely carry, grabbed your canteen and a box of C-rations, grabbed the survival kit, which contained a UHF radio that provided a radio signal of your location, and selected a route of departure that provided immediate cover and concealment. After that you had another plethora of decisions to make based upon the condition and experience of the crew and the actual or perceived immediate threat. There was little to perceive about the threat in Hobo Woods. You had minutes to clear the area and even fewer minutes to find a good place to hide. Any protracted movement would give your location away. Any movement whatsoever would have to be at night through areas that Charley knew intimately.

I got the tail numbers of the three helicopters that were going and contacted the crews to make sure they were prepared to fly. I walked to the flight line and checked the log books to ensure there were no maintenance problems that had been overlooked. One Helicopter was having avionics gear replaced. It was something simple and there was no chance that it could be redlined before the morning. I felt confident that we were ready for tomorrow's mission.

I dropped by the orderly room and found the first sergeant and clerk. The first sergeant was thumbing through the Personnel Data Card files looking for Jennings' home address in the US.

"Any word on Jennings?" I asked.

"Yeah, he's dead," said the first sergeant. "I told the son-of-a-bitch that if he didn't quit drinking, it was gonna kill him. He just wouldn't listen. He was doing real good, too. He had been on the wagon for a couple of weeks and I really thought he was going to straighten up and fly right. Hell, I don't know what more I could have done for the guy."

"Sorry to hear that," I said. "Anything I can do?"

Top appeared agitated. "No, there's nothing anybody can do now. But you do have to give me a statement about what you saw today at the temple. The MPs say they need that to close the book on this incident. So, better get it to me by morning."

"Sure," I replied. "I'll put it on your desk tonight before I hit the rack."

I didn't mention that there were others there that could have provided statements. It seemed rather cut and dried to me. It would be deemed an accidental death suffered from a fall. The report that went to his wife would probably not give the embarrassing details of the naked inglorious display that led to his death and would probably not include the fact that he was aping a gargoyle and about as drunk as you can get without passing out. Some things are better not said. While the dead rest in peace, the survivors should morn in peace.

I wondered if the first sergeant assumed any of the blame for Jennings' death. He was certainly in a position to have him hospitalized where professionals could have dealt with his alcoholism. Surely, the first sergeant must have felt that he misjudged the severity of Jennings' alcoholism and felt some modicum of responsibility. Based upon his discussion with Doc, he had taken it upon himself to "reform him and get him back on track." He had rebuked the efforts of the doctor and dismissed the comments of several people who had brought Jennings' problem to him in an effort to get him assistance.

It had been an active day, both on the airstrip and in the city. I went back to my room and finished the rather matter of fact statement amounting to what I had observed. I left out the parts that addressed the first sergeant and his lack of effort to execute actions that may have saved Jennings' life. That was merely superfluous information now and wouldn't change the fatal outcome. A chronicle of all the regretful details and missed opportunities would do little more than exacerbate this tragedy and extend the pain and suffering for those who would always have unanswered questions.

CHAPTER 4

The next morning was uneventful. The charge of quarters had awoken everyone and I double checked to make sure that the crews were up and moving. James was a proverbial sleepyhead and it often took a second well aimed nudge or wet rag to get him going in the right direction, but today no such antics were required. The pilots were dragging after a night of glee in the officer's lounge mentioning something about Lum and a few others making a scene of sorts. It was good that they could enjoy themselves occasionally.

The life they lead was not an easy one and the responsibilities were huge. Many of them were very young and it wasn't unusual to see a 21- or 22-year-old pilot. They were usually warrant officers who entered the Army on specially tailored flight training programs that graduated them as aviators and warrant officers simultaneously. As all warrant officers are, they were specialist, trained to do a specific task. Commissioned officers had leadership responsibilities and were destined to be unit commanders and staff officers. The usual hauteur noted between captains and colonels was not usually exhibited between warrants and lieutenants. The day may start with a casual salute to signify that the difference in ranks was noted but once the flight helmets went on and the engine was started, such courtesies were set aside.

All three aircraft left the flight line at 0400 and two gunships flanked us to the rear. I watched the lights of Bien Hoa flickering below us as we flew over. I could see the road running by the Hope Bar and the temple where Jennings had taken his dive. No dogs, this morning, I noted. I guessed that even they get lazy. The square was lit up a little brighter than usual and I got a glimpse of somebody pulling a cart of goods from south to north. He was probably headed for the market place where everybody went to get their food for the day.

Vietnamese homes did not have refrigerators and air conditioning or any of the other features found in most American homes. As a result, daily trips had to be made to the city market place to purchase food. Foods that could be maintained in homes without refrigeration were either dried or smoked, or canned in a way that they could be used over a two- or three-day span. Of course, the main staple was rice, which could be prepared easily over a cooking fire. That was eaten with every meal, occasionally with meat, which usually consisted of chicken or duck.

The whop-whop sound of the rotor blades at this early hour had the effect of a sleeping pill. I buttoned my field jacket at the neck to restrict the flow of air onto the chest and neck area and the warmth was much the same as the old downy comforter I was accustomed to pulling over me when I went to have a sleep over at a friend's house at the age of ten. The only heat in the old farm house was provided by a pot-bellied stove on the first floor. My friend, Jimmy Cardwell, and I slept in his upstairs bedroom. There was no heat source there and we would scurry from the down stairs shower room to the upstairs bedroom to jump under the covers. Within seconds the comforter would have you "snug as a bug in a rug" as Papa

Cardwell used to say, and the sandman would come quickly to whisk you away to the land of slumber. I got that same feeling in the helicopter, especially when I pulled the bullet proof breast plate close to me for additional warmth. The cockpit and instrument panel lights provided a flickering display of muted red and green that added to the surreal and calming moment. These solemn early morning occasions were set aside for remembering great things that were important to me and for engaging in self-debates about people or issues that I had not been able to resolve. The combination of darkness and flight-induced serenity seemed to catapult me back in time, and to places that became exceptionally vivid and almost lifelike. I could tiptoe through my rolodex of memories and pick whoever or whatever I wanted to remember much the same as selecting your own TV program without the interruption of commercials. It was a refreshing period for me that was often rewarding and often not, depending on the subject I chose to address and whether I was comfortable with the outcome of my memories.

Lately, I had been inclined to think about my parents and brother. My brother and I were a strange lot. We were separated from our parents at an early age and adopted by a doctor and is wife. There was another brother that was barely a year old who was sent to another home. We knew nothing about him at the time. I say we were a strange lot because we were. We were confused about who we were and although we were young and intellectually pliable, we were inextricably from another culture that was not on a keel with that of our adopted parents. Blood is indeed thicker than water and the genes leave an indelible signature that is hard to erase. Both he and I were learning that at the time but neither of us knew it. We didn't know if the little-known elements of where we came from were responsible for ever burgeoning character flaws.

My adopted father had been tops in his field of medicine and tops in just about anything with which he elected to get involved. He had been the youngest graduate of his medical class, a high school and college football and baseball player, and had boxed his way through medical school as a lightweight professional fighter. He was as tough intellectually as he was physically and he could not abide quitters and losers. He was a man of great intellectual wealth that had the ability to express himself with admirable oration, but loved the simple expressions that carried direct and profound messages. "Don't do it unless you're going to do it right," he would say with a cigar holder and Havana clenched between his teeth. "Anything that's good, hurts," he would say with a determined and menacing glower. "Any mistake you make that feels like it's just too good to make once, is the one you don't want to make the first time," he would say with a grin and a smirk. When we had some lame excuse about where we had been or what we had done and it was clear that we were being less than truthful, he would say "You're not going to get anywhere with that line. It's like trying to feel your way around in a nudist camp when the lights go out. You're always going to be wrong." He had his faults when he was younger. He drank heavily when his war, WWII, was over. He would down several glasses of scotch then go out on the town. According to my aunt, he came to her house in Cincinnati upon his return from Okinawa and drank himself into a stupor, then left the house and came back three days later with a new wife. The marriage lasted about three months. There was a time when other doctors in the community threatened to recommend to the American Medical Association that his license be pulled if he did not quit drinking. As the story is told, he did quit, abruptly and with little fanfare. There was no Alcoholics Anonymous or withdrawal program; he just quit. That was his style…just get it done.

He was a workaholic when the term wasn't recognized as a medical malady. He was by all accounts in that era, very dedicated. Consequently, we did not see him a lot, and his evening hours were devoted to reading medical journals and preparing for the next day's operations or procedures.

My mother was the prefect doctor's wife who had an iron-clad constitution about ethics and behavior. I heard her say "damn" once in my life and rarely ever saw her lose her temper. She was the consummate southern bell who always gave the best accounts of her family and circumstances. She had learned to hold a grudge, and maybe that was warranted, because my brother and I had gone in directions that were contrary to her plans.

My brother and I were diligently protected from the dredges of society and as a result we were not allowed to do anything that would "bring discredit or shame to the family name." That meant too that we could not do the variety of things that other kids in our community could. We were over protected and restricted from staying out after 9:30 pm. That included after football games that I played in as a member of the varsity high school team, riding bicycles on the roadways, and just about anything else that other kids could do with little restraint.

There had been an abrupt end to our relations with our parents. My brother, Danny, had elected to get married and drop out of school and I had married at the tender age of 15 after running away from home over issues related to being able to have the same freedoms as other children my age. In the process I had made some horrific mistakes that lived with me for years. When I ran out of money, I committed a series of petty thefts. Of course, I was caught and sentenced to a juvenile delinquency facility, probably with my father's approval. I escaped and was recaptured before being finally set free eight months later to make it totally on my own. It was a phase I went through. In my reality-challenged state, I believed I was impervious to the law and social mores, and it took about three years of hitting life's-lessons walls to discover that wasn't true. My parents were both livid and hurt by this reprehensible behavior, as they should have been.

Somewhere along the way I had just flipped out. I don't know how or why, but I did. Probably genetics; that genealogy thing. I have no idea what makes a 14- or 15-year-old person depart from reality in such a way that he cannot be told anything, or is devoid of the capability to listen to reason or the voice of wisdom. I just don't know.

I was introduced to the Army by a judge in Baltimore. I resided with a friend, Steve, and his family in Bowley's Quarters on the Chesapeake Bay. The next-door neighbor often called the police when we had parties that were loud and lasted long hours into the night. The police were generally nice enough, opting to give us the opportunity to take the party inside and tone down the music. A mutual resentment had developed between us and our neighbor and we were always looking for some form of sweet revenge. One evening after Steve and I drank ourselves into a stupor, we took the neighbor's tires off of his new thunderbird, placing cement blocks under the rimless drums. We hid in the woods and watched him walk to the car the following morning with coffee in one hand and newspaper in the other. Not realizing that his car was tireless, he seated himself behind the wheel and drove it unceremoniously off the blocks. He didn't think it was nearly as humorous as we did and the police didn't either. Of course, the police knew exactly where to come to round up the usual suspects. We surrendered the tires to the responding police officer and were booked with malicious mischief or some related offense. The judge suggested we would be better off in the uniformed services than on a chain gang. We couldn't help but agree with him.

Steve failed the Me Tarzan- You Jane entrance exam, but I passed in flying colors. Indubitably, the Army was just what I needed. It is an institution that has a way of making you listen and getting your undivided attention. They are in the business of making men out of boys and are especially well-experienced in the art. There were iron-clad consequences for bad conduct and failure to obey orders and I had learned the hard way. Platoon sergeants and Field First Sergeants were specialists in adjusting behavior and I had mine adjusted, both mentally and physically, many, many times. I had made the transition from child to man. Oh sure, there were a few judgment problems that lingered, but I attribute those to the innate imperfections and natural defects common to most men.

Ultimately, I had become a responsible person who was capable of being responsible for others. Quite simplistically, that is what the Army calls leadership. I learned quickly that being a leader comes with a price. It is hard work and long hours, and the greater the rank, the greater the responsibilities. It requires great listening and interpreting skills. It demands a dogged sense of enthusiasm when all the enthusiasm is gone and total devotion to the task. It means you protect and defend those you are responsible for even when they don't always deserve it.

I wanted my family, especially my father, to know that I had cast aside my childish ways and taken a meaningful direction in my life. Not being able to find a way to convince them of this had become a burdensome cross to bear. I yearned for the time that I could return home and say "I'm sorry for the hell I put you through" and hear them say "We forgive you." I knew that my successes alone would not be an admission ticket back into the family. A chest full of ribbons and a half dozen combat stripes on the sleeve of my uniform would help, but my father would look into my soul with glowering eyes to see what lay there while my mother would look into my heart. It would be an interpersonal inspection for which the only preparation would be good deeds and a sincere desire to be a good person.

I wrote letters home every four or five days. Occasionally, I would get a response. My father had written me a letter that I read in the latrine that still had walls between the johns, before making the morning trek to the flight line. I had told him in a letter written the month before that I was trying to get an R&R out of country for two weeks to see Japan or possibly Hong Kong. He had responded by saying "If you get to Japan, ask the Geisha Girls if they remember me, and by the way, don't tell your mother about this." Such a comment was uncharacteristic of my father. Was it intended to thaw the ice? In the last paragraph he said "You need to come home." There was no explanation, no rationalization, no reason, just- you need to come home. I took the comment to mean that I would be welcomed back. Of course, there would be my mother to deal with, but mothers can never turn their backs on you forever. I think God made it that way intentionally to ensure there would always be a clear path and a gate unlocked for wayward children.

I would pen a response to his letter tonight, paying careful attention to write a message between the lines that would respond to his comment about Geisha girls in such a way that my mother would not, at first glance, understand the communiqué. You had to be very careful with such undertakings. My mother made the daily trip to the mailbox so she would be the first to examine the letter with the APO San Francisco return address. She was smart enough to ask questions in the inquisitive mode, and also smart enough to know when questions should not be asked. I would probably not get the encoded missive by her completely, but she would most likely let this one slip through with a quick review. I could picture her saying to herself, "That scallywag is up to his old shenanigans." And she would be right, but these shenanigans were well-intentioned shenanigans meant to repair the cornerstone of a relationship between a father and a son. She might even smile when she read it, and laugh to herself when she dropped it on my father's lap.

The co-pilot, Warrant Officer Montgomery, who was commonly referred to as Mouse, jarred me back to reality with a comment regarding the traffic control tower at the 25th Infantry Landing Strip. "Damn," he said. "Do they have to shine that flood light right in our eyes while we're trying to land?"

The tower light flashed across the nose of our helicopter several times as we approached. Mouse had already made contact with the tower operator to let them know we were on short final, and other than to acknowledge that they had you in their sights, the light did little more than cause a nuisance when trying to land. Mouse didn't realize that he was still talking on their frequency when he made his comment. A sheepish reply came back from the tower "Sorry about that, Tiger 26."

Mouse replied with an emotionless ho-hum reply. "No problem, control tower."

All five helicopters sat down on the strip and shut down the engines. Steve and I jumped out and opened the pilots' doors. I could see a small group of men standing near the base of the tower. Three of the men were dressed in camouflaged fatigues with a small pattern much like the Koreans wore, or some of the rag tag mercenaries who seemed to dress in anything that came close to resembling fatigues. The mercenaries typically wore fatigues that were similar, but different enough to make one believe they were required to bring their own rather than have them issued from a common source. Subtle differences in uniforms could be problematic when you were trying to distinguish good guy from bad guy during combat situations. Although it was rarely aired, there were a number of "friendly casualties," which was the term used to mean good guy shooting another good guy accidentally.

By this time the group at the base of the tower was drinking coffee and they seemed to be rather jocular about something. Steve and I opened our canteen coffee we had obtained in the mess hall. It was cool by this time, but still warm enough to drink. I was frequently aggravated by some of the pilots who seemed to forget they had crews when they were being presented with food or drink while their crews stood just feet away. Such discourteous and unmannerly actions have nothing to do with rank, but it does have something to do with being a gentleman and having a little compassion for those less fortunate "enlisted swine" that protect and defend you. An officer is ordained by act of congress with the understanding that you will conduct yourself as "an officer and a gentleman." I made a note to myself that if I ever was commissioned, I would remember that one must act as congress has ordained, indeed like a gentleman.

The group moved to the helicopters where we discussed the morning's mission. We were not lifting elements of the 25th Infantry; we were taking in what appeared to be military trained civilians who could have any number of government or military associations. Often, these folks were members of Provencial Regional Units (PRU) or elements that had associations with the CIA or other specially designed alphabet units that collected intelligence. There was always a search underway for North Vietnamese and Viet Cong elements of COSVN, Central Operations of South Vietnam, believed to be in Cambodia and/ or just inside the Vietnam border near the Parrot's beak that jutted east into Vietnam. Consequently, many people went into the jungle looking for runners or document carriers that could be captured and tortured into giving information about COSVN's whereabouts or plans and stratagems. It was a risky profession, but one that was necessary.

Today's plan was that two empty helicopters with gunships flanking them would maintain an altitude of 500 feet in an effort to attract the attention of Charlie and his compatriots. They would maintain this altitude and fly around and about for six or seven kilometers making sure that their movement and intentions to land would be obvious. They would do a quick landing, commonly referred to as a touch and go, without making an insertion. By the time they were on short final to the pre-selected LZ, we would be dropping off all three personnel in another LZ about 3 kilometers to the north. The three Intel operatives we dropped off would reconnoiter the area and determine if it was safe to move away from the LZ. This type of plan only worked when the military intelligence types felt at there was good reason to believe that a particular area was devoid of any major enemy troop strengths. The area was prepped with artillery fire off and on for several days making it a hot zone for the enemy. People sniffers were dropped to determine how much movement was going on in the area and radar units would set up monitors to detect any foot traffic in the area. There were other functional kinds of equipment that could be used but they are classified systems that shouldn't be discussed. After the insertion was made, movement by the personnel inserted had to be quick and deliberate to get to checkpoints where their route of travel could be calculated by ground control elements. If responses weren't coming in as prescheduled by the ground maneuvering elements, decisions would have to be made as to what needed to be done to make an extraction. If all contact was lost, little could be done. Sending additional people into the jungle to find those that had been killed or captured was, in the vernacular, spending good money after bad. You got a sick feeling when that happened and helicopters would remain nearby for some time in the event contact with the maneuvering elements was made and a pickup could be accomplished.

We got everybody on board and started the engines. My helicopter had been designated as the one to carry the three personnel, which gave me reason to be concerned because we would be going in without gunship protection. The order was for negative suppression of the area, even if we received fire, until such time as the Ops center running the operation approved it. I pulled my finger out of the trigger housing to prevent myself from accidentally discharging a round in defiance of the negative suppression order.

We were initially trailing the other helicopters and once we were given the signal, we broke off and moved to the north as if to completely separate ourselves from the intended mission of the other two slicks with flanking gunships. Within minutes the other helicopters were gone and feelings of loneliness and helplessness crept over me. Night lights were on inside the helicopter cabin and the pilot was checking the decca position map to see exactly where we were and where we would have to set down. These were tenuous moments for a plethora of reasons. We were flying on an azimuth to get to a location where we assumed we could land. We were going to spear our way through triple canopy trees into a small clearing that was probably just big enough to get into and out of with little room for error. Unless it was absolutely necessary, we would not use a landing light and we would not put the skids down. Our passengers would probably use a pinpoint flashlight to get an idea of how far above the ground we were and jump at the appropriate time. We would have to pull pitch from a semi-hovering mode and get enough torque and speed to get us out of the area and back up into the heavens. If any one of those things went wrong, it could be a very bad hair day.

I heard the pilot over the intercom. "OK, we're right over it. Let's do a 360 in a wide circle and come right back into it."

Mouse made a minor adjustment with the control stick and tail rotor pedals and we started a slow turn to the right. "You guys ready back there?" he said over the intercom.

"I replied for both of us when I saw Steve hold his thumb up. "Yes," I said. "We've got it under control."

Under control, my ass, I thought. We controlled absolutely nothing. Our fate was in the hands of a 21-year-old co-pilot that had a reputation for screaming like a little girl when the chips were down. That really wasn't fair to Mouse because he was a good pilot, but I guess in stressful times like this you had a tendency to look for the weakest points of your circumstance. Sure, Mouse could get us in to a clear LZ as well as anyone could, but in the night when you couldn't see the trees it was difficult to fly something with churning rotor blades in between them with any degree of certainty that you weren't going to clip a limb with a rotor or a shrub with a tail rotor. Tree limbs and chopper blades don't mix well and if it happens at 60 feet off the ground, the ensuing fall combined with the flying mechanical parts makes for a tossed nut and Jesus bolt salad of deadly proportions.

We began our descent and I could see the tree line coming up and the sky line getting higher. I knew the trees were coming up quick and there wasn't enough moon to see a clearing or much of anything beneath us. We were in a black hole.

I heard Hunter say "Just hold your altitude. I'm going to take a peek."

Hunter flashed the landing light which to everyone's dismay lit up trees a few feet below us. We had not expected to see trees. Everyone thought we were 100 plus feet above the ground.

Hunter yelled "Pull pitch. We're at tree top level."

Mouse already had a glimpse of the trees through his chin bubble and pulled pitch, simultaneously adding a little right cyclic. I heard the blades hit something on the right side of the helicopter and I knew we were in trouble. Mouse was yelling "Shit" in a high-pitched voice as he tried to pull the helicopter back to the left. I could tell we weren't gaining altitude and felt the nose dip as Mouse pulled pitch and tried to give it forward cyclic to fly straight up and out of the hole we were in. He was fighting the pedals trying to gain control of the tail rotor that now seemed to have mind of its own. None of the adjustments worked. The sound of the rotor blade snapping and the raucous grinding sound of the transmission trying to free itself from its housing inches behind my back told me that it was over. I could make out the ethereal image of Steve's body as he lay gripping the center seat, probably to get away from the door and latch on to something that would provide a little stability as he prepared for what would come next. Then there was nothing but darkness. It wasn't a darkness that was just devoid of light. It was a horrific macabre darkness that seemed to be as frightening as it was peaceful, and as enigmatic as it was real.

A long dark corridor loomed before me. I was guided down it by someone who was holding my left arm. As we walked, armed personnel on both sides of the corridor came to attention. The only noise I heard was the clicking of the heels and the sound of weapons slapping legs as we continued toward a closed door that leaked light from beneath it. When we reached it, the party to my left opened the door and a hand on my back gently pushed me into the room. The door shut softly behind me and I found myself in an office of sorts. There were papers strewn across the desk in front of me and some were scattered on the floor. There were no windows or closets or any other exits. A man sitting behind the desk in an overstuffed chair turned to face me. He had the color and facial characteristics of Clark Gable.

"Well, I see you made it," he said with a strong and clear voice.

"Made what?" I asked.

"Made it here," he replied.

"And what is here?"

"Without oversimplifying the issue, here is where you are."

I was confused but happy to see I was in one piece. This cat and mouse game was not annoying but it was baffling. I was determined to know what was going on and how I got here.

"I will give you my name, rank and serial number as required by the Geneva Convention," I said, thinking that quite possibly I had become a prisoner of war.

"I already know your name, rank and serial number," he replied. I know your father's name, rank and serial number. That's not what this is all about. As a matter of fact, my good friend, you called this meeting. I just had to be here for you."

"And your name, sir?"

"Who would you want me to be?"

"A friend," I said.

"If that's what you want then that's what I'll be. You call the shots here, not me. Please sit, he said as he pointed to a chair."

"How do you feel?" he asked.

"You should know," I responded.

"Yes, I do. You feel very well. You are without pain, feeling rather well actually, and even though you are befuddled by this whole affair, you have virtually no anxiety or qualms about being here."

And he was right. I almost felt as if this was the place I needed to be. I felt comfortable, hardly uneasy, even though this could only be deemed a surreal and incomprehensible experience.

"You never answered my question," I repeated. "Your name, sir."

"Do you believe in God?" he asked.

"I'd be inclined to believe that you're not him."

"Well, let's say that I am."

"I'll play the game," I said. "I'm not sure I believe, at least it's difficult."

"It's not a game," he said with an expression that seemed to relate a more serious demeanor. "Life, and death, is not a game. You being here is not a game. You are here by your own design. You created this entire event, not me."

"Are you a good man, or someone to be trusted?" I asked.

"Good is a euphemism to which I have grown accustomed. Have you heard the expression; God is good?"

"Then if you are God, this must be heaven."

"Why?"

"Because God lives in heaven."

"Not lately," he said with a laugh. "I have been everywhere, and some places I didn't want to be."

"And why are you here?"

"You brought me here" he sighed. "This may be hard to understand, but let me explain it this way. We all make transitions in our lives; some are metaphysical, some are ideological, some are those that of our own doing, and some are not. Some are intangibles that are meaningless and some are real events that are life threatening. For the greater part, your mind controls these issues and events that lead you into these transitory periods. Then there's this other ditty called fate. Fate is a very controversial word. Are you really led upon a path by some instinctive force to an event that causes your demise? Did the actions you took or the decisions you made result in this fate? If so, it was not fate; it was a predictable eventuality for the circumstances you agreed to or permitted. For example, if a paratrooper falls to his death, it is not fate. It is indeed what could happen given the circumstances. I don't have the figures here in front of me, but let's say that for every 10, 421 airborne jumps, there are thirty Mae Wests and one streamer. You see where I'm going?"

"So far, so good," I said.

"What man doesn't understand is that everything he does is done with conscious electives. You decide what you will or will not be and believe what you want. You make all the decisions in your life starting before you are born. And as easily as you can choose to live, you can choose to die. People have been practicing self-euthanasia since the beginning of time. Spouses die shortly after being widowed. People elect to give up on life, cash in their chips, and throw in the towel. Conversely, there are many situations where people can decide to live, even in the face of the worst dilemmas. Audie Murphy, Alvin York, Teddy Roosevelt, and many others are proof of that. On the other hand, you can't fight old age. That's become an intractable issue at the round table for some time now and remains a matter of great consternation. But even old age has an extended slide rule. Life expectancy used to be 40; now in some parts of the planet it's 75. Why do you think that happened? It's because man made a conscious decision to live. It's not about immortality. There is no such thing. With the current state of gravity and air pollutants, by the time you turned 200 years old you'd have a turkey-like dewlap that hung from your chin to the ground. Not a pretty sight, Bo. Life runs its course until there is no more use for it. The planet feeds off itself. Ashes to ashes, dust to dust. When man cannot fulfill his obligation to the planet in such a way that he contributes in a meaningful way to human society, he must be returned to the earth. In a pedestrian or sophomoric way, that's just the way it is."

I was absorbing all of this with some uncertainty but was more interested or taken with the concept of the mind or will of an individual being powerful enough to overcome or reject death. Connecting death to age was not a problem for me; that was the standard, but to correlate usefulness to death sounded all too clinical.

"Then it is possible that people could live much longer than they currently do? I asked."

"Yes," he said. "That's true. Those that elect to live longer could do so. That is not to say that the old folk's homes would expand; they wouldn't. You see, good health is not the only factor in extending life. If an individual desires to live, he will do so but, generally speaking, you will not find him in an old folk's home. Think for a moment if the average life span was extended to 90 years. At some point, the lion's share of the population would be living in nursing homes and the remainder would be working to keep them there. A shrinking tax base would have everyone living in squalor and the old but healthy folks would become a burden on the under 65 crowd. At some juncture the wells would run dry, retirement programs would disappear and trade balances between nations would vacillate wildly. There is a happy balance that must be maintained. I thought man's government structure would do a better job at handling this."

"Living, at some point in time, takes an effort," he said. With the growth in industry and the advent of technology, man has grown lazy. As a result, the Americans, particularly the Americans, have recognized retirement as the end of one's work life and the beginning of the end. This phenomenon has been aggrandized as "The Golden Years" and those who enter this phase are called "Senior Citizens." It was never meant to be that way. Society is suffering because the wealth of experience, logic, and morality accumulated by the aging is leaving the mainstream of life and disappearing into retirement villages. Years ago, there were no retirement villages. There were family homes, and generations of families shared the home. There were certain qualities, conditions and characteristics such as honesty and integrity that were established and handed down from one generation to the next. The old folks who could no longer build railroads or construct houses tended gardens and made decisions in the community. They were an active, integral part of societal affairs. This commingling of people ensured there was a tenor of civility in the community and a level of respect for each other, the absence of which may spell an end to civilization as it is known today. Man in his infinite wisdom- I'm being fallacious- has decided to establish an idealistic secular end to this process. If the mean for moral and social intelligence is 70 years old, and you're quarantining aging people away from the mainstream, then you're stripping yourself of the intrinsic social and moral wealth of past generations. But I digress."

"Let me get back to the root of my lesson on life, especially as it pertains to you," he continued. "There are three divisions: mind, body and spirit. Spirit is a metonymy for yearning to see and do, being involved and the need to interact and participate. It is supported by faith and a dogged determination to lead a meaningful existence. The mind is a cognitive instrument used for a multiplicity of processes including perception, memory, thinking, problem solving, imagining, and language. It is supported and extended by a continuation of the mental processes. The body is a temple. I do hope you recognize the reference to this in the bible. It is supported and extended by a continuation of the mental processes. The essence of who and what you are must be in sync with who and what you want to be. Achieving balance and well-being is paramount to the existence of life. High spirited people constantly send subliminal stimuli to the brain. For this reason, they are active and they are in sync. They are very much alive and have a fervid desire to live. So, you see; mind, body and spirit are not only the propitious elements of life, they are indeed the core or the essence of man."

"Bo, you have these qualities. If you lean forward in the foxhole, all things are possible. You can use your mind to create and mold both your present and future at will."

"Is this like purgatory? " I asked.

"Let me preface any answers to those kinds of questions with this underlying principle. It is all about faith. Jesus was a man. The earth is inhabited by man. The bible was written by man. Religious laws, tenets, and ethical behavior codes have been created in the best interest of man. Faith is real. To say that it is not real is to say that the religious fundamentals which have resulted in a multitude of civilized generations and the preservation of civilization were without foundation. Without an unwavering belief in this faith that God, heaven, the Ten Commandments and so many other facets of religion are real, man would not have evolved to what he is now and the earth would be devoid of civilizations."

"Let me ask you a few questions," he continued. "Is your mind real?"

"Yes, of course."

"Are your thoughts real?"

"Yes, of course?"

"Do you have loyalties to people or a set of beliefs in any particular thing?"

"Yes, of course."

"Can anyone prove that any of these things exist?"

"Yes, of course, by my actions."

"So that would indicate that they have certain faiths or beliefs that will cause you to act in a certain way?"

"Yes, of course."

"Can those faiths and beliefs just as easily include the reality of God and heaven, and a set of beliefs regarding religion?"

"Yes, I suppose they could. Well, they do for many people."

"When you were a child, did you believe in Santa Claus?"

"Yes, of course. Everyone did."

"Did you have faith that he was real?"

"You bet." I smiled.

"Why did you believe he was real?"

"Because my parents said he was and there were toys under the tree every Christmas."

"What made you quit believing in him?"

"I was told he didn't exist."

"And why did that happen?"

"I would imagine it's because at some time it becomes too difficult to continue the façade, hide the gifts from Santa Claus where they couldn't be found and continue to make a child believe that reindeer can fly."

"Do you believe in the spirit of Christmas?

"Yes," I said. "It is a time of joy, a time that brings people together, and a time that is used to recognize the birth of Christ."

"Is Christmas, its spirit, and the functional role it plays in recognizing the good in humanity real?"

"But of course."

"Is the mental process that brings the spirit of Christmas and the belief and trust in people and ideals real?"

"Yes."

"Do you think that using the powers of your mind can overcome any obstacles and allow you to make choices that can save and preserve life?"

"Yes," I said.

"Do you want to live?" he asked.

"Yes, I want to live, I want to live."

The tone of Steve's voice was urgent. "Goddamn it, if you want to live, you better help me get your foot dislodged from this machinegun mount. We're running out of time."

I could not feel Steve's touch on my foot. The blood supply had been cut off and it tingled as if it were asleep. I looked around me and saw I was hanging downward at a 45-degree angle. The helicopter had come to rest on its nose. The chin bubble had been pushed into the front seats and the instrument panel was completely smashed. It appeared that the nose of the helicopter took the brunt of the crash. Even though it was still dark, I could tell that the transmission was still in place. One of the three Intel operatives was lying bloodied in the starboard door and partly beneath the helicopter. I knew in a glance he hadn't made it.

"Steve whispered, "We've got to get out of here."

"Where's everybody else?" I asked.

"They all got out except for him," he said, nodding toward the chap in the starboard door.

"They're gone, everybody's gone. They left here on a due east azimuth as soon as we crashed. You were out for about a minute. I stayed behind to get you out. Mouse has the UHF emergency radio and started sending a signal. He and Hunter are looking for the LZ we were supposed to land in so they can arrange for the other slicks to pick us up while the gunships cover them. We haven't heard them yet but they should be here shortly. Mouse didn't have time to communicate our situation to the Ops Control Center. He's guessing, I would imagine, that the intel guys we put in will call Ops and give them a sitrep."

I got to my feet surprisingly easy after Steve freed my foot. The feeling was coming back rather quickly. I rummaged under the seat and found my ditty bag with strap that held my camera and C-Ration meal. Steve took the machine gun barrel out of my weapon to make it unusable and inserted it into his its bag. He grabbed his machine gun and enough ammunition to last a while, wrapping the linked ammo over his shoulder, looking much like Pancho Villa. I took Steve's and my M-14s and all the magazines of M-14 ammunition and stuffed them into my jungle fatigue leg pockets. I knew there were other things we needed to do but they just didn't come to mind and we were in a hurry.

We were traveling in small groups. I had no idea in which direction the Intel guys went, and Hunter and Mouse could be anywhere. I didn't think, based upon what Steve had said that Mouse and Hunter could be more than 200 meters away from us. That could cause problems in the dark. We did not have a challenge and password system in effect for these kinds of situations. It certainly would help during hours of darkness if we did. If we got close to someone and didn't know who they were, we could not identify ourselves as friendlies without a challenge and password. That would create a lot of unnecessary chill bumps and could result in a firefight between them and us.

Damn, I thought, why didn't we practice this? Another hole in the training plan, I thought. Surprisingly, these kinds of scenarios were never practiced. It was up to the pilot or ranking person to take charge of the ground situation after a crash. Mouse and Hunter had "didied" (a contrived Vietnamese word for left or went). I suppose the intentions were good, but things could get hairy in Hobo Woods, and to think that this event would be an exception to the rule was ludicrous.

Steve said, "You take the lead and let's go.

"Which way is east?" I asked.

"Hell, I don't know," he snapped. "I thought you did."

"Well which way did Hunter and Mouse go?"

"I think that way," he said, pointing to the right.

"Are you sure?"

"Hell no, I'm not sure."

I tried to relive the flight into the crash sight to get a bearing on where we were.

"We made a large loop to the east and circled back to the north looking for the LZ, but I don't think that's going to help us. The position of the helicopter on the ground means nothing."

"Where's the north star?" Steve inquired with a muted but anxious voice.

"I can only see a couple of stars above all of these trees, and I wouldn't know it if it was labeled in big letters."

"Isn't there a compass on board?" Steve asked.

"Yeah, it's part of the instrument panel that's kaput."

I looked around as best I could in the dark. The area behind the helicopter was covered in vines. There were large stumps and lots of debris and helicopter parts on the left of the aircraft.

"When Hunter and Mouse left, were they moving quickly or fighting the woods," I inquired.

"They were moving quickly and disappeared almost instantly."

"Then they had to go this way," I said, pointing to the open area to the right of the helicopter. "If they would have left in any other direction you would have heard them thrashing around."

Steve began to move in the direction I had chosen. "Right or wrong, let's get the hell out of here," he said.

The first 25 feet were clear and easy enough to move through. We ran into some impassible areas and had to adjust our route of march more to the left.

"We're taking a northward bias," I said.

"Meaning what?"

"We're moving more toward the north because we had to change our course to get around all those bushes and shit. Somewhere we need to adjust about five degrees east to compensate for the move to the north."

"Let's just get out of here," said Steve.

We were both making enough noise to be mistaken as a mule train. The M-14 ammunition magazines were slapping together in my leg pockets and Steve's Pancho Villa style ammo belt was slapping rhythmically against his machine gun as he walked. I had two pairs of Army OD green cushion sole socks in my ditty bag with my camera. I took them out and gave a pair to Steve. He toned the ammunition noise down by wrapping them with the socks and I did the same with the magazines in my leg pockets.

We were moving rather well and I expected to catch up with Hunter and Mouse at any time. Thirty minutes went by and we still hadn't seen or heard any sign of the pilots, Intell guys or other helicopters. We didn't say it but we both knew we had a problem of epic proportions. The path was looking less and less like a path that someone would have taken if they wanted to go in a straight direction. We had to move in a variety of angles to keep our movement in a general direction and I was beginning to wonder if we weren't traveling around in a big loop. I had been a pathfinder and wasn't the type to ever admit to getting lost, but when the adrenaline is pumping and you're concerned that Charley is breathing down your neck, you have a tendency to throw the rules to the wind. Of course, that is precisely when you should be following the rules. We were without a compass, our noise discipline was terrible, and we had a body odor that was a no-no for the jungle. Charley had a nose for gun oil, C-Rations, hair spray, deodorant, and just about anything that didn't come in his scant and austere basic issue of equipment. Now was not the time to ask Steve if he was wearing his Wild Root Crème Oil or English Leather. We would have to worry about those things when the time came. Steve had the lead now and he came to an abrupt halt. We had come to the end of the perceived path. There was swamp on three sides of us and brush so thick you couldn't move through it without a machete, which we didn't have. Of course, to use one would be like beating drums in a library.

"How far do you think we've come," he said.

"Maybe three hundred meters at best," I replied. "Not far enough to get away from whoever's going to look for that helicopter."

"I think there's another path behind us about 50 meters back," Steve whispered. "It was hard to see in the dark bit I believe it will take us around this swamp."

"Your guess is as good as mine. I didn't see it, but if you say it's there it's got to be better than this."

Steve squeezed around me to start his backtrack along the path and tripped over his own feet in the dark. I reached down to pull him up and got a hand full of his Pancho Villa ammunition in the process. The belt snapped apart and the loose end of the ammunition belt struck his machinegun as I tried to pull him up, making a noise that resonated through the trees and across the swamp. We both looked at each other as if we were two schoolboys that had really done something wrong. I had that feeling of abject anticipation you get when you break your mother's favorite living room lamp and quickly look around hoping she is somewhere out of earshot. It is described as the Oh-No second, when all your senses come alive because you know you've done something terrible and you will find out what the consequences are in a mere second. We both knew that the metallic snapping noise of the ammo belt was hardly what you'd expect to hear in the jungle. We had broken one of the major rules of survival in a hostile environment. Neither of us said anything. We just looked at each other in silence as if we were waiting for an echo.

"Jesus," Steve whispered. "If Charley's out there, he had to hear that."

"We better get off the path and stay quiet for a while," I said.

Steve eased to his feet and we started back down the path. Steve was walking as if he was barefoot on glass and I followed closely in his footsteps. We found a small separation in the trees and vines and Steve glided into it with me close behind. It was a cubbyhole of sorts, just large enough for two people to sit.

We had our night-eyes by this time. Our eyes had adjusted to the darkness and we could see objects and shadows that were within 15 feet of us, but seeing took a back seat to hearing in this situation. Charley could hear a rat pissing on cotton at 100 meters and if he had heard the clanging of the ammo, he would be hunting for us in a stealthy and vigorous way. Capturing a couple of helicopter crew members would be an enormous prize for a Viet Cong soldier, especially one who was fourteen or fifteen years old and had been force-marched away from his village and summarily brainwashed into thinking that Americans were evil, sadistic cannibals with an appetite for babies and young people. The North Vietnamese propaganda machine had created these horrific lies to boost recruiting efforts and introduce a horrible consequence for being captured. Evidently, it was working. We were killing and capturing more young people than we had in the past, many of which became KIAs because they refused to be captured.

We had been motionless and speechless for about 10 minutes. We had reduced activity to a point where you didn't have to take your pulse rate; indeed, you could hear it as well as the sound of your breath. We were hearing monkeys and other jungle critters but there was something predictable about the sounds of their movements, and I felt I could discern their sounds as opposed to those of a more deadly two-legged creature.

We were both alerted to a sound that had something different about it. It was the kind of noise that made you know it was something that had weight associated with it. Neither of us moved but I could hear Steve's breathing. Was it because we were inches apart or was it because it was loud? I didn't know, but I instinctively put one finger to my lips to indicate he should be quieter.

Seconds became minutes and minutes seemed like hours as we sat motionless. The silence was broken by whispered Vietnamese words that seemed to be within an arm's reach. I heard one voice say "You see anything?" and another closer voice say "Nothing here."

Now there were footsteps within feet of us. I tried to keep my eyeballs quiet as I moved them from left to right but I sensed they were making noise and turned my gaze to the path some two feet ahead of me. Beneath the vegetation that concealed us there was a barely perceptible shine to the flash suppressor of my M-14. I wanted to move it but I dared not. Beyond the flash suppressor there were two feet. One foot was pointed in my direction and the other was pointed down the path we had just traveled. Everything seemed to stop. The world stopped turning and I refused to even think. Even the thought process could result in a noise and could trigger that mystical sixth sense in the enemy that stood at my feet so close he could spit on me with a dribble. The feet remained for an eternity. Finally, I heard the voice further away from us. "Let's go," it said. The feet remained for a few more seconds as if they were having second thoughts about leaving. Perhaps Charley's sixth sense was working but he wasn't listening to it, I thought. The turn of the foot signaled an end to the silent madness. The footsteps away from us were quiet, but loud enough to let us know that the immediate danger was dissipating with the sound of each successive step.

We lingered without saying anything for at least five minutes. There was always the chance that we had not outsmarted Charley and he might have sensed our near presence and merely withdrew to a place where he could watch us expose ourselves. When we were convinced that the immediate threat had departed, we eased our way back onto the path and started anew in the same direction that Charley had left. We returned to the point where Steve believed there was a new path, and after determining that it looked usable started down it. The moving was easier on this path. Daylight was beginning to trickle through the trees and we realized we were becoming a lot more visible than before.

I was alarmed that we hadn't seen any helicopters or any indication that someone was searching for us. We were in no position to try to send smoke signals or in any way expose ourselves. The triple canopy jungle prevented anyone being able to spot us from the air and our only prayer was to find Montgomery and Hunter, and hope the little used UHF emergency frequency radio had enough battery power to transmit an SOS signal.

It was possible that the command-and-control element for the Intel operation would not want to send any rescue elements into the area where the insertion was made for fear of compromising the operation. If we were the only people in distress, and there was no reason to think otherwise, any rescue operations in the area of the insertion would cause a convergence of forces by Charley to the affected area which could result in detection of the Intel operatives. The 25th Infantry could send in ground forces to try and find us, but this was Hobo Woods, and any response would have to take into account the need for expanded air support and artillery. Artillery, which was usually plotted along the route of march and in locations that would typically be deemed enemy avenues of approach or enemy-held terrain, would be hard to plot because they would not know our location and might inadvertently target us.

I was betting that there had been a command-imposed delay of three to five hours, sufficient to let the Intel operatives move at least a kilometer, or a click as it is referred to in military terms, away from the crash site before they executed the first phase of a rescue operation. If I was right, we were a couple of hours away from getting help. If I was wrong, we were going to have to find a way out of Hobo Woods, and the odds for that were damned small, almost like betting on a horse with no legs.

The ever-increasing daylight was making us cautious. We finally agreed that we would have to find a hiding place and try to stay camouflaged to the greatest extent possible. There was a hill that loomed ahead of us and we found a position on higher ground that gave us limited observation of the sky above us. If a helicopter did fly over within a 500-meter area, we would be able to see it. Certainly, we could hear it if it was within a click.

An hour passed, then two, then three. I wound my Army issue Elgin wristwatch to make sure I was tracking the time right. It was not looking good for the home team, I thought. I was somewhere between angry and dejected, emotionally. Steve, in his normal quiet demeanor, had little to say. When we did talk, it was in whispers and we kept all conversation brief. We were hungry but neither of us wanted to open a C-ration can for fear of the smell attracting attention. Just tearing the wrapper on the little C-ration package that contained cigarettes, matches and toilet paper could create enough noise to make it an unnerving situation, even if no one heard it but us. I rolled to one side to urinate and worried intently about the smell which took on an aroma that can only be described as a hideous stench. Strange, I thought, it never smelled like that before. This, I concluded, was my first piss in Hobo Woods, and I was hoping it would be my last.

I had started contemplating what actions would be necessary to get us out of Hobo Woods when I heard the distinctive sound of a helicopter. It sounded like it was far away and it was so faint initially that I wondered if it wasn't just a by chance flight of an aircraft that knew nothing of our dilemma. If it got close enough, I would be leery of jumping up to run for an opening in the trees to try to wave it down. We probably wouldn't have that opportunity, but for now there was hope. The sound of the rotor blades came closer and finally I got a peak of it somewhere around 800 feet above us. The urge to jump up and start waving my arms was overwhelming. I knew that would do little to identify our location. Steve remained motionless and looked at me with a helpless, gloomy expression. He was just as bewildered and angered with our situation as I was. Stunned and dejected, we watched the helicopter fly past and then away from us. We could no longer hear the sounds of the rotor blades that for a brief second had given us a fleeting sense of salvation. We both fell silent as the feelings of hopelessness overcame us. We sat side by side, both too depressed to comment on what may have been a missed opportunity.

We began to discuss what we could do to reveal our location to a passing aircraft. We toyed with the idea of climbing a tree to place something on an upper branch that could be seen from above. Neither of us had anything white or of a color that would stand out to a passing aircraft. We were OD green through and through; OD T-shirts, OD underwear and green jungle fatigues. If there was any emergency marking material it would be in the survival kit that Montgomery and Hunter carried away with them. The only other recourses were to climb a tree and get bare-chested or fire a few tracer rounds at the next aircraft that flew over us. Tracer rounds were not part of the usual ammunition inventory for Viet Cong or North Vietnamese. Our machinegun ammunition usually was constructed to fire four rounds of non-tracer followed by one round of tracer. If we reconstructed the belt to fire ten rounds of straight tracer, a savvy pilot or door gunner should quickly grasp the unique arrangement of tracer fire and conclude that there was a certain irony about this event, especially if the rounds were fired horizontal from a treetop location. If the rounds were fired in the direction of the aircraft during daylight hours, they would likely not be seen because of the angle of fire. The firing of the tracers would have to be done well ahead of the aircraft, preferably perpendicular to its flight, to get their attention. We would be relying on attentive pilots who would see these tracers through their chin bubble or crew members who would observe them from a door position. Of course, when the tracers were fired, we would be sending a message for a click in every direction that there was fresh meat for the taking in Hobo Woods. We would be lucky to have ten minutes to get extracted. Otherwise, we would be fighting an inexorable and determined opponent in his back yard with nowhere to run. It was a last ditch, best guess plan that had some ugly repercussions if it failed. If a helicopter saw the tracers and merely reported it without coming in to extract us, we would be, as the expression goes, toast.

We were discussing the mechanics of the plan when another helicopter flew over, this time at an elevation of about 800 feet. It appeared to be the same helicopter that had previously flown over. Although we could not make out the tail markings, I knew they were similar. If it was the same helicopter, it was an indication that someone may be searching for us. We watched it intently knowing that it would be useless to jump up and wave our arms. The likelihood that we would be seen was miniscule. The helicopter dropped in altitude and when it had passed us by about 200 meters, the pilot did a hard right tail rudder followed by a hard left tail rudder which made the helicopter twist right and left.

"Damn, Steve," I said. "Are they trying to tell us something?"

"Yeah," he said excitedly. "They know we're here."

"Is that it or are they trying to direct us to an LZ?"

"Get the tracers ready," I said.

Steve quickly disassembled the ammunition belt and reassembled it joining five or six rounds of tracer fire.

I heard the helicopter fly away and this time I could tell from the sound of the blades that it was not making a long loop to return as it had done before. I had raised myself to my knees in our covered position to watch the helicopter's flight. Steve suddenly grabbed my arm and pulled me back to a seated position. He pointed off to the left at a path that came down from the hilltop. I could instantly make out four people coming down the trail. In front was a Viet Cong. Behind him was Montgomery. His hands were tied and a rope tied around his neck was tied to Hunter's neck directly behind him. Hunter's hands were also tied, and behind him walked another Viet Cong. They had been beaten rather badly and Montgomery walked with a limp.

I looked at Steve and he knew what I was thinking. If we took out the VC it might hamper our chances to get extracted but Hunter and Montgomery would be little more than numbers in a history book. If we didn't kill them, they would kill or maim Montgomery and Hunter when it became obvious that a helicopter was landing to make an extraction. I made a decision that I hoped wouldn't be one of my last. I pointed at myself and held up one finger, then pointed at Steve and held up two fingers. I would shoot the lead VC, he would shoot the one behind Hunter. Steve prepared his machinegun and I raised my weapon to aim at the lead VC. Steve knew to follow my lead and waited for me to fire. The M-14 bucked ferociously in my hands. Steve fired a split second later. The lead VC was shot through the head and went down in a heap, falling at the feet of a stunned Montgomery. The trail VC was shot in the neck. The bullet pierced his jugular vein and blood spurted almost instantly from the gaping hole. He began to make a hoarse and throaty sound that reminded me of a horse in pain. Hunter, who had been a college football player, pulled Montgomery back towards him to get enough slack in the rope to kick the VC in the head. The kick was lethal and would have killed him without the aid of a bullet. Steve and I ran to Montgomery and Hunter and Steve used his knife to cut them free. We all began to run back down the trail in the general direction that the helicopter had taken previously. If we had guessed right and accurately interpreted the helicopter's waggle to mean there was a suitable LZ ahead, there was a chance we would be eating in the mess hall tonight. If we were wrong about the pilot's intentions, we might be scrambling for bugs to eat in a cage, if we were lucky.

The adrenaline levels were high as we ran in the direction of the possible LZ. The path was taking us to higher ground and the trees were thinning out as we moved toward a rockier terrain. I told Steve to fire the remaining tracer rounds above the trees in our direction of travel if and when the helicopter returned. We were moving to higher ground now and the sweet sound of rotor blades coming from behind me was hardly a distraction. This time the helicopter was coming in at 500 feet which told me that they knew we were here. Steve fired the remaining tracer rounds and the helicopter dropped to a lower altitude. As he flew over our position, he blinked his landing light several times. When the pilot reached a point one hundred meters ahead of us he began to ascend and rolled left to make another loop. His message was clear; the LZ was a hundred meters ahead.

I was in the lead running well ahead of Hunter who followed some twenty meters behind me. The path took us up a gentle slope to a point where the trees continued to thin out. For the first time I could see the LZ. It was tucked in between rocks and trees about sixty meters ahead of us. There was a saddle in the middle of the LZ which was about 75 feet wide. There wouldn't be much of a problem getting the helicopter in and out unless Charley decided to rain on our parade, for which he had grown notorious.

Steve was bringing up the rear, devoting as much time to rear security as he was to pushing a wounded Montgomery in the right direction. I was aware that the helicopter was on short final to the LZ. I could hear the flapping sound of the change in the angle of the blades indicating that it had begun to flare as it slowed to find a resting place. What I didn't know was that Charley was also watching and admiring the helicopter with a lust and zeal quite different from my own.

The first round to strike the helicopter tore through the transmission housing just ahead of me. I heard the loud popping noise as if someone had slapped the side of the helicopter. Steve began firing indiscriminately as he brought up the rear, feeding the Pancho Villa belt into the weapon with one hand while firing with the other. The door gunner began firing his machine gun from the door mount and yelled for us to get on board. I knew the pilots had to be anxious to get out of there. The helicopter was taking hits now from several different angles and at some point would have to lift off if they expected to get out of there in one piece. I pushed Hunter down beneath the spray of bullets being fired by the door gunner and he got on board. Steve ducked under the tail boom and approached the right door where the crew chief was also firing. He came in from the other side of the helicopter and helped me pull Montgomery into the floor of the helicopter. Montgomery stiffened as I pushed him in and fell on top of him. The pilot was pulling pitch while the co-pilot kept his hands near the controls. If the pilot was hit, he would take over. We were sliding off the ground cushion and into the air. The chin bubble exploded under the copilot's feet. I could hear the pilots yelling back and forth but could not understand what was being said. Steve was lying in the floor firing his machinegun into the trees on the left side of the helicopter. We took several more hits from ground fire over the next ten seconds.

And then it was suddenly over. The helicopter was flying almost defiantly up and away from a kill zone that belied its name, and there was nothing but cool air flowing through the open doors, which in some quaint way wafted away the fear and hopelessness we had all experienced. Hunter had some nasty cuts and contusions suffered at the hands of the VC that would heal in due time without hospitalization. Amazingly, none of the pilots were hit with anything more serious than flying plexiglass. Montgomery had a through and through gunshot wound to the back of his thigh that had entered and exited his leg as he was pushed onto the helicopter. It struck the butt plate of Steve's machinegun where it was imbedded.

Montgomery was alarmed by the burning sensation and had to be held down until we found the entry and exit wound and assured him that he would live. And this time, he didn't scream like a little girl.

We arrived back at Bien Hoa the day after our harrowing adventure in Hobo Woods. We were debriefed and questioned extensively about the crash and everything that led up to it. Evidently, two of the Intel operatives managed to stay with their plan and had continued their mission. The helicopter had tangled quite gingerly with the trees and we didn't get the number of casualties one would expect from such a crash. Still, one man was dead and by this time his family was probably being notified that he wasn't coming back. The aircraft was destroyed and probably the body of the Intel operative was destroyed with it. I didn't like to think that he would be listed as simply missing in action. Regardless of the controversies surrounding this subject, the Army is not so callous, nor does it tend to lie or in any way camouflage the truth about such matters. If the service the dead man worked for, whatever that was, elected to do so, they could have but I don't see the need.

Hunter had kidded Mouse Montgomery about his injuries. Aside from telling him that in supplement to being a hero, he had been a prisoner of war, got a purple heart and a million-dollar wound that got him out of country, all within the span of 24 hours, he reminded him that he had not "screamed like a little girl" when the chips were down.

Steve and I were in relatively good shape. We had both taken physicals against our objections, but Craig and Doc Quackenbush were adamant about such things. Our frayed, bloody flak vests were replaced with new ones. The old ones were hung with great ceremony on the wall in the platoon shack. Most notable was Steve's, which bore the damage of two glancing rounds. We had spent the evening downing a few shots of a variety of different brands of alcohol. Everybody seemed to show up with their private stock of liquor, some legitimately happy to see us alive, and others who were of the very prominent but-by-the-grace-of-God-there-go-I group downed the alcohol with us, exhaling a sigh of relief that indeed, it was us that drew the flight and not them.

We were put on stand down for 48 hours. I commented to Steve that I didn't think I could live through another stand down. He laughed in his usual quiet way.

The morning after had arrived and I woke up about seven in the morning. When I got to the mess hall Cookie was cleaning up after the breakfast meal. He saw me when I sat down at the table just inside the door where I usually sat.

"Sarge, you are one lucky son-of-a-bitch," he said. "How many choppers do you have to ride into trees and mountains before you get the picture?"

"Just one," I replied.

"And which one would that be?"

"The wrong one," I said, laughing to myself that he had taken the bait.

"You're gonna be sorry," he said, while shaking his finger at me in a motherly way.

"Then I'll still be alive. I have to be alive to be sorry."

"Then your mama will be sorry she didn't kick your ass and keep you out of this man's Army."

"I think my mama is happy I'm in the Army," I countered.

"If I had a kid like you, I'd be happy that you were in the Army, too. One day you'll have a kid, and if he does the dumb things you do, then you'll be begging him to come home.

"Doesn't your old man want you to come home?"

"Well, he didn't," I said. "But he does now."

"Then he's a lot smarter than you are, Hardin. Get the fuck outa Vietnam before Charley filets your ass or you wind up with a Jesus nut for a crown."

I was amused at Cookie's jargon. He was the quintessential, dogmatic Mess Sergeant who would never be known for mincing words. He was egregiously direct and happy to bare his opinions in a loquacious way. His command of military colloquialism was evident in anything he said. The Army had made him what he was, and he was the Army.

I often wondered how people like Cookie, the unit commander, the first sergeant, and I would fare when we got out of the service. Was there an afterlife that was anything like the Army? Were civilians even remotely attuned to aggressively meeting goals and objectives? What would we do without the advantage of rank? What were the consequences for subordinates who did not tow the line, follow orders and show a level of respect for their superiors? I could not picture myself in an environment where consequences were selective and behavior was optional. For me it was all about having a mission to accomplish that was as difficult in its design as it was rewarding in its completion. That was the Army way. You do great work, and you get recognized for it.

Steve came into the mess hall looking well rested. It was time for both of us to look back on the events of Hobo Woods with a refreshed and healthy perspective. I felt clear headed, given the night before. Cookie graciously brought me a cup of coffee and when he saw Steve, he returned to get another cup. Steve sat in the chair across from me. He had been by the orderly room to pick up his mail, which stuck out of his leg pocket.

"Letters from home," I asked.

"Yeah," he replied. "Haven't even had a chance to see who they were from."

"Are you tired?"

"Not really"

"Got any aches and pains you didn't have before?"

"Everything is fine except for a few cuts and bruises. It could have been a lot worse. Terribly worse."

"Yeah, I guess we were lucky," I said. "Do you remember going down?"

"Sure," he said. Every second of it."

"I blacked out when we hit the trees," I said. "Don't remember anything until you were pulling on my foot dislodging it from the gun mount."

"I didn't black out, but I'm convinced I had some hallucinations," said Steve.

"How so?"

"Well, when we first hit the trees, everything was spinning around and people and equipment were flying all over the place. I saw you flying out the door into the trees. I thought you had been thrown free of the helicopter. I expected to find you on the jungle floor. When we finally quit moving, which was a Godsend, you were lying on the jump seat with your foot caught in the gun mount. The Intel operative went out your door. I watched him leave. When he left, you weren't anywhere to be seen. I checked the Intel operative that was crushed under the helicopter to see if he was alive. He wasn't. I talked to Hunter and Mouse for about ten seconds and told them I was going to look for you. They got their gear and left. When I went back to get my weapon, you were there on the seat."

"I don't remember a thing until you started pulling my foot out," I said. I remember the landing light was turned on and I saw the trees beneath us. I knew Mouse was flying and trying to get us out of the tree tops. That was the end until you were pulling on my foot."

"Maybe I was out on my feet, as the expression goes," he said. "But if I was, I don't remember it. I never had the sensation that I was stressed out. It's just really eerie. If you had been dragged around outside of the helicopter with your foot caught in the mount, it would have surely broken your foot."

"Who knows," I said. "I guess anything is possible. I had fleeting visions of being somewhere else, as if I were dreaming. I don't have so much as a bruise on my ankle. My jungle boots must have taken the brunt of the pressure. As soft as they are, you would think I'd have scars or something."

Steve chuckled. "You were saying something like 'I want to live; I want to live.' Do you remember that?"

"No," I replied. "Not at all."

"Well, I think we have some lifelong friends in Hunter and Mouse," said Steve. "We were lucky to be able to hit both Charleys with two shots. If they had been able to get off a few rounds from their AK-47s, it could have been bad. Hunter or Mouse could have been shot, not to mention us. That machinegun is not the weapon of choice for that kind of skirmish either. The damned thing got heavy and I was hanging on to the ammunition for dear life when we were running. I almost lost it once and I had to reseat the ammunition in the tray. The belt kept breaking because I couldn't keep the slack in it."

"I'm glad you were able to hang on to it," I said. "The volume of fire you put out when we were trying to load the helicopter might have made the difference."

"You want to try to get to the ville today," Steve asked.

"I would like to try. I'm almost a little worried about going down there, although I would like to see Hoa."

Steve laughed. "Believe it or not, getting to see Fifi sounds like something I would like to do. She's pleasantly naïve enough to be entertaining."

"Maybe she always will be."

"Nah," said Steve. "Probably not. In due time, she'll be like all the rest. You got lucky with Hoa. She has a good head on her shoulders and she has this zest for learning. She seems content with everything, takes everything in stride."

Steve's prompting was sufficient to make me think about venturing to the ville. It would be good to see Hoa, and visiting the Hope Bar would do much to make me remember that pleasure is always better than pain. Over the last few days, I had endured quite enough angst and mayhem, and the soft arms of a woman and a breast to lay your head on sounded especially inviting to me. It was probably something about that motherly instinct that as a child you seem to find appealing after you hurt yourself.

Steve saw the wheels of my mind turning. "Let's go," he said.

"Why not," I responded.

We arrived at the Hope Bar in the back of one of Cookie's mess trucks. The driver signaled when it was safe to exit through the flaps of the large canvas tarp. We found the Hope

Bar just as lively as we left it. Papasan was playing records from a turntable he had acquired on the black market.

"Papasan, who is that?" I asked, trying to determine the identity of the group that cut the record.

"I don't know. I buy it from GI. He say number one record."

I read the album cover. The names Lester Flat and Earl Scruggs were prominently and colorfully displayed.

"Oh, yeah," I said. "You did well," I lied.

The record had a worn album cover and may have been ancient, but if Papasan got what he thought was a good deal then I wouldn't want to burst his bubble. Although there were ample country and western fans around, rock and roll ruled at the Hope Bar. It was still early in the day and there was a better than even chance that when the evening arrived and the bar was a little livelier, there would be an outcry of dissatisfaction when the Bose speakers were pumping out fiddle music. Humperdink, Tom Jones, the Who, and the Beatles were the rage in music- no offense to Lester Flat and Earl Scruggs.

I walked down to the other end of the bar where Big Mama was busily chipping ice.

"How are you, Bo?" she said, with a proud look on her face. "You look happy."

I sensed that there was something I should acknowledge but wasn't quick to grasp it, then I did. I had never heard her say "how are you, Bo" or "you look happy."

"Big Mama," I said. "You said that very well."

"Thank you very much," she replied. "Hoa teach us English. Pretty soon I talk like you."

"Toc Lam," I replied, meaning very good.

"No" she shook her head. "You no speak Vietnam to me anymore. If you do, I no learn English."

"OK, whatever you say," I promised.

I spent a few more minutes praising her desire to learn the language. I knew that her motives, to a great extent, were rooted in money. If she could speak English, she would know a lot more about what was going on around her when GIs filled the bar, she could settle disputes between the girls and the customers, and she could increase her knowledge of what she needed to do to increase her profit margins. And of course, Papasan would not be buying more Flats and Scruggs records.

"Do you know where Hoa is?" I asked.

"Without hesitation she said, "You go her house." She smiled a large smile exposing a nasty looking medial, facial, distal cavity in her right canine tooth.

There was a message in the smile but I didn't know what it was. I gathered that she wasn't working and was still at home. I excused myself and found Steve who had adjoined himself in conversation with Fifi at the other end of the bar.

"I'm going to see Hoa," I said.

"You gonna be a while?" he asked.

"I don't think so."

I caught a cyclo outside of the bar. We arrived at the entrance to the Vietnamese Army Compound where Hoa resided. I paid the driver and made my way through the guarded entry point and down the long corridor of shanties. Hoa's was distinguishable from the rest because a part of the wall next to the entry door was made from Budweiser beer cans. I knocked on the door as a force of habit. Regardless of where you are, there is a reason to act chivalrously, I thought. I heard Hoa say "come in" and I ducked to enter through the doorway.

The room inside was almost dark; just light enough to see your way around. Items had been placed around the walls and floor where light usually streamed through the cracks casting little flicks of light reminiscent of a disco lounge. I felt the bamboo mats beneath my feet. The bed, which took up most of the space in the room, was covered in several layers of Mosquito netting and I could see the angel like body image of Hoa behind it.

"I was told you were maybe dead," she said in a low monotone voice. "I cry and cry and cry. Then your friend Craig come yesterday and say you alive."

"I was very lucky," I said.

"You take clothes off. I want to see your body and know you are alive."

I obeyed without hesitation. I took my clothes off and found the opening in the mosquito netting. Inside, Hoa was lying on the bed completely naked. Two candles were lit on a small stand that sat next to the bed. When I got to the bed, she grabbed me and pushed me onto my back and sat upright on my midsection.

"You scare me," she said.

"I scare me, too"

"If you die, I kill you," she said, giving up on using the correct English.

"If I die, I kill me." I laughed quietly.

"It's not funny, Bo."

"I know," I said. "But it's over now, nothing to worry about."

Suddenly she was crying. The tears were streaming down her face, falling onto her breasts and then to my stomach. She leaned forward and hugged me. She stretched her legs down over mine and laid on top of me for what seemed forever. The warmth was surreally overwhelming, and seemed to place a vast and cleansing expanse between now and the despicable inhuman events of two days before. Her long, coal black hair fell gently around my neck and chest, softly embracing my skin. Eventually, she arose to a sitting position and grabbed a cloth from the table. After dousing it in an oily substance, she began to rub every part of my body.

"This protect you from evil," she said, as she continued crying and rubbing my body. "Better I do this than a priest."

She was still crying when she straddled me with her hips and guided me inside of her. The tempo went from slow to fast, and slow again. In the hours ahead, we enmeshed ourselves in each other as though this would be the first and last time either would experience something on this level. Much later with both of us exhausted, she lay on top of me. With her lips near my ear she said "Bo," tell me you want to live."

"Yes," I said. "I want to live. I want to live."

CHAPTER 5

The sun rose early the next morning. Steve and I had returned from Bien Hoa around eight the evening before. I was up early today, wanting to get back into the routine to which I had grown accustomed. I checked flight schedules with operations and the operations officer had expressed surprise in seeing me. "I thought you were going to take it easy for a while," he had said.

Easy, I thought. Take it easy and miss something? I doubt it. Maybe Cookie was right. It was possible that I had gotten a little too deep in the groove. I knew I hated down days and could not abide sitting around doing nothing. I'd much rather be behind the machinegun feeling the wind in my face and totally involved in the day-to-day operations of the war than be sitting idly by waiting to hear the stories of the day. And there were many. In the course of a week's time, there would be a dozen notable events worthy of record.

Operations was preparing for MACV missions in the coming days. They were always unpredictable. Military advisors and their Vietnamese counterparts would board the helicopter for the purpose of accomplishing a patrol of their assigned area of responsibility. Essentially, they were going to check for VC roadblocks, any unusual terrain reconfigurations such as foxholes or smoke coming from areas where they didn't expect to see it, or any indication of movement in areas that had been declared free-fire zones. Advisors and their counterparts had carte blanche authority to fire at will at suspected or confirmed targets. Generally speaking, for these missions we took gunships with us that had mini-guns, nose mounted 40mm belt-fed grenade launchers, and rocket capabilities, so if a target was identified, both the slicks, which were armed with machineguns and rockets, and the gunships could take it under fire. It was not unusual to shoot elephants that Charley may have used for transporting supplies, people who happened to be in a free-fire zone, or road blocks that showed any indication that they were hostile. There were no command decisions made from afar about which targets to destroy. The military advisor or his counterpart would quickly determine if something was out of place or inconsistent with what they expected to see and the order would be given with a nod of the head. On several of these missions, enemy patrols were sighted, and in some instances, Charley took multiple casualties. There were stories that prisoners had been tossed out of helicopters by MACV or Intel Ops personnel, but I never saw it happen nor can I remember any fist hand accounts of such activities.

Company size operations were much different. The entire unit would be deployed to a pickup point to load and insert. Task force construction of fighting forces had become especially popular with infantry units which allowed field commanders to tailor units to size and configuration that best suited the mission. Major considerations included geography, estimated size of the enemy force, speed of the ground element, aircraft support and a variety of other factors. For these reasons, ground elements were often inserted in a variety of different locations and in varying sizes, the theory being that it is easier to fly them in rather than have everyone placed in one location then maneuver to other locations. If Charley's intelligence elements were accurately obtaining and communicating information relative to insertion dates and times, we could encounter ground fire and strong resistance getting into LZs. Charley was definitely at a disadvantage when combating battalion size operations. His usual fighting force of as few as six and as many as 50 had to be well covered and concealed in order to avoid the prepping artillery prior to the insertion and the gunship strafing of LZ perimeters. If he made it through this barrage, he had to worry about breaking contact and fleeing the area once the insertion was accomplished. Charley's departures or retrogrades were further exacerbated by blocking forces that could be brought into place to contain his movement and eventually squeeze him into areas where his entire force could be eliminated.

I was fairly certain that the history books would not accurately and properly record the capabilities and heroics of the American military and the futile plight of the VC and North Vietnamese forces. Charley was horribly outmatched. He could not use tanks or aircraft and had to rely on mortars or explosive devices to destroy targets that were not line of sight. He did not hold formations or run up the colors; he couldn't. He survived on stealth and could move only when he was not under the watchful eye of the South Vietnamese or American Military. His only hope for winning this war was to gain sympathy and status from the American anti-war minions and persevere against the superior power and capabilities of the American military establishment. In reality, I don't think he thought he would ever win, but he did count on not losing.

News was continually trickling through Armed Forces Radio and other sources pertaining to the enormity of the anti-war movement in the states. I knew that what we were hearing, and to a great extent discounting, would be pretty potent fodder for the North Vietnamese Forces and the VC. Their propagandists would use this kind of information to their distinct advantage. It would be much easier for the VC to recruit young impressionable people from farms and villages if you could convince them that they would be heroes, not just to their country but to Americans who were now opposing their own military. There were also indications that higher ranking Republic of South Vietnam Officers, even generals were hedging bets on who would be victorious by becoming agents of the opposition. Many had been arrested and the general trends of a country in political and military disarray were beginning to emerge. Thanks to the insane upheaval of values and patriotism in our own country, the enemy was getting a big break. As a reaction to anti-war sentiment, the U.S. had initiated a pacification phase that served only to let Charley improve his logistical and ground operations capabilities that would become very significant in the final phase of his campaign to overwhelm existing South Vietnamese Forces and take the capital of South Vietnam. Stopping the bombing on North Vietnam contributed to the enemy's campaign by sending a message that we were weak and growing tired of the conflict. I did not like what I saw and couldn't fully comprehend what was going on. As confused as I felt, I had a gut feeling that this war was not going to be like so many others the U.S. had fought and won so gallantly.

Operations had recently picked up an FNG. Word had it that he was a professional football player. Every morning he would be out on the PSP running back and forth. He had quite an array of different exercises and running techniques that he used. I watched him carefully, wanting to ape his style and gain his size and agility. Evidently, he was a loner and liked it that way. The only time I ever saw him was in the operations section or out on the PSP running and doing sit-ups. On the one occasion I had tried to converse with him, he made it clear through short and impassive responses that he wasn't interested. There are people like him in all walks of life, I thought. I wondered if this kind of reaction was more prevalent in a combat zone. There were a lot of people who just didn't want to become friendly with others in Vietnam. Some people came here right out of civilian life and may not have liked the war, but were convinced they had a role to play and a debt to pay as a citizen of the greatest democracy in the history of mankind. I wondered how you could quarantine yourself from relationships of any kind and spend a year as a recluse. But people did it, and I believe they did it at the risk of losing that part of the psyche that enables you to relate with other members of the human species. I know it had to take a gargantuan effort to mask the most natural and atavistic characteristic of human behavior, that being to interact with others.

On the days when I didn't fly, I would exercise or read. I had an incline board in my room and about 100 pounds of weights that I had accumulated over two plus years. I had a wall full of books and several boxes that were loaded with paperbacks. The unit had a resource for books. I don't know if it was a non-descript support group, the USO or part of the military PX program, but we always had a rather handsome supply. Many of my books were sent to me by pen-pals. Those that I intended to read again, I kept. Those that I didn't, I took back to the orderly room to be handed out to others. On down days, if I wasn't exercising, I was reading.

Today was no exception to the rule. I found a good book and a folding chair and went to the patio located just outside of my room at the west end of the barracks. The lights inside the barracks were poor to non-existent so I usually read in my OD green boxer shorts on the patio where I could see.

We had recently begun hiring local women to perform house cleaning duties. They had been labeled "hooch maids" by the GIs. The hooch maids would see me on the patio reading, and those that spoke a little English would initiate conversations. Of course, with the hiring of hooch maids we had received the usual warnings that they could not be fully trusted. We were told to report any unusual or suspicious incidents that would indicate their presence had ulterior motives. I found that humorous. Many of these hooch maids were young women. The GIs joked around with them and had their fun. The hooch maid had no access to sensitive material other than an occasional map which would have no markings of any consequence. Most of our missions were day missions. By the end of the day, anything found on a map was history. Extended missions took us out of the company area and on those occasions, there were no maps to be seen in the company area. The hooch maids washed our clothes, picked up after us and kept the place clean. Without them, we were a bunch of slobs. Mine was an older married woman who would often throw a fit when I messed up the room after she had cleaned it. Her antics were more about personality than anything else and I knew she liked me. She would bring me Chao Yai (something similar to a Chinese egg roll) from time to time and I would give her little items that she probably sold in the market place. There were so many things that they didn't have such as can openers, razors, mouthwash, and many other trinkets that Americans had taken for granted for years. It was a way to make her happy and when I wrote home for a few things I needed, I would always include a request for inexpensive items I could give to my hooch maid.

I got into my book and was baking in a very hot sun that no longer had any effect on me. I had grown accustomed to the heat and had a tan that was three layers deep. Anyone who had been in Vietnam for more than a month was tanned well. They had been through the acclimation period which consisted of losing your appetite and a lot of weight, then getting a tan, and finally getting in shape. There was much to do aside from your regular duties. Periodically, sandbags had to be filled and new bunkers constructed. When ammunition arrived, it had to be inventoried and placed in bunkers and conex containers, and we were always moving people around and constructing new buildings. The engineers were spread thin in Vietnam and most of the immediate work was done by the unit. There never seemed to be a shortage on talent. People became known for their talents. We had John the artist, Ralph the carpenter, Jim the plumber, and a host of other folks that had special construction talents. We had a karate expert, musicians, tumblers, athletes and actors. Collectively, we were capable of anything. It came in handy.

I hadn't been in Vietnam very long when the decision was made to construct two new, large sandbag bunkers. It was a 6-week project so when we weren't flying, we were filling sandbags. In the process I lost about 50 pounds. I believe it was a combination of being new in country and filling sandbags that resulted in this dramatic loss. I needed to lose the weight, particularly the excess fat, and never gained it back. The self-imposed exercise program and the heat kept me at a trim 210 pounds. I was thin, virtually devoid of fat, and in the best shape of my life.

I was in the middle of the second Chapter of a dry book when one of the operations clerks came to the patio. He related that Arseneaux needed to see me about an upcoming mission. I asked him if he knew anything else and he said "no."

Dang, I thought. The Ops building is a mere 50 meters away. If it was that important, he could have walked over here. I rose from my seat and went inside the barracks, a little agitated that Arseneaux couldn't save me the trouble of donning a uniform and reporting to the Ops building. If this was some ridiculous less than urgent message, I would express my displeasure to Arseneaux when I got there.

When I walked in the Ops building, I didn't see Arseneaux. Lieutenant Johnson, an Ops Officer, saw me enter and motioned me to his office in the back of the building.

"Hope you're getting rested up," he said.

"Yes Sir, I'm taking it easy today," I replied. "I'm not sure I like the way you said that, though. Sounds like you're getting ready to put me to work."

"Well, maybe yes, maybe no. You see, what I've got for you is strictly voluntary. We've got a request from the 25th Infantry to provide three helicopters for Long Range Reconnaissance Patrol (LLRP) support. Evidently, they are going to be using these guys to probe areas around enemy flanks to ascertain enemy strengths and capabilities, potential LZs, and all that jazz. They specifically requested seasoned troops with field time, and of course you came to mind. All the pilots will have at least six months in country. They wanted to know if we had a flight doctor. Obviously, they don't understand that a battalion flight surgeon is not going to come along for this kind of mission. I talked to Doc Quackenbush. Hitechew's replacement is in and he doesn't mind if we take him along. He is a trained door gunner and seems to work well with the pilots. He'll be able to provide any immediate medical support they need. They don't seem to have any problems with that."

"Have you talked to Craig about this?" I asked.

"No, I didn't, but Doc did and he said he would go if you went."

"Excuse me Sir, but why doesn't the 25th Infantry have enough of their own helicopters?" I asked.

"We asked that question," he replied. "It seems as though they have a shortage. They got a bunch shot up near Vo Su and they've had an outbreak of dysentery and hepatitis, which put a bunch of their people in the hospital. Additionally, they want aircraft with different tail boom markings. It seems that Charley has been pretty successful matching tail boom markings to units in their area and all indications are that they can predict the size and type of the incoming force based upon tail boom markings. That remotely makes sense. They fly the same kinds of operations day after day, primarily large insertions and Charley is getting wise. Additionally, they have picked up a dozen Vietnamese Air Force (VNAF) Pilots and they're unsure about how well they can be trusted."

"The latter seems to be a more compelling reason," I said.

"You're probably right."

"When does all this kick off?"

"Day after tomorrow," he replied. "They will provide rations and quarters, but I wouldn't expect much. I'd be inclined to take along a box of Cs and a dozen pair of clean underwear and socks."

We both shared a laugh. Clean underwear and socks were kind of a standing joke in the unit. We were accustomed to washing out what we had and letting the wind dry it out. Actually, a lot of people didn't wear underwear in the field, certainly not tee shirts. The OD green boxer shorts were the wear of choice in the barracks area. In the helicopter, perspiration quickly dried in the wind.

"How long is the mission?"

"Three weeks, more or less," he said.

"Does my platoon leader, Major Merrill, know?"

"Yep. All that's been coordinated. Scherer will take over your platoon while you're gone."

"Sounds good to me," I said. "I'd just like to get an operations briefing before we go so I know some of the particulars."

"You got it," he said.

"Thanks, Sir"

"No, thank you," he replied.

I left the Ops building and headed down to Craig's med station. I most certainly wanted to be at the briefing. I always felt as if it was a mistake to exclude crews from the mission or Ops briefing. Too many times we were left in the dark regarding mission requirements. The mission we were just on that resulted in a crash and escape might have been a little easier for all concerned had we been briefed on the geography, and had some idea which way we needed to go to get out of the area. As it turned out, we took the right paths to a pickup point, but that had been a guess. I had a compass in my room that I intended to carry with me on this and each successive mission. I never wanted to find myself in another situation where I had to guess my way out.

My infantry experience was that every man should know what the mission, goals and objectives were. For the infantryman, the Five Paragraph Field Order, through successive briefings, detailed the objectives and actions of every man, and maps were always used to depict terrain and show the location of enemy forces. There was absolutely no guess work. If you got lost, you knew who was supposed to be on your flank, a rally point was selected for those occasions when all went awry, and the chain of command was clear. Beans, bullets, and resupply were covered in detail. Absolutely nothing was left to the imagination. Conversely, in helicopter units, crews did not attend briefings and pilots were not prone to describe the mission unless you asked. The responses were pitiful: it's a milk run, no big deal; gotta pick up a bunch of 1st Cav guys and insert them; going to Vung Tau to get some maintenance done; or, working with MACV. Lum Edgars was better than most, and I gathered his experience as an enlisted man caused him to be that way. He would tell you how many people were being inserted, he'd get out a map and show you where we were going, and check to make sure there were rations and the proper equipment was on board. He knew that it was to his benefit to do so; many of the others did not.

Craig was writing a prescription when I arrived. "Well, well, well," he said. "They finally realized they needed me around to watch you."

"I doubt it," I replied. "Doctor "Q" probably wants to replace you with a WAC. You're getting short and he's dreaming of a replacement with a kinder and gentler facade that will have the guys lined up begging for prostate exams."

"Yeah, I'm getting short," he said. "And that's exactly why I don't want to go on this one. But this place isn't big enough for two head medics and I've probably worn out my welcome anyhow."

"Doctor Q overheard our conversation and chided Craig in a mocking voice. "You're just too quick to give those prostate exams, with no gloves, no less. Marquis De Hitechew, I'm beginning to wonder about you."

"He taught me everything I know," said Craig, nodding his head in Doc's direction. "We practice on each other. What's a little peanut butter between friends."

"It is approaching the lunch hour," I laughed. "I hope we're not having peanut butter."

"Nope," mused Craig, thoughtfully looking up as if to remember. "I think Cookie's doing noodles today. That's noodles as in midget intestines."

"You got bowels on the brain," I jeered. "Hope you don't have a bowel pal."

"Not one that makes you howl." He joked.

Doc Q spoke quietly but succinctly. "This is a place of business, and I do have my reputation to think of. One day someone will be investigating me to see if I'm the kind of doctor they want in a big wealthy partnership or as the Surgeon General and one of you twits will relate this conversation and everything I've labored and toiled for will go right down the drain."

We both looked at him strangely as he smiled and left the outer office. He was joking, of course. He was a remarkable person and everything you'd expect a doctor to be. He always had that calm demeanor about him that was enviable and certainly worth emulating. He rarely misspoke, and except for the nuclear physicist that worked in the battalion 3 shop as a strategist, he was the smartest man on campus. According to Craig, he had seen him mad only once, and that was at a chap named Friedman. Friedman was the company jack of all trades who fixed pipes and cleaned up unscheduled messes at the behest of the first sergeant. Friedman had no concept of safe sex and proceeded to contract back-to-back cases of venereal disease. The rule was that if you contracted venereal disease, you would be confined to the company area for 30 days. Friedman contracted venereal disease repeatedly, each time within minutes of his last healing. Craig had made a virtual pin cushion out of Friedman's butt, injecting him with shot after shot of penicillin. After the eighth or ninth series of shots, Friedman proclaimed that he only had one episode of venereal disease, but had endured nine relapses. Doc Q took exception to this self-diagnosis and yelled loudly enough at Friedman to scare him. He told him that the next series of shots would be given to him in his eyeballs and if that didn't work, he would have to be exiled to the infamous island where people are sent who cannot be healed.

Of course, there was no such island; it was a myth. A lot of people believed that it was real. Stories abounded about GIs who had contracted all kinds of weird venereal diseases that caused their penises to split open, turn black, or fall off. Doc Q convinced Friedman that it was real, and Friedman believed it until the day he left. He never came back for more shots. Craig tried to drive the spear in a little deeper when he told Friedman, who was just a few days from going home, that oftentimes they would make people believe they were going home when they were really going to "the island." When Friedman asked me if that was true, I validated Craig's remarks. In retrospect, we probably overdid it, and I'm relieved Friedman didn't follow Jennings' example and take a plunge off a Buddhist temple.

Craig was humoring me with a story about our illustrious pathfinder detachment. It seems the Air Force, who was responsible for maintaining and operating all the retail liquor stores, called class six stores in the military, got in a shipment of San Miguel beer. The pathfinders made multiple entries into the tent between the rounds of the walking guard, and managed to extract two pallets of the highly prized and scarce nectar without being detected. The guard was there because similar thefts had occurred before. The pathfinder detachment commander was advised of the incident and impressed upon the detachment the need to put the beer back or face the consequences. The pathfinders then spent the greater part of the next night sneaking the beer back into the tent while avoiding the guard that circled it. One of the pathfinders left a note that read: We'll be back. The Air Force was livid and knew the pathfinders were the usual suspects for such underhanded tomfoolery. The Air Force Investigative Service wanted the Army's Criminal Investigation Division (CID) to open a case on the incident and identify the offenders. The CID said there was no offense because it was never officially reported and no beer was missing.

Craig and I had a friend, Vic Perry, who was in the pathfinder detachment. We surmised that he, if not wholly responsible, was at the nexus of this band of merry thieves. In Vic's egotistical eyes, it would not have been thievery; it would have been putting the suds of San Miguel into the hands of those most deserving. The stealth and planning of such a stratagem would have been a labor of love that illuminated the high degree of professionalism exhibited by the pathfinders both on and off the field of battle; a mere test of their skills and ability to be versatile in the types of missions for which they should always be prepared.

"What do you think?" I asked when Craig had finished the story.

"It's got Vic's fingerprints all over it," he replied.

"Is he in trouble?"

"Nah, you know Vic. He'll come out smelling like a rose. He's invincible, incorrigible, and insane. I understand they're going to be restricted to the barracks for one month. And, of course, that's excluding missions, which will mean they will feel the pain for about a week. I think most people are looking at it as the smooth shenanigan of a modern-day Robin Hood and his band of merry men."

"And the Air Force is saying: Curses, foiled again," I quipped.

"Nope, wrong era. That's Simon Legree, or the four stooges, or old movies, or something like that. The Air Force is saying: Shit, how did those bastard slip through our fingers?"

Vic Perry was totally unlimited by conceptual restraint. He was a gregarious soul and, in the vernacular, the life of the party. When he was off-duty, he had a beer in his hand. When he was on duty, he wanted a beer in his hand. He was one to make jokes and the raconteur of great stories. His father was an Army major. After his parents divorced, his mother eventually married an Air Force Sergeant. Vic wasn't happy about his mother's choice and made no bones about his aversion to any mention of the Air Force. Stealing the beer probably was a way to get back at his mother, who he proclaimed to be trailer trash, and the man she married who Vic thought was at the root of the divorce. His mother and step father lived in Macon, Georgia. When he drank to excess, he would talk about going back to Macon and kicking that "zoomie's" ass.

If he was ever afraid, it didn't show. Pathfinders were required to land in the LZ ahead of or with the first lift of helicopters and clear it for landing. The risk factor was high and the chance for getting wounded or worse was somewhere between probable and imminent. Although the LZ may have been prepped with artillery fire and strafed by helicopter gunships, there was still a chance that Charley would be there. On more than one occasion, Vic got pinned down by enemy fire and was able to come out unharmed and smiling. He was quick to volunteer for difficult missions and would often be difficult to control in an LZ.

Pathfinders used the clock method for securing LZs. When the helicopter dropped them in the area to be cleared, pathfinders would maneuver to 12, 3, 6 and 9 o'clock locations. If their areas were clear, they would report it to the team leader who would in turn give the signal for the helicopters to land. If a pathfinder encountered enemy resistance, he would use a radio code to alert the rest of the team if he was able to do so. Vic had a tendency to venture further into his assigned sector than he should. If he saw an opportunity to get a kill by moving further away from his pre-designated position, he would not hesitate to do so. The correct procedure calls for reporting the enemy citing, giving his location, and relying on the gunships to remove the threat. The rationale behind the procedure is that if there is more than one enemy and they are positioned in depth, any attempt to maneuver into the area would probably be fatal for the maneuvering element, and the temporary 360-degree security circle would be compromised. A loss of any one of the perimeter clock locations could jeopardize the safety of the other pathfinders as well as the operation.

Vic had been warned several times to hold his position and essentially follow orders. When it became obvious that he was not, he received Article 15 administrative punishment and reduced in rank. Shortly after receiving the Article 15, operational procedures were changed eliminating the requirement for pathfinders to be the first personnel in the LZ. As it was explained by the Battalion Ops Officer, Charley had become wise to our procedures and was using tunnels and natural terrain features to get behind pathfinders, which resulted in an increased and unacceptable mortality rate. Thereafter, pathfinders went in with the first lift of soldiers, employed smoke to mark specific landing areas for succeeding lifts, and basically managed traffic in and out of the area.

Vic had toyed with the idea of requesting a transfer somewhere that he could "get some action." Although he desired to be in the thick of things, he knew that the pathfinder detachment was a cherry assignment and the benefits were many. You might be working for three or four days then be off for a week. Sometimes the detachment had to make two or three-week vigils on battalion sized operations, but most of the time they were of short duration. When he was in base camp there was beer to drink, clean sheets to sleep between, hot food, and the ville was just a mile away. The need and appreciation for creature comforts outweighed the need to be locked in mortal combat. He wisely elected to stay with the detachment.

Thereafter he had some near misses but never lost another stripe to the best of my knowledge. On one occasion he went to the ville and had too much to drink. He met the "girl of his dreams" and elected to bring her back to the barracks, which was off limits to all non-assigned personnel except the hooch maids. Their first sergeant had a habit of coming through the barracks every morning and rousting the troops out of bed. He did so by physically grabbing any part of the person available and shaking him awake. He go to Vic's area and smacked what he thought was Vic's butt while yelling for him to get out of bed. It wasn't Vic's butt; it was the butt of the girl he had brought in the night before. She lurched up in bed, but by that time the first sergeant had continued further down the rows of double beds ahead of him. She woke Vic who was sleeping on the other side of her. Realizing that he had made a serious mistake, he then had to determine how he would get her back to the ville without being detected. While he was trying to find transportation and someone that would attempt to conceal her at the MP main gate checkpoint, the girl decided that she needed to go to the bathroom. Vic put her in a uniform, which hung on her like drapery, pushed her hair under a military cap, and several pathfinders bunched around her and escorted her to the latrine. Vic managed to return the girl to the ville without discovery of this impulsive undertaking; however, he indebted himself to several people who received hush money in the form of beer and cigarettes for several weeks.

Craig put a rubber band around a blood sample that was going to be sent to the lab and held it up to the light. "This one ought to be interesting," he said. "This fellow's got something really wrong with him and we don't know what it is. He's itching and scratching to beat the band, he's running an intermittent temperature, and his vision is impaired. I talked to a friend at the Bien Hoa hospital and he said they had a similar case that resulted in the soldier being shipped to Japan for observation where he eventually died. They're sending the meat wagon over this afternoon to pick him up for further testing. I have a bad feeling about this guy. He doesn't look well, his skin color is almost jaundiced, and he's got those glazed over eyes and poor motor skills that make you think he's losing his brain functions."

"Too bad," I said.

"Yeah, it is. There are people like you that come to Vietnam and have very few medical problems, and then there are guys like this. He's been in country for two months and he's really messed up with something. I often wonder if there isn't something distinctly genetic in each of us that predisposes us to the kinds of diseases we'll contract. I believe that one day blood pathology will tell us when we are going to die and the quality of life we can expect. Although there have been great leaps in technology and science, we've still got a long way to go. With all that we know, there is still a lot we don't know."

"One thing I do know is that we're leaving in two days for the Tay Ninh area," I said, reminding him that we had some work to do. "It looks like they are counting on you for medical support."

"I'll bring my little black bag," he retorted. "I'll bring along some suture kits, lots of four by fours, a whole bunch of tape, a couple of tourniquets, and the basic patches and glue, and of course everybody's favorite, tetracycline."

"I doubt we'll need any no-sweat pills," I laughed.

"Well, I'm bringing a year's supply just in case. "If there's a desperate wicked city woman abiding in a local ville and a box of gourmet C-rations on the helicopter, there will always be a need for tetracycline."

"I would be at the briefing," I said. "I'll let you know when it is as soon as I find out myself. We're going to be separated from the rest of the unit. I doubt we'll get any mail before we return. Hopefully, the 25th Infantry will provide hot meals at Tay Ninh. I'm losing my taste for C-rations. Even the infamous "Ham and Lima Beans with Juices" are beginning to turn me off. The world must be coming to an end."

"I noticed that a lot of people here think it already has," said Craig.

I rested too well that night. It was a long, deep sleep that left me groggy. Perhaps I got too much, I thought. I made the briefing at the Ops building at 1500 hours and started getting my gear ready. Scherer was taking over my job as the platoon sergeant during my absence. He would probably not take flights, which meant the Crew chiefs would not be getting an occasional break, depending on how frequent the missions were scheduled. There wasn't much said at the briefing that would give any indication of what we would be doing other than "make insertions as directed" and "stay on call to make extractions." Times and dates had not been established for the insertions. Meals would be provided but there were no dedicated quarters, meaning that wherever you could find a tent to sleep in, that would be your quarters. It wasn't unusual to sleep in the helicopter when you could. Oftentimes guards were provided to walk the airstrip. If you got up to go to the latrine and the guard mistook you for the enemy, and he could in the dark- that could be a problem.

Early the next morning I met Craig at the helicopter. He got the weapons on board and loaded the ammunition trays. Steve was there to help. Craig and I did the usual pre-flight inspection. Craig had managed to find a water cooler which he had loaded with his private stock of grape Kool-Aid. I kidded him about the Kool-Aid. Usually, grape Kool-Aid was the mix of choice for Vodka. It wasn't available in the PX so the troops counted on families sending them enough to make it through the month.

The pilots, WO Larson and Lieutenant Chien, arrived and did their pre-flight, and in due time we were flying in the direction of Tay Ninh. It was still dark and I watched the streets of Bien Hoa disappear slowly in our wake as the pilots set an azimuth for Ngui Ba Dihn (the Black Virgin Mountain), which was just a little east of Tay Ninh.

Eventually, the rhythmic sounds of the rotor blades cast their spell on me and my mind began to wonder. I began to examine my feelings for Hoa and wondered what would happen to her. My feelings for her ranged from big brother to lover and I wasn't sure of what I really wanted them to be. She was a soul caught in a time warp, I thought. But aren't we all, I wondered. Doesn't each of us go from one chapter or segment of our lives to the next? Surely, it was not possible to have a long-range plan that included another being at this age, in this country, in this war. Neither of us knew where the other would be tomorrow. Was I being unnecessarily or inadvertently cruel to this woman?

I had not seen a display of emotions from her before like I had just experienced. Our intimate times had always seemed to be something we both needed and shared equally, as if we were surrogates for someone yet to come. I had seen her cry when she was sad or worried about money or her family, but never had she displayed an exclusive and inimitable need for me. I often felt as if I was the single brother that had married his brother's widow so she wouldn't be alone. She had shocked and dismayed me when she expressed a need for me to be there with her, an undeniable concern for my well-being, and the notion that it should have some degree of permanency.

But the future was limited to the next hour and the next mission. Indeed, you could be foolishly intrepid enough to take living for granted, but it would be wise to place an asterisk next to it. I concluded that it would be prudent to decide not to make decisions about anything that didn't require a decision, or in any way prognosticate the future. Futures are inundated with hope. People who have hopes have an innate sense of fear that their hopes will not materialize. And in Vietnam, fear is not your friend.

Our flight of three helicopters arrived at Tay Ninh a little after daybreak. The area was dotted with tents and artillery pieces that covered several acres. There were rows of helicopters lined up along the PSP and one bore on its tail boom what appeared to be the marking of our battalion pathfinder detachment. Craig and I tied the rotor blades down and took care of the usual necessities. When the pilots went off to share war stories with some of the other pilots, Craig and I got together with Joe Ford and James Carson, crew chiefs for the other two helicopters, and their gunners. We were sitting around engaged in idle conversation when Vic Perry walked up to the helicopter carrying two cups of coffee. He handed one to Craig and one to me.

"What in the world are you doing here?" I asked.

"We got here yesterday," he said. Seems they want to win this one so they called the 145th Battalion Headquarters and asked specifically for me."

"Ah, your reputation precedes you," teased James in a voice that was supposed to sound like W. C. Fields.

"If only they knew what we knew," said Craig. "They would have asked specifically for you to stay in Bien Hoa."

Vic laughed. "Hey, they've got hot coffee over in the mess tent and the cook actually made some honest to goodness donuts that actually taste like donuts."

"I'm getting excited," said James. "How often does this happen, I wonder."

Vic continued. "The 25th Infantry Commanding General is supposed to be here shortly to kick off the operation with some great words of wisdom. The operation is supposed to start tonight, according to our detachment commander. He says it's pretty loose. They're going to be using a lot of jump teams to leap frog through the area and try to avoid using the search and sweep concept because of the difficult terrain. Most of the Area of Operations (AO) is heavy jungle and swamp. There's a little high ground here and there and the basic concept is to prep and seize the high ground and send probes into the low-lying areas. They want to cut off and squeeze Charley using this kind of tactic. Of course, the word is that the hard-to-find COSVN Headquarters may be out there somewhere. The Intel guys have been intercepting a lot of Charley radio traffic, and they believe that there may be some NVA there as well. We've got two pathfinder teams here. One team has two FNGs on it."

"Oh my God," screeched James. "You mean you can't do it all by yourself?"

"James, you're such an asshole," Vic retorted.

"Where are the Long Range Reconnaissance Patrols or LRRPs as they are commonly referred to?" Craig inquired.

"If they're who I think they are, they're over there," said Vic, pointing to several men sitting under a tent with the sides rolled up. "I was talking to them this morning. One guy is a know it all; one guy is an American Indian who doesn't say much; and one guy is an FNG. The other team is overdue. Evidently, they're putting it together from company resources."

"Well, this could be interesting," said Craig. "They want experienced people to insert inexperienced people."

Vic laughed. "When I asked about their pathfinder unit, they said they didn't have one yet. It appears that the aviation assets were sent over without a pathfinder detachment."

"Man, that can't be right," I said.

"It is what it is," replied Vic. "By the way, the guns are back here in Tay Ninh West. They've got a helluva assortment of howitzers and four deuce mortars. The detachment commander is worried about trying to fly around rounds en route to the LZs. They had the command briefing this morning and the Artillery Liaison Officer (ALO) said there may be some minor delays in delivery because of the multitude of LZs they intend to use. They've pre-registered about 150 different targets. The ALO has a target list."

"Well hopefully we won't have any problems," I said.

Big operations like this troubled me. Anytime there were multiple aircraft in the sky concerned me. The operational equation was suddenly loaded with helicopters, jet aircraft support, men with bullets, ALOs with lots of big bullets to fire at targets and men with automatic weapons. I had seen a lot of accidents in my tenure in Vietnam, and I knew before this operation was over there would possibly be people killed by our own artillery rounds, accidental discharges, and the infamous oops-I-thought-you-were-a-VC shootings. Anytime there are lots of people shooting and lots of machines flying and lots of booms and bangs, it is a pretty safe bet that somebody is going to get hurt. All you could do was hope it was the enemy instead of your own people.

Craig and I left Vic and the others in the middle of one of Vic's favorite war stories and walked to the tent where the lone LRRP team was located. We introduced ourselves and confirmed that we'd be working together. Two of them, Patello and Krasinski, were from New York. The other, Runninghorse, was an Apache from Arizona. Patello was the classic "New York Yankee" with a heavy accent, often vociferating ostentatious characterizations of the war, Nixon, and just about anything else for which he was a self-acclaimed expert. Krasinski was the FNG and hadn't been in country long enough to develop any opinions about anything. I could sense his uncertainties. I had those same uncertainties when I was an FNG, not to mention butterflies that through metamorphosis became pterodactyls. Runninghorse was an interesting fellow. I mentioned to him that my grandmother on my father's side was a Cherokee Indian. He said that his was too. I replied "then we have something in common," to which he retorted, "I doubt it." He showed virtually no emotion. You got the sense that he was not angry or outspoken, he was just honest.

"How long have you been in country," Runninghorse inquired.

"Over two years," I replied.

"What made you stay so long?"

"Didn't have anything better to do in the states for one thing, and I kind of got addicted to the place."

"I know what you mean," he said. "I'm thinking about staying longer but I haven't really made up my mind. The outfit is alright, but I think I'd be interested in staying longer if I could find a job that gave me better living conditions. The worst reservation is nothing like this place."

"What intrigues you about Vietnam?" I asked.

He smiled. "Now we have something in common."

Craig and I got another cup of coffee from the mess tent and spoke with the team for a few more minutes. They were pretty well briefed on the operation. They were missing their fourth member. I thought it strange that they would operate with only three people. The handbook on LRRP teams was written around four people with specific responsibilities for each member. Using only three would mean a shortage in firepower and tactical capabilities but they could compensate for that by staying a little closer together and walking single file in areas where front and rear security was needed. I didn't see any smoke grenades amidst their gear and asked Patello about it. For once in the course of the conversation he was gracious and said they had forgotten to include that in the pre-combat inspection. He sent Krasinski, who was junior in grade, to obtain one for each man.

When Craig and I returned to the helicopter, Vic was keeping the group entertained with story after story of great conquests of "Georgia Peaches," specifically those of the non-fruit variety. He was particularly proficient at describing the anatomical features and conquests of women in such a way that it was easy to see that it was probably nonsense. You found yourself drawn into the environment he created and could get a rather vivid picture of these Cleopatras and Helens of Troy he painted so well. If you questioned the need for him to enlighten us with these cherished tidbits of romantic gallantry he would say, "It's a dirty job but someone just has to do it."

The pilots returned and informed us on some of the details of the operations and the part we would play in it. The truth was nothing much had changed. We were on call and the plan was to drop LRRP teams into LZs sometime after dark. The LZs had been prepped and the teams knew that many, if not all of the LZs, might not be suitable for landing, which meant they would have a five- or ten-foot leap from the helicopter to the ground below. That is a real detriment at the onset of a mission, particularly if someone should strain an ankle or break a foot. The problem then becomes getting the injured party back in the helicopter. The immediate solution for LRRP team members is to toss their gear out first to free themselves of the extra weight.

Lieutenant Chien was from Sacramento, California. Like most Asians, he could be funny, and often poked fun at the "dinks, gooks, and slant eyed bastards." He always said this is no place for a "Chink" until one of Chiang Kai Shek's units showed up to support the war. I had the occasion to be with him when we visited the unit prior to supporting them. Surprisingly enough, he caught the attention of some of them, but many of them paid little attention to him walking through their midst. "Hell, I ain't no half-breed," he said. "What's wrong with these Chinks, anyhow? It's hard to show off when they don't even recognize me. You'd think they'd see my name on my uniform and say Damn, there's one of us. Dumb Chinks probably can't read. Maybe they think I'm a Spic. Do I look Spicish?"

He would often drink too much and had a tendency to fall asleep in the cockpit. We were making a return trip from Vung Tau where we had picked up some parts. Major Shelby was flying and Lieutenant Chien began to snore with his head drooped forward onto his chest. I unbuckled my seat belt to move forward and nudge him awake. Shelby waved me back and told me to buckle in tight. Within a few seconds he dropped the pitch and we were auto-rotating straight down. As Chien awoke, Shelby began yelling "My God, we lost the rotor." I was quite sure from Chien's reaction that he had soiled his pants. Shelby laughed all the way back to Bien Hoa. I never saw Chien sleep again. He may have been awake for three days.

Chien had picked up an extra box of C-rations. "Hey, I got me one with the chocolate candy and a B-3 unit, or is it B-1? And guess what Hardin; I met another guy from Sacramento."

I looked at him, somewhat amused at the way he expressed this discovery.

"Yeah, I know what you're thinking. You think he's another Chink, right?"

"I didn't say that."

"Well, he is. He's a Captain in the 25th Infantry Artillery."

"Well, that makes sense to me, LT. He probably started his career making firecrackers and just moved up to the big booms."

"Hardin, you number hucking ten GI, you know that?" he said jokingly in a contrived Vietnamese accent.

"No, me number 2, excrementally speaking." I retorted.

Chien didn't give up. "No, you big smarty pants. Too smart for your own good. I oughta have you court martialed."

"Oh, I get it, LT. Now you want to play the rank card."

"No candy, no B-2 or B-3 units for you, Hardin."

"Now I'm really broken hearted," I jeered, holding my hand over my heart.

"Serves you right for messing with me," he said feigning a punch to my midsection.

"I don't know about you, LT. I just don't know about you."

LT laughed and began opening his C-Ration unit. "Better eat," he said. "It may be my last supper."

Craig said, "Best I get a picture of this. Maybe someone will make a painting out of it and we'll be famous."

Vic piped in. "Not without a naked woman in it. The last supper didn't have a naked woman, but I understand from some very reliable sources that Michelangelo purposely left Mary Magdalene out of the picture. Actually, she was sitting at his feet with her hand on his thigh. Didn't go with the theme; it expressed some sexual overtures that would have undermined the significance of the last supper. Hey, picture this! Judah had the hots for Mary Magdaline but she had the hots for Jesus. To get to Mary, Judah had to take Jesus out of the picture. He found a way to get enough cash together to take her out on a serious date, and at the same time get rid of his competition."

Craig laughed. "Such sacrilege, such horrifying sacrilege," he said.

"Just fast forward that whole event into the world we know today," said Vic. "We'd have cops running all over the place investigating everybody. Let's see, we got bribery, debauchery of some sort, and finally murder. The trial was a joke. Pontius Pilot says I can find no fault with this man but do what you gotta do. Jesus got a speedy trial but man he could have used a change of venue, don't you think?"

"Now even more sacrilege." Craig said.

"Vic, maybe you should rewrite the bible," I said.

Vic Smiled. "Maybe I'll get to it this weekend when I have nothing to do."

WO Larson paid little attention to all of the joking and horsing around. He was a quiet sandy to red-haired Midwesterner who was usually quiet. He was the diabolical opposite of the loquacious and outgoing LT Chien. He was so tranquil and composed that you often wondered if he was awake, particularly when you were on a twenty- or thirty-minute flight. When he was at the controls, you saw virtually no movement and the head stayed so straight you thought someone had strapped a dummy into his seat. He was a kind and gentle person given to occasional cheerful or factual remarks but never was he ostentatious or insincere.

"What do you think?" I asked Larson in an effort to get a response.

"About what?"

"About the mission," I said, attempting to find something about which he could converse.

"It could be exciting," he replied. I really don't want to go in after dark unless we have to," he added.

"Hell, I don't want to go in during the daylight, or dark, or dusk, or at dawn," said Chien. "Did I miss anything?"

"Well one thing we know for sure," I said. "Charley knows we're here by now. I don't know how many soldiers he has out there but by now he should have been able to muster a force that can shoot at helicopters. There have been half-track 51 cals reportedly spotted on and around Ngui Bah Dinh. They leave some pretty large holes in helicopters and will do terrible things to rotor blades and Jesus nuts."

Vic said "Glad it's you and not me. We're going in with the first lift tomorrow. I think they're putting the LRRPs in tonight."

Craig and I decided to get everything ready rather than wait until the last minute. We tied down anything that could move with straps and did another check of the helicopter fluid levels and safety wire. The LRRPs joined us about 30 minutes later and sat in a circle next to the helicopter. They had all their gear with them and checked to make sure there were no loose items dangling from their rucksacks. They were going to be going with us, and their other team, which was now in tact, sat next to the helicopter behind us.

Patello was talkative, talking about previous missions. Krasinski was wide eyed in awe of Patello's stories. Runninghorse didn't seem to be interested and used a stick to doodle in the dirt in front of him. I could see that Krasinski had his doubts about this mission or possibly his courage was beginning to leak.

Training for LRRPs was often given in country to make up for the shortage of personnel experienced in trying to keep the teams manned. The training was sketchy and often did not include long range patrols and techniques taught in stateside training programs. Most infantry battalions had recon teams in their combat support companies but that they had proven to be insufficient in number to support the requirements for jungle warfare. As a result, additional LRRP teams were trained and assigned to each company and were considered battalion assets when multiple teams were needed. In most units, particularly those that had been in country for a long time, LRRP team members were drafted from the company infantry platoons. Obviously, the platoons did not want to give up their best men, and frequently those that were volunteered were not the best qualified. Brigade and division size units with Ranger battalions had ready resources of LRRP teams to the extent they were available in the numbers needed for multiple operations.

Although we had not been given a time of departure, I knew it was near. The LRRP teams had begun putting on their facial camouflage. LT, who had left the ready line to attend a briefing, returned and said we'd be leaving in 15 minutes. I untied the rotor blade and gave the LRRPs instructions on how to exit and enter the helicopter. Patello's facial expressions told me he thought I was being condescending or found my remarks all too plebian for someone of his vast experience. I covered the possibility of them having to jump if we could not touch the skids down. Runninghorse was taking everything in stride, clearly listening but looking at the helicopter as if he was rehearsing everything in his mind. I could tell that Krasinski was a deer caught in the headlights. I could tell that he was already imagining the worst possible scenario and would need to calm himself before we got to the LZ. I looked at all of them and said "I'm sure you'll do fine" with a final reassuring look in Krasinski's direction.

In minutes we were airborne. It was just about dusk. LT had advised me that we would take the long route, meaning that we would fly around a while to confuse Charley. It was getting cool and I tightened my flak vest to keep the cool air off my chest. Krasinski, who was sitting at my feet, looked up at me occasionally to see if he could see the fear in my face that he was experiencing. I knew that this wasn't going to be easy for him. He was going to spend a night in the jungle with the bad guys. He'll get over these fears, I thought, after he has a few missions under his belt, but I could never picture him being another Patello. I could see that Runninghorse was confident. He didn't appear to be the type that could have his confidence undermined easily. I concluded that Krasinski should follow his lead.

Krasinski tugged on my pants leg to get my attention and handed me a letter. "I forgot to mail this," he said.

"No problem," I replied, as I pushed the letter inside my breast plate to the pocket beneath it.

We were finally on short final to the LZ. As we made the final turn, I could see that it was remarkably large, about 300 meters long and 100 meters wide. We were to land at the south end and the team was supposed to exit the helicopter and make their way west. We came in quickly over the trees with the intention of dropping our cargo out quickly and efficiently. Patello and Runninghorse were crouched in the ready position. I noted that Krasinski was struggling a little trying to get to his feet.

As Patello and Runninghorse exited the helicopter we began receiving fire from the east. I heard the first rounds hit the tail boom. Chien had not seen three people exit the helicopter and turned in his seat to see if we were clear to leave. Krasinski still sat at my feet. I reached down to grab him and push him out, thinking he might need a push to get his mind and body in sync with the mission. Craig had already started firing in short bursts to the east. When I turned Krasinski's head around, I saw blood pouring from his forehead. Chien saw Krasinski's face and knew he'd been hit badly. He pulled pitch and the helicopter surged forward. Most of the fire was coming from Craig's side on the east. I saw Patello and Runninghorse disappear into the west wood line. When we were 100 meters away from the LZ, I fired into the tree line north of where we had dropped off Patello and Runninghorse. My intentions were to stop the movement of enemy, if any, in the area north of where we had left them. When we reached an altitude of 200 feet, Craig left his weapon and examined Krasinski. He was dead.

Chien reported to mission control by radio that we had one dead on the helicopter and had inserted two into the LZ. There was silence for a moment, and then a voice came back. "Land at the medevac pad upon your return," it said.

The trip back was strangely solemn. Complex emotions always infused the cockpit when we became the flying sarcophagus that carried a soldier on the first leg of a trip that would inevitably return him home. Krasinski still sat with his head leaning back against his rucksack. His eyes were still and lifeless, and his side touched my leg. I kept it there to steady him and keep him upright. In any war, there are unambiguous and painful times when reality cannot be distorted or in any way obscured. Indeed, this was such a moment.

Krasinski had expressed to me through his actions and demeanor that he had that ominous, gloomy feeling that I had seen in the eyes of others before him. His fear had proven to be the instrument of his death. He had hesitated but for a moment upon our approach to the LZ, and perhaps it was that moment of uncertainty that killed him.

If Krasinski wasn't ready for this, he shouldn't have been sent, I thought. Patello should have seen the timidity, the uncertainty and the fear. But someone like Patello wouldn't care. A weak team member would make him look all the stronger, and once again he could boost his own ego at the expense of others. Runninghorse's Indian heritage may have caused him to believe that every man runs the gauntlet to his own destiny. That would be an idiosyncratic Indian trait, would it not? I could tell he was someone who wouldn't waste his time making judgments or meddling in the affairs of others. It was not his place as he perceived it. Wasn't that just a little selfish? Wouldn't that be considered as aberrant thinking in an institution that trains men to watch each other's backs? There was a miasma of misgivings and shortcomings that surrounded the death of this man, I thought. It was often cloaked or masked by the nature of the mission, a shortage of personnel, the need for a body count and so many other issues related to the "big picture," to wit: closing with and destroying the enemy.

When we landed at the medivac pad, there were people standing there to carry Krasinski away. I imagined they were thinking that this would be the first of many. The body snatchers were always so damned clinical about their work. They unloaded bodies as if they were cargo intended for dry storage in a warehouse; two or three to a gurney if they felt it was necessary. There was no reverence that I could discern. But I wasn't a body snatcher, and I didn't know what they endured or how they felt about having to grab someone's decaying flesh, or opening a body bag and pulling its inhabitant out in three or four pieces.

When the body was removed, a medic asked me if there was anything else. I remembered the letter I had in my jacket pocket and decided not to give it to him. Krasinski had kept his commitment to his country, and I would keep my promise to him. The next morning, I found a company clerk from one of the units and gave him the letter to mail.

CHAPTER 6

We had been at Tay Ninh West for two weeks. The operation was going well. Surprisingly, the basic theme of the operation, to squeeze Charley between maneuvering elements, was working quite well and casualties were low. It was hot as Hades, as the expression goes, and canvas lister bags which were scattered sporadically around the base camp often ran dry. We were flying about three hours each day. Insertions were no longer needed at night. Once the squeeze was in place, Charley found himself trapped and there was no need to sneak around and find him in the dark. We knew where Charley was and he knew that we were cognizant of his positions and capabilities. There were tunnel complexes in and around Black Virgin Mountain, which provided him with some temporary relief but they would soon be searched. Enemy forces that were positioned in areas away from the mountain had to learn how to deal with the ever-increasing accuracy of artillery and mortars. Although Charley had grown fairly proficient at using the terrain to protect himself, the 25th Infantry was finding it easier to flush him out of areas that had heretofore been impenetrable sanctuaries.

Helicopters were bringing in prisoners on the hour. They were pitiful looking, but still deadly and always rather haggard looking, as one would expect. Their eyes were red and they appeared to be malnourished. They were all virtually expressionless as if told to appear that way. They squatted in circles with their hands tied behind their backs and blindfolds over their eyes. Military Intelligence personnel and their interpreters intermittently appeared at the base of the lookout tower where the prisoners were being guarded to escort one or more of them to tents to be interrogated. Vietnamese interpreters had ways of extracting information that were exclusively their own and unique to more conventional American methods. The age-old empirical techniques consisted of whatever it took to obtain the information based upon the level of will and pain threshold of the individual being questioned. Even the most stubborn and recalcitrant were soon separated from the information they tried desperately not to reveal. Craig and I noted during our own studious period of observation that there were 18 prisoners at the base of the tower. Periodically two would be taken away for questioning and two would return, but sometimes two were taken away and only one returned. At the end of several hours there were six prisoners at the base of the tower. It became a game of sorts to ascertain how many had returned after questioning and how many remained that had not been questioned.

"I think they've all been questioned," I said. "The six that remain are the lucky ones who decided to talk."

"It could be that they didn't talk but are being held only to be called back and told that their compatriots told different stories and they are dead meat."

"Nah, the six that are there are safe," I said. "Look, no bruises or contusions."

"Well, it could be that they are the ranking group and sung like birds and their stories are being corroborated by the peasants, or enlisted swine, whichever you prefer."

I laughed. "The six that are there are a mix of swine and officers who have been thrown together to insult the officers in such a belittling way that they will be forced to talk."

"Let's try this," said Craig. The six there are undercover minions of Military Intelligence who are extracting pertinent and usable information from their unsuspecting comrades."

"Nope, they're not talking."

"Just check out the body language, innuendos and exchange of eye signals; all the telltale codes of thought and info exchanges."

"Perhaps they're all that remain," I said, and had no real reason to believe otherwise.

We waited for a minute, then two, then ten. No one came to retrieve anymore prisoners. One of the prisoners was beginning to wobble. With his waning strength, he had the awkward appearance of a drunken duck, trying desperately to maintain his balance. The Vietnamese guard stepped forward and kicked him in the leg while scolding him sharply. The prisoner tried to steady himself to no avail and fell back on his buttocks. The guard yelled at him again and the prisoner attempted to return to his squatting position, this time falling forward to his knees. The guard saw that it was useless. The prisoner had been without water for an eternity in the hot sun and was sapped of all his strength. Within moments he would fall forward and lose consciousness.

"That boy needs some water," said Craig.

"And a week in Bermuda at an all you can eat buffet," I added.

"Depends on how you look at it," said Craig. "On one hand he's an animal that would have tortured and killed any one of us for no reason at all. On the other hand, he's still a human being that's fighting for his life."

There is certainly nothing perplexing about his antipathy for Americans now, I thought. Did he deserve to die in this manner? Should this kind of cruelty be acceptable? Were we playing tit for tat? I knew of many situations where Americans had suffered hideous injustices and extreme cruelty at the hands of VC and NVA soldiers. I didn't know this man's story. He may have been the worst of the lot, but there was a piece of me that wanted to take him a canteen of water. I guess that's why they call it a piece, I surmised. It's floating around in my psyche with no affiliation to an ideological base, or any good sense of direction. But we must do what must be done to win this war, I concluded. And it was not always pretty.

I noted a helicopter coming in from the east that appeared to have our company tail boom marking. As it flew closer, I could see the distinctive tiger on its nose and knew that it had a tail number from my platoon. Craig was watching it too and pointed at it as it landed.

When it had landed, I saw Steve Hall, one of the platoon crew chiefs, dismount and walk in our direction. He had seen our aircraft markings and knew where to find us. Steve had an air of pretentious arrogance about him that left you with a malaise of angst and disgust. He was the kind of pugnacious character that you just didn't like to be around. I kept him busy most of the time when he wasn't flying on jobs that would keep him away from normal average people.

"What's going on, Hall? I asked. "What brings you out here?"

"They want you back at Bien Hoa, Sarge," he replied in his usual straightforward manner. "You got personal problems back in the states."

"Who told you that?" I asked.

"The first sergeant. He wouldn't give me any more information. Just said you had to come back right away. You gotta get your gear and get on that helicopter. They're not staying. Just came to drop me off."

Hall went back to the helicopter that brought him to get his gear. I looked at Craig. "Dang," he said. "This trip was bearable with you, just barely of course. But I don't think I can put up with Hall for another week. "

"Well, it may be shorter than that. I don't think they're going to need us for the mop up, and I don't believe they're going to be using any more LRRPs."

"What an asshole that Hall is," said Craig. He was giving Doc a ration of crap one day. I wanted to knock the piss out of him. He's an obstinate bastard who won't keep his mouth shut."

"I'll see you back at base camp," I said.

"No problem," he replied. I hope everything is alright."

"Yeah, probably nothing to worry about."

I picked up my gear and went to the waiting helicopter. One of the maintenance mechanics was crewing and he helped me get on board.

"You know why I'm going back?" I asked. He held his hands palms up, to indicate he didn't.

I could not begin to imagine why I had to return. Perhaps someone was sick or possibly a car accident. We had a tail wind and managed to return within an hour. I left the flight line and dropped my gear off in my room and went to the orderly room. The first sergeant looked up from behind his desk as I walked in.

"You've got to go to the Red Cross office," he said.

"Do you know why?"

"I haven't the foggiest idea," he replied. "Marshal here will drive you up to their office on main post."

When we got to the Red Cross office, I signed in on the clipboard put there specifically for that purpose and took a seat with several other people who were also waiting. It wasn't long before someone called my name and I followed him back to a cubicle that was small and strewn with miscellaneous paperwork.

"Are you Beauregard LeRoy Hardin?" he asked.

"Yes, I am," I said.

"Is your father Dr. Robert H. Hardin?"

"Yes."

"I regret to inform you that he passed away on October 25. It was a heart attack following a short illness."

I was stunned but emotionless. I couldn't imagine him not being alive. Indeed, he was the life of the family, the virtual godfather of a generation of Hardins that looked to him for money, guidance and acceptance. He set the standard for the local medical community and a family that depended on him for everything. He was the raconteur of great jokes and stories, the person people would crowd around at the country club table to hear him speak, and a respected man in the community whose scholarly wisdom was often sought after and never questioned.

"What is today's date?" I asked.

"It's the 5th of November," he replied.

"How come it took so long to find me?" I asked.

"We were informed two days ago. You were in the field. You need to sign here," he said, as he pushed another clipboard across the table to me.

On the way back from main post I remembered my father's letter and the comment regarding the need for me "to come home." He was a heart surgeon and he knew he was dying. He just wanted to express the need for me to be there but didn't want to ruin my day with the truth. He would do that, I thought. It was his style. Preserve and protect the living and honor the dead. I'm going to miss you Dad, I thought, but at the time I really didn't realize how true that would be.

When I returned to the orderly room, the first sergeant said he was sorry for my loss and explained that he was told there was a death in the family but wasn't told who it was. He went on to say that I had a flight going out in three days. He turned to the pass board and said "I'm signing you out. As far as I'm concerned, I don't expect to see you until you return. You've got two weeks in the states and if you need to take another week, I'll carry you on leave until you return. You need anything?"

"Thanks Top," I said. "I'm fine."

I didn't like the feelings I was having. They were strange, completely out of character for me; a lot of guilt, a lot of remorse, and a lot of uncertainty. I hated the notion that anyone had to feel sorry for me and wasn't pleased with the looks I got from passersby. Word had traveled fast and most of the company knew by this time.

I wasn't really sure what to do with myself. I didn't want to be alone and I didn't want to be thrust into a crowd and engage in the usual disingenuous small talk. I felt anxious and morose, and agitated and angry all at the same time. I wanted to cry and was angry that I couldn't. Crying, I had decided, was a trait that was unbefitting of the moment in this environment. I didn't mind if someone else did, but regardless of the number of psychiatrists that said it was good for the soul or inner self, it just wasn't part of my repertoire of emotions. In time that would change. I would just have to work this out.

I went to my room and fidgeted. "Fidget," I pondered, must be a word of southern origin. Both my mother and grandmother would constantly say to the children "Quit fidgeting." My fidgeting must have bothered them then as much as it did me at the moment. I couldn't contain myself. I was reading a page from one book, then another. I was reading a letter then looking for another one. I was suddenly aware of the fact that it was hot and I was perspiring. I went to the latrine and washed my face then returned to my room where I continued to perspire. I was slowly growing tired of me fidgeting. I must change the environment, I thought. I could not abide staying in my room for three days waiting for a flight back to the "real world" and I could not tolerate these restive feelings. Exhausted with the moment and my intractable impatience, I decided to go visit the Hope Bar and Hoa.

The Hope Bar was quiet. There was no music playing and very little activity inside. Papasan had closed the side windows to block off the tantalizing view of the alley ways on either side of the building. A fan over the bar intermittently interrupted the flicker of a solitary light fixture, which was working on about 30 volts and gave the appearance of a very old ten-watt bulb. The intermittent light and slowly swirling fan gave Big Mama, who stood behind the bar, an angelic image as if she were standing in a soft blinking haze. The light behind her shadowed her face and I could not recognize her at first. I squinted my eyes in an attempt to focus in on her.

"I couldn't tell it was you," I said.

"It is not me," she said as she laughed. "I am a ghost."

"I always thought so." I replied.

"No, I lie. I am too old to be ghost."

"How old is too old to be a ghost?" I asked.

"Thirty," she said. "But I am thirty-one," she lied.

"I wouldn't take you for a day over twenty-nine," I lied back.

"Bo, you full of shit, you know that?"

"Sure, because I'm not a ghost," I said. "Do ghosts shit?

"I can't remember," she laughed. "I am too old to remember."

"I need a drink," I said.

"What you want, whiskey?"

"Your best," I said.

"I have a bottle of Imperial, very old, maybe two days."

"That will be fine."

Big Mama poured me the drink and I threw a stack of military script notes totaling 30 cents on the bar. The drink was hardly imperial whiskey. If it was it had been so badly watered down that you could hardly taste it.

"Big Mama, this is bad stuff," I said.

She took my drink from my hand and pulled a bottle of Johnny Walker from under the bar.

"Here, I give you some of Papasan's hooch. I don't like it when he drink too much. He all the time want to fuck me."

"What's wrong with that?" I asked.

"He fuck number ten thou."

I decided not to provide a follow up to Big Mama's comment. I wouldn't want Papasan to come in and surprise us while she was airing out his sexual shortcomings in detail. She probably wouldn't care, and would yell at him the way she usually did when he got upset. But she wouldn't give up.

"He like very fast rabbit."

"Be nice," I said.

"I know you fuck good. Hoa say you fuck good."

Her inference to Hoa caught me off guard. I really didn't think Hoa was the type to discuss intimacies in public.

She continued when I said nothing and looked at her in amazement. "She don't say with words, Bo. She say with her eyes. I know these things. Just like I know you have problems right now. I see it in your eyes. What your problem?"

"My father died."

"Oui cha," she said. "That too bad, number ten. You go home?"

"Yeah, in three days."

"You tell Hoa?"

"I haven't seen her yet," I said.

"She no come here today. Maybe you go her house. She had to go to doctor about her toe."

"I will," I said.

I finished my drink after talking to Papasan for a while. He was worried that the military script might be changed to a different color in the near future, which would make the old script worthless, and he had several hundred dollars worth that he wanted to dispose of. He suggested that I should get several hundred dollars in Piasters and buy the script from him. I told him I probably wouldn't be around long enough to accommodate him because I was going home for a few weeks. I promised him I'd do what I could.

When I got to Hoa's place, I heard the sound of water coming from within the thin walls. I knocked on the door and she said she was bathing. She said to come in but made me promise not to look. I lied to her and said I wouldn't. When I entered the door, I could see her in my peripheral vision crouched down in the familiar Vietnamese squatting position. She was completely naked. She was washing her hair over a bowl and the long black draped languidly downward to the top of the bowl. Her body was wet and what little light was in the room seemed to careen off the drops of water that rolled slowly down her back onto her buttocks. I sat on the bed three feet away from her and raised a cupped hand to each side of my face.

"You look at me," she said accusingly.

"Well maybe a little but not too much."

I could see her injured toe. It was bruised and the nail looked as if it was somewhat lifted from its normal position.

"What did you do?" I asked as I pointed at her toe.

"I walk like elephant. I hit my toe table leg at the Hope Bar."

"Does it hurt? Do you want me to kiss it for you?"

"No, It doesn't hurt," she said. "You don't kiss my dirty feet."

"Some people like to kiss feet."

"Some people crazy."

Another cultural glitch, I thought. Vietnamese are not a foot-admiring people. It is an insult to sit with your legs crossed showing the bottoms of your feet, particularly if you have just met someone.

"I have bad news," I said.

"What is bad?" she replied.

"My father died about two weeks ago."

"You go home now?"

"I will for about two weeks."

"I'm sorry for you," she said, looking genuinely saddened at my news.

"It will be alright," I said.

"My plane leaves in three days. I'm going to Knoxville, Tennessee to talk to my mother and my brother. I'm sure they are very upset."

I saw the doubting, or possibly questioning look in Hoa's eyes. I knew what she was thinking. Was this a way out for me? Was I using this as an excuse to leave and never return? I had been there for years and she didn't know for sure when my tour would end. Neither did I.

She stood straight up and came to me. Her breasts rested against my face as she pulled my head into her chest.

"Bo, promise you come back to me," she said in a despondent voice. "I need you. You don't need me but I need you. I don't think I could live here without you. You promise me you come back."

"Of course, I will," I said, feeling sorry for her and the fear and doubt she harbored.

She lay down on the bed and pulled me down next to her. She reached over and began to rub my chest. It was the custom to rub the chest of someone who was mad, sad or anxious about something. I never appreciated it before but I did now. Her right hand moved slowly up and down my sternum and soon the uneasiness and anguish began to subside. The fidgeting had disappeared and I felt as if I was gradually regaining control of my faculties. The warmth of her next to me and the slow rhythmic rubbing of my chest eventually got the better of me. The worry and heightened emotions over my father's death combined with the trip back to Bien Hoa had made me very tired. In a few seconds I was asleep.

I awoke several hours later. The mosquito nets had been pulled down and there was a small candle lit on the stand next to the bed. Hoa lay on my shoulder and she was sound asleep. I looked at her long black hair and petite body. She was magnificent, I thought, and the dim lighting illustrated and highlighted the curves of this vivacious woman who at this moment was perfect. I pondered moving my hands to the curves and breasts that lay next to me. Sex would be great, but this was not the night for it. It seemed almost sacrilegious given the circumstances. I pulled her body a little closer to mine. Her lips parted slightly as if she was trying to say something then she pulled her knee onto my chest slightly below the hand that still rested lightly on my sternum. I leaned to my left just enough to blow the candle out without waking her and went back to sleep.

The next morning was picture book perfect. We made love in every conceivable way for what seemed to be hours. We bathed each other using the large bowl intended for that purpose and shared a breakfast of eggs and bread retrieved from a local vendor by the next-door neighbor's son who was glad to get the twenty piasters I gave him to make the trip.

I felt human again. I left Hoa with a gold ring that was given to me by my father with the promise that I would retrieve it upon my return. I could tell that she felt I was being honest and although she was sad that I was leaving, she felt, as I did, that our relationship had progressed immensely. In the last two weeks we had found in each other something that wasn't there before, but neither of us could put a name on it, or perhaps we were afraid to try.

I returned to the base and gathered my things, dropped by the orderly room to pick up my money from the company safe and checked with the Operations room to see when the next flight was leaving for Saigon. I left Bien Hoa on a flight later in the day and arrived in Saigon in about 30 minutes. The next day I boarded a Pan Am flight for the states.

Boarding the aircraft was a surreal experience. Everything was so clean. The lights were bright and the luster of the seats and carpeted aisles appeared luxurious after living in such an austere environment. The stewardesses were both enormous in size and carved works of statuesque art. It had been two years since I had seen a European or American woman, deemed "round eye" by the GIs, and a woman that exceeded a height of five feet appeared to be an Amazon. I was equally amazed at the crispy clean uniforms they wore. There were no fashion statements in Vietnam. Clothing consisted of jungle fatigues for the duty day and evening ware was flip flops and cutoffs. My ill-fitting Khakis I had pulled out of mothballs for the trip home seemed hardly adequate for the occasion. Were it not for the other GIs in similar attire, I would have been asked to leave the plane.

The flight home was marked with the usual gaiety of those who were making their final departure from Vietnam. There was singing and yelling and even crying from those who had completed their year and now reveled in anticipation of the home-comings that lay ahead. I took two small pills from my Sleep Ease bottle I had found at the PX and downed them without water.

I awoke in Alaska as the plane touched the ground. We were going to have a two-hour layover before continuing on to the states and I relished the opportunity to get off the aircraft and into the airport. It was cold in Anchorage but we only experienced it briefly as we walked from the aircraft into the airport. I remember stuffed animal heads and a few larger animals that were completely stuffed. They were done tastefully, I thought, as I walked by them into what was less than an impressive lounge. Several of us sat down and ordered something exotic. I guess we were all trying to make up for lost time, experiencing behaviors and environments to which we had grown completely unaccustomed.

An older gentleman sat down at the same table and began to ask us questions about Vietnam. He was polite as he was inquisitive, and in the course of the conversation we learned that he had been a deputy secretary of sorts in the Kennedy Administration. We were all impressed. There was no reason to doubt this chap. He was well spoken and very polished. I remember that he had a way of looking at you that made you believe he was really interested in what you had to say and was committing every word to memory. I don't remember who he was but I remember that I was envious of his people skills. He was caring, enthusiastic in a subtle but ingenuous way, and had the aura of a very distinguished general.

We spoke for quite a while. The soldiers at the table told war stories, none of which appeared to be enhanced with camouflaged truth, and the gentleman listened intently, occasionally asking questions or nodding his head in agreement.

Eventually we were alone. All the others had left to join a few girls who had meandered in and found a nearby table. He leaned forward to suppress his voice where his comments could not be heard. "I have a proposition for you, my friend," he said. "You may not like what I have to say but hear me out without getting too upset. You have been watching young men die for a long time. You have labored tirelessly to win a war that is at best frustrating. The people of the US don't have the stomach or the commitment to stick with this to the end. It is going to wind up as a source of embarrassment for the administration left holding the bag in the not-too-distant future. We, my organization, don't like this notion any more than you do, but we have concluded, unequivocally, that this war will prove to be a historical cancer for America. It will be our most humiliating loss ever to a band of ill-equipped and unequally trained fighters whose only edge, is that of will or perseverance. Our defeat, no matter what it is called, will tell third world countries everywhere that political war can undermine the efforts of superior American combat technology. There are too many potential battlefields on our horizon, too many struggles that will absorb the lives of our soldiers, sailors, and marines, if the outcome of this war is what appears to be a certainty. My group is not a peace-loving group like some might think. We have worked closely with politicians in an effort to gain their support to use the kind of munitions needed to win this war. A voting constituency that wants this war over at any cost, unfortunately, adversely affects them. We cannot count on their support in any capacity. We have explored other options, but none have had the surgical acumen needed to excise this certain malignancy that will inevitably malign and degrade the world's recognition of America as a super power. There is but one solution to this problem and it is one that none of us like. We have to play an absurd game of politics that ends this way. Either America fully supports the war and we end it militarily, or the fighting man demands a withdrawal from this war based upon non-support from the people. The catalyst for both hypotheses is you, and people like you, who are willing to establish an unparalleled and never-seen-before dialogue with the American people. We believe that if we create a conduit to the American people for the people actually fighting this war, we can find a quick resolution. Quite frankly, we hope that solution will be a quick, decisive defeat of our enemy by our military, and that it will be so magnificent that none will ever question our political resolve in the foreseeable future. The only way to assure historical opulence is to force America to make a choice of only two alternatives. At this time. we are locked in a standoff that clearly advantages the doves and pushes the hawks into political and historical obscurity. Only people like you can put an end to that. You have to speak out in a way that makes clear the enormity of the situation. Let me say that whatever you do, you will be well paid for it, and if at any time you want out, you can leave. I am prepared to make you a near perfect deal, but you will pay a price, and there will be times when you regret it. I am not hiding anything, I mean not to be deceitful, and I will be the first to tell you that this whole venture will serve to embarrass you and those close to you."

I was beginning to get the point. It was clear that he and his group had an agenda that included some form of political tomfoolery and rather elaborate scheming that was clearly beyond my capability to understand. I listened carefully, all the while keeping an ear keyed on the airport public address system that would announce the departure of my flight. I was curious about what role he envisioned me played in this proposal and continued to listen. The gentleman continued.

"Let's cut to the chase, as the expression goes. Assume for a moment that you went into that bathroom and changed clothes and went your own way, instead of the Army's way. I would assure you that you would have the time and money to visit your home or whatever your intentions were, then I would ask that you would become a part of our campaign or cause as I have described it. We would use some media propaganda to show you as a disgruntled soldier who has grown weary of fighting a war that is not fully supported by the American people, and characterize your plight as one that parallels the thoughts, feelings and opinions of every Vietnam soldier, sailor, and marine. The Army will consider you AWOL but not the American people. They will see you as one who could no longer fight a war with two enemies; North Vietnam and a dysfunctional political system. With the right media coverage, we will characterize you as someone that wants to get the attention of the American people and gain their support for this war. Your position will be that quick and decisive military planning strategies aimed at mass destruction of the enemy will end this war and bring the fighting man home. In the interim, you will be well paid and protected. Five thousand a month ought to hold you over. There's a bonus when this is over, and a law firm ready to provide legal services that you will obviously need sometime in the future. We will keep you hidden and away from both the Army and others who would like to shut you up."

I heard the announcement of my flight departure over the loud speaker. We would be boarding in 15 minutes. The gentleman acknowledged it, turning his head toward the speaker.

My retort to his proposal came without any thought. "I'm impressed but I think not," I said. "I agree with many of your thoughts and ideas, and I'm inclined to believe that some of your prophecies may come to pass, but I come from a family of fighting men and what they think of me is important. I have good friends back in Vietnam and I am obligated to return to them. They need me and I need them. My military life, especially in Vietnam, is not at all complicated. I know what I'm going to wear, where I'm going to be, and what I'm going to do, with very few exceptions. I think you may have a hard time finding a young soldier who has political views on the war. Most of us are driven by things that are totally unrelated to your cause. We appreciate camaraderie, given the situation, even if it's experienced when immersed in a lethal undertaking. We are driven primarily by sex and booze, which have become the rewards du jour for doing a good job in the field. We take great pride in reveling in our accomplishments, which we relate in what has become known as war stories. We could give a damn less about the political aspects of war. We are young and foolish and look forward to the moment when we can engage the enemy. We take crazy chances both on the battlefield and in the whorehouses. We hate memorial services and take great pride in getting decorated with little ribbons like the ones our fathers have on uniforms that are hanging in attics a long way from here. These are our reasons to live. The only reason we would take a stance against the flower children or the politicians is if they did something to degrade us or piss us off. Vietnam is a crazy enigma. It is 5000 revolutions per minutes of life and death. It is the creation of the aged and the deadly playground of youth. I have been there for two years and hope to stay until it's over. I guess you would call me selfish and uncaring, given your position on the matter, but I know where my heart is. It is with the Vietnamese people who are ruthlessly slaughtered and with those who must slaughter the slaughterers. It is with my buddies who cover my back both in the jungle and in the ville. It is especially alert to a passing flag, making my chest swell proudly while trying to control tear ducts as it did with my father and generations of fathers before him. This is my war and I love it. My government has made Vietnam my home and I intend to stay there. I want no interruptions except the sound of artillery and the rattling sound of machineguns that are making mincemeat out of the enemy."

I turned to walk away. "Got to catch my plane," I said.

"Yes, I think you do," he responded with a note of resignation in his voice.

I boarded the Pan Am in a long slow, moving line of men who seemed incredulously different, as if they had already reconnected with a world left behind and were now content. Everyone returned to their same seat as if they had gained some form of ownership from sitting there on the first leg of the flight.

The freedom bird shuddered a bit and strained ever so slightly to lift its cargo. I began to ponder coming home and wondered what awaited me. Most of my schoolmates had moved or were involved in things that I couldn't relate to. I thought about the country club and the good times I had there. It seemed so long ago, and it was. I hadn't been there in years and based upon some of my subtle lifestyle changes, I probably would be somewhat out of place in such an environment. Sometimes people change. I knew I had, and for the worse. My values, compared to what they once were, had really gone south. I had wanted to be a doctor like my father, or a lawyer like my uncle. I had made a mess out of things succumbing to the aspirations of the "wrong crowd." I had made the mistake of getting married young. A hundred fights and 2 children later, to make a very long story into a very short one, we had agreed to divorce. There was nothing amicable about our agreement. She had taken most of the money I had and I got all of the bills. She was in the throes of getting the divorce, at least I thought she was, and I had wrongly assumed that I could play the role of a single man until the paperwork caught up with me. In retrospect, I could see the errors of my youthful ways but it was all history now. No reason to apologize for being infinitely stupid, I thought. Indeed, it was time to move on to more positive and honorable accomplishments.

Somebody in the seat behind me tapped me on the shoulder and offered me a drink. I grabbed my cup and watched an old soldier, a lifer like me, pour Jack Daniels into it. I said thanks and we spoke for a while. It was an uncomfortable conversation. I was turning my head back to the rear to both speak and reply. His situation was much like mine. He was going home on leave as a result of a death in the family. He had been in the 1st Cavalry and had extended for a Special Forces assignment. He extended for 6 months in order to get the assignment and a 30-day free leave came with the extension. It was just another one of the great presumed freebies that come with being a soldier.

Before long there were a dozen or so people conversing back and forth across the aisle. We went through Special Forces' bottle and started on someone else's. The stewardess was busy bringing drinks to people. The small two-ounce bottles were getting ordered in threes and fours and before too long, the laughter and joviality we had all enjoyed in little post exchanges were now present in the Pan Am cruising at 30,000 feet. The war stories came with a rush. Each story was better than the last. An assault by one VC became an assault by a North Vietnamese company. We were playing one-up-man-ship. I waited knowing that someone would tell one that would be truly unbelievable and before too long it was told. But no one challenged the prevarication of facts. No one really cared. Questionable war stories told in drinking circles were not a manifestation of one's true character or capabilities. War stories were treated much like ghost stories or tales of turmoil passed from one generation to the next that seemed to get better each time they were told. Those who told them well gained in stature. It was the guy that didn't tell war stories that worried me. But no such guy was present in this gathering of revelers and before too long the entirety of the airplane was chatting and laughing.

The stewardesses had loosened up, and had grown tired of running to the galley every time there was a call for another two-ounce bottle. They parked a cart with several hundred bottles in the middle of the aisle and were tossing the bottles 10 and 15 feet to waiting hands. When a young soldier nearby said he was out of money, they declared that drinks were on the house and began passing them out to whoever needed them. In the course of a conversation with Special Forces, a stewardess placed a cup of Johnnie Walker on my tray. I didn't see her set it down but another chap did and brought it to my attention. A group in the rear began to sing a hundred bottles of beer on the wall and a larger group objected. Eventually the singing subsided. The last distinguishable voice heard in the group of singers was that of a stewardess.

This lasted for several hours. Before it was over, the stewardesses were drinking and laughing with the crowd. One sat on my lap and someone snapped a photo, which was given to me. It seemed like it was alright to laugh again. It was laughing without fear, laughing without reservation, laughing without care. It dawned on me that laughing was a carefree act and these people had discovered that they had left the twilight zone of fear and apprehension behind and entered a world where they could laugh again freely.

The evening ended like it started. Little by little the chatter subsided, overhead lights went out one at a time, and the snores of sleeping men rose in a chorus. I believe they slept well…for the first time in a long time.

The bumping along the runway of Travis Air Force Base awoke me. Others had already moved to the windows to get their first glimpse of California. For many it was the end of the line. Some were staring hard at departure areas to see if they could identify awaiting loved ones. They couldn't. Windows were dark and identifying anyone would have been impossible. Emotions ranged from high, for those only moments away from seeing loved ones, to low for those who had another plane or two to catch. I kept my seat knowing that there would probably be a little anxiousness on the part of those who were in a hurry to get off the aircraft. I had a way to go, first to Atlanta via Pan Am, then on to Knoxville via Republic Airways. I still had 8 or 10 hours of traveling including layovers. I felt a little excited for those who were meeting wives and mothers here at Travis. One young fellow kept saying "Jesus, Jesus," in an uncontrollable way. Another was fighting back the tears. These are moments that folks do not forget. I didn't know then just how important they were or what an impact they would have on the lives of those who experienced them. Some were about to have their every wish come true but some were in for big surprises. Many girlfriends had found other boyfriends but continued to write, opting to delay the bad news until the soldier had returned. This was cruel, I thought. People get over terminated romances in due time. It is better to spend 6 weeks in mourning in Vietnam than the first 6 weeks back in country. For some returning crusaders, the visions of long nights in a motel, or a walk on the beach would be mercilessly wrenched from their repertoire of wishes and desires. Many came back to wives who had made other romantic arrangements. Yes, these were moments to remember, and they all happened miraculously in the middle of the "make love-not war era." The hemisphere was divided both in military perspectives and romantic dogma: a guerilla war in the east and a love-in in the west. It could be confusing, indeed it could.

The ground felt good to walk on. We were being herded to another holding area where customs would in-process those who were getting their baggage and going no further. I sat with several others in an area where vending machines and coffee were available. A long two hours later we boarded the aircraft en route to Atlanta.

The flight to Atlanta then on to Knoxville was spent sleeping and looking out the window at fields and cities below. My brother and two of is friends picked me up at the airport. True to form, my brother had an evening lined up for me, which included a meal which really didn't interest me. I had gorged myself with all the heavy carbohydrates and sugar I could stand. I felt bloated and uncomfortable and was able to talk them out of going to a restaurant. We were going to the Stonebridge Inn on the outskirts of east Knoxville where food was served and a band provided music for dancing. When we arrived there, the first order of business was to order a drink, then another and another. Sometime in the middle of the evening I heard my brother say, "Just have a good time and don't worry about anything." And I didn't. I found a girl that was as interested in dancing as I had suddenly become and she moved to our table to be close and convenient. Several friends and acquaintances from years gone by also moved to the table. A singer by the name of Buddy Rich was playing piano with accompaniment. The music was good and the woman was big, all of five feet three inches tall. Those at the table didn't quite grasp my reference to her as a round eyed Amazon. We danced every slow song which seemed to be about every song played. My brother decided to award me with the sobriquet of "Jungle Bunny." I don't remember leaving the bar but I vaguely remember someone helping me out of the backseat of the round-eyed Amazon's car and into my brother's.

The next morning was what you would expect; a head that hurt and the startling sensation you get when you wake up somewhere and don't recognize anything around you or remember how you got there. It was my brother's house. I could hear my brother and his wife, Ann, arguing in the kitchen about the hour we got home and our condition when we arrived.

"Well Ann, he just got back from Vietnam," he said. I told you we were going to take him out for a few drinks. I'm sorry if it lasted a little longer than what I anticipated, but dang, he just got back from Vietnam."

"Yeah, he just got back, but you didn't," she said. "I bet you were dancing and carrying on like that drunk in there lying on the floor."

I was lying on the floor. There was a blanket thrown over me and I was minus my shirt and shoes. It was a one-bedroom apartment but there was a couch. I wondered if I had missed the couch.

"And look at him," Ann continued. "He's got to be on drugs. Hell, he's lost sixty or seventy pounds. You've read all that stuff in the newspapers about GIs being on drugs over there. Nobody gets that skinny without something being wrong."

"He's not on drugs," said Danny. "I know my brother. He doesn't do that sort of thing."

"Well, I tell you what," she said. "I'm going to work and I don't want some drug addict staying in my house while I'm gone."

I elected not to say anything but thought it would be wise to make myself known rather than to let this conversation become any more vile and inaccurate than it had become. I moaned and stretched sufficiently to be heard and made my way to the kitchen.

Ann gave me a hug and said, "It's so good to see you, Bo. Welcome home."

"It's good to be here," I said. How have you been?"

"Just fine," she replied. "I'll get you some coffee."

"I have to apologize about last night, I said. "Sorry about getting in so late and keeping Danny out until the wee hours. I hope I didn't get him in trouble."

"No, that's alright she said. I know you just got home and all."

Danny said nothing but listened carefully. He winked at me as if to say "everything's copasetic." Danny had to go to work and excused himself, telling me he would see me about one o'clock. He intended to take a half day off from the car lot where he sold cars. He hugged me and bid us farewell.

"What did you intend to do today?" said Ann as she sat my coffee down on the table before me.

"Just thought I'd rest a while and watch television."

"Well, I have someone coming over to clean the apartment today. If I could drop you off downtown, then Danny could bring you home; I believe that would be better."

"Sure Ann, no problem," I said.

I made a quick decision that I wasn't going to tolerate this kind of treatment. I knew no one owed me anything but I didn't deserve this. I wasn't angry, just disappointed, and possibly a little troubled that she could reach these terribly wrong conclusions without giving me the benefit of the doubt.

I cleaned up and packed my bag and met Ann at the car where she was waiting impatiently to go to work.

"You're taking your things," she asked.

"Yeah, I'm going to do some laundry and buy a few new clothes." I lied. "The ones I have aren't really worth keeping."

We drove almost in silence to Henry Street and I told her she could drop me off there. I said "Thanks for the ride" and got out of the car. I went to the YMCA and got a room for three days.

I called my mother from my room. When she answered there was an awkward moment of silence.

"Mom," I said. "Are you there?"

"Yes," she said.

"Are you OK?"

"Yes."

"I thought I'd come and see you."

"Where are you?"

"At the YMCA."

"I don't think that would be convenient."

I had heard that expression before. "Not convenient" meant I don't want to see you. I was surprised at her response. Danny had told me that she had been drinking since Dad's death, which was something I had never seen her do, and not to be surprised if she was under the influence when we saw her. I tried to find another way to divert what appeared to be a catastrophe, at least for me. I decided to act like I didn't comprehend her poignant remarks.

"Well maybe we could meet somewhere."

"No, that wouldn't be convenient either."

I was losing my patience which is something one should not do with this strong-willed outspoken woman.

In a desperate attempt to resolve this situation I said, "Mom, what is the problem?" That was a mistake.

She became boisterous and vicious in her tone and quickly retorted. "I'll tell you what's wrong. You killed your father, that's what's wrong. You left this family and went to Vietnam when he needed you the most. He worried about you every day. You killed him just as sure as if you drove a knife into his heart."

I said nothing and there was silence at her end. What could she expect me to say?

"I'm sorry, Mom," I said, and the phone went dead. I felt helpless with this turn of events. Nothing is more demoralizing or destabilizing than having a parent angry with you when there is a death of another parent. We are all psychological children until our parents are deceased, regardless of whether you're ten or sixty. Acceptance is one of the needs we are born with, and it remains forever until the surviving parent is no longer alive. I knew my mother was demonstrably headstrong when it came to matters such as these. I had seen her refuse to talk to her twin sisters for years over a matter so trivial that it could have been cast aside and forgotten rather than resolved through unnecessary discussion. Blaming me for my father's death represented a conundrum that would not be resolved easily. It would take time and time would be my ally. She needed time to think, and the hurt she felt combined with the new affinity for alcohol would extend that time.

I called my brother and advised him of the conversation as well as moving out of his apartment. He apologized for Ann's conduct and said he wasn't surprised how Mom had reacted. He asked me to meet him at the lawyer's office for the reading of the will he had set up for the two of us. I did so and learned that except for a trust, which had been established for my brother in the event that my parents predeceased him in death, there was nothing specifically earmarked for us. I didn't think there would be. My father was a proponent of hard work and believed that wealth without work was a sin. After the reading I went back to the YMCA and my brother went back to work.

Returning to the small room at the YMCA was difficult. I had become lethargic and aggravated with the outcome of this trip. I could never have predicted what occurred, but I should have been aware of the possibilities. Staring out the window from the fifth floor of the YMCA at an overcast and gloomy day made the day's events even more ominous. I decided there was no need for me to stay in Knoxville. There was nothing more I could do. I had the feeling that I had violated the inner sanctum of my dwindling family at a time when my presence merely added to the unrest and confusion, and it would be best if I left. I packed my bag in two minutes, checked out of the YMCA and got a taxi for the airport. Inside of three hours, I was on a plane bound for Philadelphia with a ground connection to Fort Dix, New Jersey, where the Army would arrange a flight back to Vietnam.

I reviewed what had happened on the flight to Philadelphia. The journey home by the prodigal son had not gone as intended. Other than the greetings of a brother with his own life and agenda, there were no extended arms or salutations. Perhaps I had expected too much, I thought. It was quite possible that my prescient father had foreseen this outcome and dutifully warned me in the letter that said "You should come home now."

The states, Knoxville and the civilian way of life seemed strange to me. In some ways it was as if I was watching an old movie in black and white that could not keep my interest. I was out of place, a geographical alien and mislaid extraterrestrial in a country I could visit but had no other claim of origin or familial rights. Had I laid the foundation for my own exile? Was my ambivalence the result of my own misguided expectations? I didn't know, but I knew I was in the wrong place. Home had become a metonymy for survival, but to live I had to return to Vietnam.

The flight back to Vietnam was precisely what I expected. I caught an Air Force C-141 out of McGuire Air Force Base which is adjacent to Fort Dix for transportation and support purposes. There were about 100 men on the aircraft, most going to Vietnam for the first time. Duffel bags were stacked and tied down in the cargo area and fabric and metal jump seats were in place for the passengers. They were uncomfortable and sleeping in them was almost impossible. Many of the young soldiers who were going for the first time began to question those of us who had already been there. There were men that aspired to heroism and predicted their heroics in pre-fabricated war scenarios, moving like Sergeant Vic Morrow in the television serial "Combat" to destroy enemy bunker after enemy bunker. There were others who were truly frightened by the prospect of being in a combat zone and were not afraid to admit it. There were several more mature soldiers who made no prejudgments and were satisfied with waiting to see what the future held.

I had learned that you could not prejudge soldiers or predict how well they would do in a combat situation based upon their youthfulness or personality traits. You just had to wait and see. Some went to the field and rarely complained, while others you would expect to take everything in stride were the biggest complainers who found fault with their leadership, living conditions, and the Vietnamese people. A lot of young men became very mature men and the soldier that was picked on as a child often became a force to deal with when a weapon was placed in his hand. Those that were unreliable and untrustworthy before they came in the service, a.k.a. losers, who did not change their behavior afterwards, became even bigger losers because they now had two enemies: the enemy we were fighting as well as their own peers who could not rely on them to fulfill their part of the mission. Their backs were never covered.

There was one young soldier who was especially inquisitive. He had red hair and looked like he was sixteen. His pimpled face and ruddy complexion made me think of Opie on the television show, Mayberry RFD. When a seat next to me became vacant, he sat down to talk to me.

"What's it like over there, Sarge," he asked.

"Well, it's what you make it," I answered.

"How long you been there?"

"About two years."

"Did you ever kill anybody?"

"Yes, a few."

"Was it like in the movies?"

"Nothing like in the movies," I said. In the movies you get a bird's eye view of everything the good guys and bad guys are doing. In the movies there are no equipment malfunctions and weapons never have to be reloaded. In the movies there are heroes that are clearly observed destroying the enemy and taking prisoners. In Vietnam, it's not that way. You don't always see the enemy and it's hard to know where everyone is all of the time. There are equipment and communications malfunctions because of the intense heat. Sometimes the only person who knows you're a hero is you. If everyone is fully committed, heroic actions are not always observed."

I was purposely vague in my descriptions of battlefield activities. There were some things that an FNG has to learn slowly. I could have said, "Most of the time you will not see the guy that is shooting at you. Most of the time you are more concerned about mortar attacks than you are snipers and well concealed enemy. Most of the time, a bullet that strikes you or someone else has inscribed on its side "To whom it may concern," and there will be many times when one of your own will shoot at you in error."

"When do I get to my unit?" he asked. "Do I have a choice? I want to be in the 82nd Airborne like my father was in WWII."

"You'll probably go to Camp Alpha in Saigon for a few days. They will give you an in-country briefing and some new equipment, and then you'll be assigned to a unit. You can request a unit and they'll accommodate you if they can. It all depends on the personnel needs of the field units."

I remembered my first night at Camp Alpha. I was put on guard duty and the cadre scared the dickens out of us with stories about guards who were walking the perimeter being killed by sappers and snipers. The perimeter was an interior perimeter almost a kilometer away from the outer perimeter and we were actually in no danger. I'm really glad they didn't sneak up on us to check our reaction. That could have been devastating. In my frightened state I would have fired every round in my M14 magazine and started looking for rocks after leaving a green and brown trail in the area of my hundred-meter dash. Months later I heard that a new arrival at Camp Alpha had indeed fired at a moving shadow that he thought was surely a VC, courtesy of an overactive imagination. I also recollected that when we landed at Saigon, an NCO boarded the aircraft and announced that the airstrip had been receiving sniper fire. Consequently, everyone was instructed to get his duffel bag and run as fast as they could to the in-processing tent. He led the way, of course with no duffel bag over his shoulder, and a hundred people almost killed themselves trying to get to the tent before they were shot. In-processing was completed in record time.

"When do I get my weapon," Opie continued.

"Too soon," I said. "And I bet you'll be glad to give it up at the end of your tour."

I wondered if he would, in due time, have the same attitude I had about weapons. They were there for protection and to kill someone. I had seen far too many accidents with all types of weapons. We had a lot of near misses within the company. Late one evening at the conclusion of a company mission, the chap in the room next to mine opened his wall locker to store his handgun on its top shelf and discharged it, sending a .38 caliber round within inches of my head. On another occasion, a door gunner had slammed his machinegun feeding tray shut which caused it to fire a burst of rounds, killing a nearby soldier who was waiting to be inserted. Even the people you'd last expect to have problems experienced weapons malfunctions and near misses. Some of our armorers were working on a 2.75 rocket launcher system and touched the wrong wires together, sending a rocket flying by the head of a door gunner who was sitting on the front part of a skid right in front of the rocket. There were numerous stories about dumb mistakes with weapons that had cost someone his life. Weapons were not to be toyed with and they were as great a liability as they were necessary for protection. The maxim "You live by the sword; you die by the sword" was just as applicable off the battlefield as it was on the battlefield.

Opie said "Thanks" and departed.

Another soldier who was returning to Vietnam and had overheard my discussion with Opie sat down in the chair Opie left empty. "I can't remember being quite that anxious to get there," he said.

"I know I wasn't," I replied. "Regardless of the training I had, the aspect of being in a war was strange and a little scary for me. That combined with the television I had seen relative to guerilla tactics and sneak attacks made it appear that whether you survived or not was a hit and miss proposition. I was being assigned to Bien Hoa and I had seen a lot of news film about the airbase getting hit and ostensibly overrun. The thought gave me cold chills as well as the news related to Viet Cong serving in the ranks of the South Vietnamese Army. I had the feeling well before I arrived that I was going to be looking over my shoulder wherever I went. I guess I had a doomsday attitude. How about you?"

"I don't know," he said. "I'm not sure how I felt. I know I wasn't as strung out or as hyperactive as our red-haired friend."

"I guess a lot of it has to do with how you're influenced or inspired by military training, environment, and the amount of news you get" I said."

"Probably," he replied. "I'm from a small town near Hattiesburg. I was in awe of the heroes that were coming back from Vietnam. We have one high school and most everybody's father served in WWII. The attitude there is you're expected to serve your country. I felt it was the right thing to do. I had heard all the war stories from the old timers and I guess I wanted war stories of my own. I was assigned to the 101st Airborne when I got in country and they require you to go through a basic three-week course before you go to your unit. I took all that in stride, I think. I always felt that I wasn't alone wherever I was. We didn't hear a shot fired in hostility for the first two months. It was boring as hell. Hasn't been much better since."

"Why are you coming back?" I asked.

"My father died," he said. It was really good to be home, regardless of the circumstances. I've got four more months left. I had jungle rot on both feet and I lost some soft tissue. The doc says I'm more susceptible now to catching it again. I think my last four months are going to be spent in the supply room. I guess I'm ready for that, except the time will go by much slower. In the field you forget about time. It doesn't really matter to me. Why did you go home?"

Damn good question, I thought. Why did I go home? There was the obvious answer and the prophetic answer, and there was always the answer derived from one's interpretation of what was accomplished during my short stay. I didn't like any of them.

"Just to visit," I replied.

"How long did you stay?"

"A week," I said.

"Gosh, that was quick!"

"I needed to get back."

We had short stopovers in the Philippines and Wake Island and just that quick, I was back again. At the Saigon airstrip there was an orderly withdrawal of the new arrivals, which didn't include the threat of snipers on the runway, and those returning from leave were sent to the main terminal to arrange flights back to their units. I was lucky enough to catch a ride on a helicopter from the Rattlesnakes, which was the unit directly next to ours on the airstrip. In about an hour, I was standing in the company orderly room.

The company clerk, Specialist Alvin Smith, looked up from his desk. "You're back?"

"In the flesh."

"Why so soon?"

"I missed you guys."

"You're kidding me."

"You bet I am." I laughed. "No, the truth is I took care of my business and wanted to be back here for Columbus Day."

"When is Columbus Day?" said Smith.

"I wasn't sure but I knew you'd know, so that's why I came back."

Smith smiled. "You're hooked on this place, aren't you? You're afraid you're going to miss something. It's not the cuisine or the palm trees and beaches; it's just this place. You just have to be here. If I'd have bet on when you'd return, I would have lost money. Doc Q said you'd be back ahead of schedule. He was right. You just can't stay away from this place."

"Pretty good perceptive analysis but you're wrong," I said. It is the cuisine and the palm trees and the sunny beaches. Be a good company clerk and give me the sign in sheet."

"No need to sign in," he said. "You never signed out. Top was going to forge your signature but he said it wouldn't make any difference unless you died. You've been present for duty."

"Now I know why I came back so soon," I laughed. "I was never really gone. Tell Top I'm back, unless he thinks I'm still here."

"You bet, Sarge," he said.

I went back to my room after I checked my mail slot. I had no mail. I rarely did. I wondered why I even had a mailbox. Well, no news is good news, I thought.

After talking to a few people in the company, I determined there had been no new incidents during my absence. Craig had returned the day before and he was nearing the end of his tour. I would hate to see him go. I was going to miss the satire and friendly cynicism. He would do well back in the states. His combo of aloofness, nonchalance, and wittiness seemed to fit in well in all the local social classes. The pilots liked him, and I'm sure Doc Q found him to be a refreshing and entertaining reprieve from the average not-so-well-informed, garden-variety GI.

I had time to think about Hoa. More and more it seemed that the psychological and emotional roads kept leading back to her. I felt a need to see her, not just to make sure she was alright, but to share with her some of the feelings I had about some of the recent events. She had a unique and simple way of putting things into perspective. Maybe it was the Asian approach she took to life's little ups and downs. Ostensibly, she believed that problems should be seen for what they are in a simple and understandable way, and simple solutions should be employed to address them. Nothing fancy about that, but at the root of a simple solution is the need to admit that you are often wrong. Philosophically, such admissions differ from the Eastern approach, which suggests that you are not always wrong, but may not always be right. Asians unhesitatingly admit they are wrong and are quick to both admit it and ask for forgiveness. That is hugely significant in a country where people are enormously concerned about saving face, particularly when most have little more than face to save. Hoa would tell you when she was wrong, but she would never dream of telling you that you were wrong. She believed she had no right to do that. If you raised an issue she felt needed redressing, she would say "You must think about that," for it was yours to redress or rectify in a clear and simple way.

Her ability to speak of someone without making or expressing judgments was another of her admirable personality traits. It was her view that everyone had the right to decide what was wrong or right and act accordingly, so long as it didn't impact someone else in a negative or harmful way. She would put a small finger to your lips if you began to berate someone, or give you the infamous Mona Lisa smile when she felt you were talking foolishly or garrulously without cause, or in an unkind and unbecoming way. She said so much without words, preferring self-restraint over indulgence and graciousness over hostility. Indeed, she was a remarkable woman.

It was hard to believe that she was from a small hamlet in an area where farming was carried out with poor uneducated people who were devoid of utilities and other fundamental services that Americans take for granted. Within that hamlet there must be a level of politeness and refinement that parallels the regal sophistication of our own aristocracy. It may well be, I thought, that in its rush to achieve great industrial and technological superiority, America had left in its wake the need for decorum, good manners, and respectability between all people.

For the first time I had to admit to myself that Hoa was special. She continued to excel, even in a climate of clouded ethics and morals where greed triumphed over humanity in a demeaning and revolting way. I was beginning to understand her in a way I hadn't before. I knew she was important to me, but I didn't want to admit or feel anything beyond that. What I did know was I looked forward to seeing her again.

CHAPTER 7

I checked with operations to see if I could get some indication of what the company had planned for the next few weeks. We were on standby for two battalion or brigade size operations but no date had been confirmed for when they would start. The maintenance people were having a fit over parts. Evidently, the kinds of parts we needed for routine periodic inspections were not coming in on time and several aircraft had been redlined because of it. There was a shortage of pilots because several had left due to injuries and several more had "derosed" which is a contrived military acronym meaning one has reached their date of rotation and left. Having a preponderance, or anything close to it, of new pilots was a matter of great consternation for the seasoned pilots. The new pilots had to go through the shock of seeing things blown up in close proximity and viewing the residue of carnage on the battlefields before they could be trusted to make calm and deliberate actions in the cockpit. Shaking or unstable hands on aircraft controls, which were so sensitive that an inch makes the difference between flying and dying, could mean disaster for everyone on board and those around it. For that reason, new pilots were tested rather well before being trusted at the controls during a combat operation. They started out as co-pilots, regardless of their rank, and became pilots when they had shown the kind of mettle and capability it takes to keep your mind on flying while bullet holes are appearing in your windshield and people are dying in the floor behind you. In the process, there were a lot of white knuckles and new and exciting, involuntary expletives being thrown around.

I dropped by the infirmary to see Craig. He was pulling a needle out of someone's butt when I arrived and turned to looks at me with a smile.

"You want some of this?" he asked as he held the syringe high for me to see it.

I laughed. "What's on special today?"

"Same as most days," he retorted. "Penicillin and the whole range of fixes for naughty boys. This stuff won't help you though. You need 150 volts of shock treatment to the medulla oblongata. What the hell are you doing back here? You barely left and now you're back?"

"It was the palm trees and beaches and cuisine I couldn't live without," I replied, remembering my conversation with Smith.

"Screw that," said Craig. "Not you" he said to the patient that was pulling up his pants. "You don't need to screw anything for at least three weeks. As a matter of fact, you should just close up shop till you get back to the states. How long is that, anyhow?"

"Hell, I just got here," he said with a look of disbelief.

"Well in your case, a year would probably be too soon. My exam of your uncircumcised penis makes me conclude that any time you go skinny dipping, you're going to get another dose."

"No shit?" the young patient replied.

"No shit," said Craig. "Now get your butt and all the attachments out of here."

"Another day at the clinic," said Craig in a resigned way. "Hey, you haven't heard the latest. Doc Q and several others are going down town with some other Vietnamese and civilian doctors to test the whores for disease and give them injections. The goal is to register the working girls so the white mice (Vietnamese Police) can control them and suppress the raging levels of venereal disease. If you don't have a card, you won't be able to work in a brothel.

"What about all the girlfriends and marriages of convenience?" I asked, referring to marriages between GIs and Vietnamese girls in Vietnamese ceremonies that weren't recognized by the US Government.

"Well, if I've got this right, they will also require cards," said Craig.

"Does that mean that people like Hoa will have to get a card?" I asked.

"Probably wouldn't hurt," Craig replied. "I'm sure that would be a little embarrassing, not just for her but you as well. I guess the standard is that anyone who sleeps with a GI, regardless of the reasons will have to be carded."

Having to forgo the embarrassment of getting an exam to obtain a prostitute's card would be a reprehensible and shameful slap in the face for Hoa. She was not a prostitute but anyone that saw me come and go could with good reason think otherwise. People who knew Hoa thought highly of her but that could change if she was labeled as a card-carrying prostitute. The affiliation between the military that ran the compound where she lived and the white mice would lead to some form of inquiry. I could see where difficulties could arise.

"I'll talk to her," I said. "Is there anything you can do for me?"

"Well, this whole thing is still in its embryo planning stages, but if I can I will. You didn't need to ask that question. It's just that it has to happen in the next week. In case you forgot, I'm so short I can sleep in a matchbox."

I laughed. "Thanks," I said. I just can't see Hoa lining up with all the prostitutes waiting to get a card. I'm not sure she could handle that."

"I know she couldn't," said Craig.

"I'm going down there tonight," I said. "I'll talk to her about it."

"What are you going to say?" asked Craig.

"To tell you the truth, I really don't know. How do you tell someone that they have to admit they're a prostitute if they want to keep seeing you?"

"Very carefully," Craig replied, "and with great finesse and diplomacy."

I had no idea how I could explain this to Hoa, and I had no idea how she would accept it. How do you tell someone that a condition of our relationship was to succumb to an embarrassing examination of your genitals and admit that you are a prostitute? The white mice wouldn't make it any easier. They would be asking for cards as items of identification when they found a girl walking on the street late at night, or at any time she was in the company of a GI. I would have to be discreet and tactful, but the facts were unassailable and she would have to make a decision.

Craig and I were interrupted by Arseneaux from the Ops Building.

"They need to see you over in the Ops Room, Sarge," he said, somewhat out of breath. There's something going on at Dau Tieng.

I left the infirmary and headed for the Ops building. Lieutenant Johnson met me at the door. We've got to move fast on this one. We're trying to scramble enough helicopters together to meet a commitment in support of the 5th ARVN Division. They're out near Dau Tieng and got hit with a sizeable ground force. Maintenance is working on two of your choppers and should have them out momentarily. We need everything we can get up in the air as fast as we can. Merrill just left here and is headed for the BOQ. We're trying to get in touch with him so he can muster all his pilots here.

"No problem," I said. "I'll check the flight line and Maintenance Bay and get back to you ASAP."

In minutes I had the available crews together and we were headed to the flight line with gear in hand. Steve went to secure the weapons and I dropped by the maintenance bay. They were rolling out one helicopter and the other would be out on the flight line in five minutes. I went back to Ops and advised Lieutenant Johnson that we would be ready to go as soon as the pilots were on station. Ten minutes later the pilots had arrived and the rotor blades were slowly revving to full speed. We left with six slick helicopters and two gunships. Two more gunships would follow when the pilots arrived. Steve had opened an extra box of ammunition so between us we had six thousand rounds.

When we arrived in the area of Dau Tieng, we were directed to go into a holding pattern about two clicks away from the action. We could see from our vantage point the unmistakable signs of warfare. There was smoke arising from a number of areas and I knew from my experience that most of it was coming from the south end of the Michelin Rubber Plantation airstrip. Several times we had flown over this area and taken pictures of rather lovely European ladies near the main house who were probably French, lounging by the swimming pool. I was sure they wouldn't be there today. From the looks of the area, it was a hot zone. If American advisors were with them, we would have someone to communicate with on the ground and would eventually know where we should land or what kind of support would be required. Eventually we were told to fly from north to south and place suppressive machinegun fire west of the yellow smoke and east of the red smoke. They requested that we fire rockets at any suspected improved positions that we saw. The ground troops had created a corridor for us to fly down. They would be in the corridor and the smoke would identify their left and right perimeters. Steve and I heard the instructions that were given to the pilots over the intercom and I verified with the co-pilot, WO Larson, that we had heard the instructions and understood the requirement. The flight leader decided to go single file down the middle of the corridor so both machineguns could fire simultaneously. The corridor was big enough to place suppressive fire out at a thirty-degree angle from an altitude of two hundred feet but we would have to rely on the gunships to fire their deadly inventory of rockets and grenade launchers. They would fly on the outside of the smoke marked perimeter and mix it up with whatever they could find. On the return trip, we would fly outside of the perimeter and attack enemy positions using 45 mm grenade launchers, commonly referred to as a pooper, and rockets. Gunners would be allowed to fire at targets of opportunity as long as they were outside of the perimeter. We would continue with the assaults until we were contacted and told to do otherwise.

On our first run, the plan seemed to be working. When the enemy became preoccupied with the assaulting helicopters, the ground troops had time to reposition and re-arm. We took some fire and most of the helicopters reported hits but none was so damaging that the mission couldn't continue. I knew we had been hit twice in the tail boom and once in the chin bubble but the pilots who were watching pressure gauges didn't indicate there was a problem. When we made the turn to fly the route outside of the perimeter, we could see the enemy moving below us. This was indeed unusual. Charley was usually dug in well and rarely did you see him moving to escape a trail of bullets that stitched the ground around him. I could not believe the number of kills we were getting. I was walking tracers behind one VC then the next. The problem was in the number of targets. One reasonably good target gave way to an even better one and it seemed that they would never end. The pilot was having a virtual field day with the pooper, watching the large rounds float lazily into confirmed positions below us. The trees were sparse enough to watch the actual explosions in some areas.

We made the second loop through and around the perimeter when one helicopter took a hit in the tail rotor. The pilot said he didn't know how badly it was damaged, and the flight leader told him to get to the closest landing strip. A loss of a tail rotor requires a high-speed landing. The main rotor provides for the movement of the helicopter in any desired direction, and the tail rotor prevents the tail end of the aircraft from swinging in the opposite direction of the main rotor. When a tail rotor is inoperative, the pilot must land the helicopter at a speed sufficient to keep it moving forward so it will not spin. It requires a high-speed skid landing which can be tricky, and particularly alarming to its passengers. I knew James was the crew chief on this particular helicopter and he would certainly have a story to tell.

We made the third loop over the area and all indications were that the enemy was retreating. We were not receiving as much ground fire as we did in previous runs and the presumption was that the mini-guns on the gunships had chopped them up pretty badly or they had ceased to move and taken cover anywhere they could find it. The gunships spotted several trucks moving outside of the perimeter and cleared their destruction with the advisors on the ground. The first gunship rolled in and fired rockets and mini-guns. The truck continued to move forward for another 100 feet and then exploded. Several men jumped from the back of it and they were taken out by the second gunship that followed close behind.

When we finished the third run, two Air Force F-105s appeared on the scene, flying overhead at a remarkable speed. In minutes we were called off to enable the 105s to make runs along the corridor perimeters. I watched as the two aircraft rolled into position and dropped an arsenal of 500-pound bombs on the outer perimeters. We knew that the Air Force had been delayed by the inability of the unit advisors to call for assistance, which was probably a communications glitch between them and their operations center. Had the Air Force been advised, they could have provided on target assistance in minutes, which would have saved many lives, and American ready reaction forces may well have had the time to establish blocking positions to prevent the VC retrograde from the plantation area. I watched in awe as the jets made three runs, the third with napalm which oozed forward majestically pushing a wave of lethal fire over the terrified enemy.

When the jets had exhausted their loads, we were still circling to the east. The advisors on the ground requested medivac assistance from the flight leader. He acknowledged that each helicopter would pick up one load and fly to an ARVN hospital about 15 minutes away. The plan consisted of one helicopter flying into the south end of the airstrip to pick up the injured while the others stayed in formation. The gunships, which had little ammunition left, would provide cover for the landing helicopters.

The formation had moved closer to the landing area and I could see bodies stacked along either side of the airstrip. There was a multitude of wounded soldiers, many of which lay on stretchers, but most were just lying on the ground holding makeshift bandages to their wounds. There was a village nearby and many of the civilians had also been wounded and were intermingled with the ARVN soldiers. Many were attired in the traditional black pajama-like clothing, making it impossible to distinguish them from VC. The flight commander saw the mélange of people in the landing area and gave the order not to take anyone on board who was not a uniformed ARVN soldier.

When the first helicopter went into the landing area a mass of people converged on the helicopter making it almost impossible to land. The pilot continued lowering the helicopter down, forcing the people out of the way inch by inch. A few were almost caught beneath the skids and several ARVN soldiers began to muscle the crowd away from the helicopter. The crew began pushing away civilians, sometimes prying their fingers from doorposts and chair legs. Soldiers began using their weapons to beat back the crowd while wounded soldiers were dragged and carried to the helicopter. The onslaught of soldiers and civilians attempting to board the helicopter continued even when it began to rise from the pad. Hands hung to the skids until it became impossible to do so and the helicopter tail boom came dangerously close to several people as the helicopter labored forward. When the helicopter was finally airborne, the pilot radioed that "It is pretty bad down here. Use extreme caution." I watched the next helicopter go in with much the same results. The crowd was becoming larger with each successive landing because more and more people had become aware that helicopters were landing and there was a way out. Each trip in became more difficult for the crews and I wondered if at some point we would cease to attempt the medivacs. I watched one helicopter dip forward on take-off, trying to get enough of a ground cushion to get airborne. A number of the people in the crowd ahead of it were knocked down or fell to the ground. Some were struck by the chin bubble as the helicopter tried to gain the pitch and forward speed to become airborne.

We were the last helicopter to land. People had become frantic. Several ARVN soldiers ran forward moving the crowd with kicks and swinging rifles. They brought several seriously wounded soldiers and one that appeared to be dead. The massive mob was so large you could actually feel them pushing the helicopter. I heard a thump and felt the helicopter briefly shudder. I looked to the rear and saw a woman lying beneath the tail boom. It was obvious that she had tried to move from one side of the helicopter to the other and in the process had been struck by the tail rotor. From what I could see, her face was a mess. Just as we were trying to lift off, a man approached the helicopter carrying a baby. He held the baby out to me in outstretched arms. Tears were rolling down his face and he was yelling something in Vietnamese that I could not understand. Larson had turned in his seat to see how the loading was progressing and saw the man and the baby he held up for me to take. I looked at Larson briefly and saw him shaking his head. The man persisted even as the helicopter began moving and attempted to put the baby on the floor next to my feet. I put my hand on the baby and pushed it back in his arms as we slowly rose away from him.

When we were airborne, I looked at Steve. I could see the look of resignation on his face. I had seen it before and would probably see it again. There are times when you just have to hate yourself, even if the events and occurrences that generate the hate are beyond your control. This was such a moment.

As we flew away from the landing area and back over the plantation to gain altitude, we took a single hit in the bottom of the helicopter. It penetrated the floor where the wounded soldiers lay bleeding and in pain. Other than the pilot turning slightly in his chair to make sure everyone was alright, little attention was paid to it. It was Charley's last insult to these ARVN soldiers, I thought, and the last those deceased would ever experience. I felt the piercing stare of a soldier who lay awkwardly twisted in the pile of bodies, with his head and torso just below my knees. His body was still and his eyes gazed directly at mine. They were the eyes of a dead man who had died at my feet. Another soldier had an obvious "sucking" chest wound, which was releasing air from his lungs. I was sure the lung would soon collapse, if it had not done so already. I could see he was near the end as he garnered the energy to make futile gasps, while the involuntarily reactions of his body tried to idle through the loss of oxygen and continue to run. I could not leave the machinegun to aid him. If we received ground fire, I would need to be there to respond instantly with the same kind of deadly force that had befallen those at my feet. In a few seconds his body abandoned the effort and he relaxed utterly and absolutely, in the way that only dead men can. Now the sullen and lifeless stares of two dead men found my eyes and penetrated my mind with their final poignant thoughts. "Just look what they've done?" they said. "Don't let this be in vain!" Finally, I turned away from the communiqués of the dead eyes' that had absorbed and captivated me. As I reoriented my weapon and attention to the land below, I experienced an indescribable feeling. It was something between sadness and exhaustion, and it remained for as long as the haunting eyes of the dead still begged for a response that I could not give.

We landed long enough to unload the dead and wounded. The Vietnamese corpsmen rushed onto the tarmac and roughly dragged the wounded and corpses from the floor of the helicopter. Those that showed obvious signs of life were put on stretchers. The others were handled like sacks of flower. It was their way of doing things and I didn't question their motives or their procedures. They had their problems, and we had ours.

The trip back to Bien Hoa was solemn. I learned through the pilots that James' aircraft had made a successful landing and the tail rotor operated well enough to get them on the ground with little difficulty. There would be war stories to tell in the little PX, and James would be vying with the other crews to see who had the best one. The beer would flow and there would be tales of profiles in courage which would be enhanced with greater amounts of beer. The magnitude of a war story seems to be directly proportional to the amount of beer consumed. But like Craig said after one such evening, "The only difference between a war story and a fairy tale is that a war story begins with 'Man, this is no shit,' and a fairy tale begins with 'Once upon a time."

When we returned, Steve went through the usual routine of removing the weapons and ammunition form the helicopter. The maintenance men were soon climbing over the helicopter checking for holes. They would have a long night ahead of them. Patching the skin was done easily but tracing the path of each bullet to find other damage that it may have done was time consuming. Doc Q or Craig would often come to the line to see if there were any medical problems that needed immediate attention. On one occasion, a mechanic asked Doc how he could be a Captain making great money when they essentially did the same thing. The mechanic explained that he conducted examinations, repaired lines like arteries, replaced parts, and stitched up gaps and perforations in the skin of the helicopter. Doc just smiled and asked "But can you do it with the motor running?" It was hard to get over on Doc.

We finished on the flight line and headed for the little PX. I dropped my gear off and found James, Craig, Steve and Vic at a corner table. They had saved a seat for me and I sat down next to Craig.

"Well, you missed a good one," I said.

"No, I didn't," he replied. "I don't want to miss anything. I'm short, remember? Heard you took some hits."

"Yeah, three or four," I said. I expected it to be a lot worse. You could actually see the bad guys this time. We hurt them bad. We fired them up and the Air Force jets made crispy critters out of them."

"Steve says he felt like he was lucky to get off the ground, with all the people clinging to the helicopter."

"Yeah, it was bad on the ground. I trust we broke Charley's back. He'll spend the next few days dragging his dead away. I was amazed at the size of the force. I've never seen Charley come to the ball park with that many people. I don't know what the final body count will be. They'll probably have to create an estimate."

"We fired 3500 rounds," said Steve. Your barrel is kaput. We're going to need a lot of new parts to get back in the air. Not just machinegun barrels either. Evidently, we took one through the nose in the middle of all those avionics and radio parts. I'm surprised that we still had communications."

"We lead a charmed life," I joked. "Craig, you should have been there," I continued. "When everybody was trying to get on the helicopter, some Vietnamese woman ran right into the tail rotor. I heard a thump and looked back. She was lying under the stinger and her face was fini."

"Facial injuries are bad," Craig replied. "In this country she'll never be able to get anything done to correct the damage that was done, if she's still alive, which I doubt. There are a lot of nerves and blood vessels that can cause you a lot of grief. They don't have the talent in the remote areas of the country to handle injuries like that."

"How many did you nail, Sarge?" asked Steve.

"You know it's funny in a way," I replied. "There were so many there wasn't time to watch the effects of the rounds you were firing. I'd get a target and fire several rounds at it then another would pop up and I'd fire at it. I just kept moving the machinegun from target to target. I never really was able to say conclusively that my rounds hit anyone and made them a casualty. I know I did, but I was too busy moving from one target to the next."

"You had the hot side going in," replied Steve. "The right side had fewer Charleys, and I could see the effects of the machinegun fire on every target I fired at. This one bastard took off running and I walked the tracers behind him for about twenty meters before I finally caught up with him. He went down like he had been nailed to the ground. There was a machinegun nest at the north end of the right side. Evidently when we started firing from the helicopters, the ground forces were able to fire and maneuver in their direction. The machinegun nest was preoccupied with the ground forces and when we flew over it was like shooting ducks in a barrel. I took out the guy on the machinegun then I got the other two. I saw one VC jump from a hole and shoot at us. I think that was the round that went through the chin bubble. I covered him up with a burst of twenty rounds and saw him go down. It was incredible."

James appeared to be listening intently but was unusually quiet. I remembered that his helicopter had been hit in the tail rotor. What happened with the tail rotor?" I asked.

"I'm still shaking over it."

"Over what?" I asked.

"Landing that bird with no tail rotor."

I pressed him for an explanation. "What happened?"

"We got to the airstrip in about 10 minutes. When we decreased our speed the tail boom started to turn. We knew the tail rotor was turning but the pilots concluded that it really served no purpose. We came in at about 50 knots and the goddamn chopper is trying to twist all the while. The pilot started yelling at the chopper to stay straight as if he could talk to it and make it listen to him. I thought for a minute we were going to turn sideways and completely lose it. My asshole was sucking buttermilk. The blades tipped a little bit and then the whole bird began to wobble like a top. The pilot started pushing down on the collective like he was trying to auto-rotate to China. On second thought, we would be auto-rotating to the USA cause we're on the other side of the world, aren't we? The gunner tried to loosen his seatbelt in order to jump out when he thought it was safe, and in the process, he was thrown out. I heard the tail boom smack right into him as we made another turn to the left. I thought the skids were going to break and finally they did. The rotor blade dipped again and hit the PSP and shattered into a thousand pieces."

"I thought you guys walked away without any problems," said Steve.

"You believe everything you hear?" retorted James.

"Not all the time," said Steve with a smile indicating he doubted the veracity of James' colorful description of what had happened.

"Well, you shouldn't cause I was just kidding."

"Don't wild and crazy war stories cost a round of beer?" asked Steve. "What's that term you use when someone is stretching the truth, Sarge?"

"You mean terminological inexactitude?" I replied.

"Yeah, that's it," said Steve. That thing that Sarge said.

"Hey, I was just kidding," said James. But I was gonna buy everybody a beer anyhow so sit tight and I'll get us a round.

Everybody got a good laugh from James' crash and burn fairy tale and the night progressed with more stories and eyewitness accounts of death and destruction. The gunship crews came in and added to the ever-increasing number of machinegun forays against an enemy that we had all learned to hate. I wondered if Charley was in his little PX telling his own war stories about the courageous way he was able to withstand the American attack and the number of South Vietnamese Soldiers he had been able to kill.

Killing your own people never set well with me. I could never understand how brother could be pitted against brother to achieve some form of political hegemony. The US civil war came closest in comparison, but the issues there were industrialism, slavery and a burgeoning divide in cultures in a country so new that the people had not yet acclaimed or realized their sovereignty as a nation. Vietnam was 5000 years old and was rich in history and culture. It had, as a country, fought numerous wars with its neighbors.

The Viet Minh had fought and defeated the French at Dien

Bien Phu in a battle the French could have never won. The problem with the French was that they seized what they could economically and gave nothing in return. In Asia, that works but just for as long as it is tolerated. The French still had a financial stake in the country and their long history there was evident in the architecture and language. Saigon and the other larger towns were permeated with villas and many Vietnamese products were produced by French companies. Billboards with French people smoking French cigarettes dotted the landscape. Many Vietnamese people spoke French and just as many spoke Chinese. But in no way did Vietnam mirror the melting pot of people contained in the USA. In Vietnam, there was, essentially, a homogeneous society of Vietnamese people. Some spoke a different dialect or were multi-lingual but they were for the most part Vietnamese. The French maintained their financial separatism and did not let the Vietnamese participate in industrial undertakings. Over time, many of the laws changed in ways that required the French to marry Vietnamese to retain their holdings. Stories abounded about French property owners who had a Vietnamese wife of convenience and a French wife with which to share a bed.

The conversation around the table had turned to subjects relative to getting back to the states. It always did. The day's war-like activities and events had become passé and the traditional music consisting of a number of old favorites and The Green, Green Grass of Home now played from a cheap rendition of a jukebox that sat in the corner. The group was growing melancholy, remembering other times and other smells and sylvan settings from North Carolina and other places in the land of the big PX. People were describing cars that sat on blocks in a garage awaiting their return and some boasted of their insatiable sexual desires they would attempt to fulfill when they returned. This was usually the time that I bid them adieu, but tonight I decided to stay a little longer. I honestly liked the stories about families and girlfriends and people back in the states who awaited the return of their soldier sons, husbands and fathers. It was refreshing to see these men in a more personable façade. It gave me an insight into the kind of people they really were out of uniform, and said a lot about their ethics, their values, and their hopes for the future. It also showed, all too often the fear and uncertainty of young men who were perplexed with the situation they found themselves in, and the extreme helplessness that many of them felt. Some honestly thought they wouldn't make it back. They never said those words but it was easy to read between the lines. I do believe some people made an effort to get involved in activities that would keep them active, such as going to the ville or joining in exercise or down time functions. Those that demonstrated they might be excessively depressed or a threat to themselves or others were referred to the battalion chaplain. The hardest time for most was during the first few months in country. It was hard for the FNGs to watch the short-timers color in one of the remaining ninety days on their short-timers calendar. The truth was the short-timers were probably more anxious than the FNGs. The much-touted hypothesis was real, I thought. Time drags when you're young and flies when you're old.

    I rose early the next morning and joined Cookie at the mess hall for a morning cup of coffee. The cooks and kitchen employees were scrubbing everything squeaky clean under Cookies discerning and watchful eye. We chatted for a while. Cookie had received a letter from his ex saying that she had erred in her judgment to leave him and wanted to know if they could put things back the way they were. He scoffed at the notion that she should be so bold and laughed several good horse laughs to exemplify his feelings. "She probably thinks there's a chance she can collect the SGLI insurance money if

I get zapped," he laughed. He was particularly talkative and I spent the next hour or so nodding my head to indicate I agreed with everything he said.

I went by Ops, and except for Arseneaux, the place was deserted. "We got nothing going on today, Sarge," he said. "Half of everything we have is headed for maintenance and the rest will sit idle for a while. We've got a couple of runs to Vung Tau to pick up parts, but they're loaded already."

"I don't need to go anywhere," I said. "How's your sexercise coming along?"

"Had to give it up. I told my girlfriend back in the states and she's concerned that I might become just a little too proficient and attract some female that would take advantage of me."

"Yeah, there's always that danger," I replied. Dang, I thought. He said that with a straight face.

"Good idea; very good idea," I said.

I dropped by the medical station to see Craig. He was putting the final touches on a bandage to a hand injury when I arrived.

"I'm too short to carry on a long conversation," he said. "People keep coming in here like they think I've got nothing but time on my hands. Everybody decided to get sick and injured on my last workday in country. I've got to get to the transfer point tomorrow and I haven't even had time to pack."

"What have you got to pack?" I asked.

"Nothing really," he replied. I already shipped my hole baggage. I just want to do it slowly and I thought I'd take one more trip to the ville before I left. You've got to go with me to make sure I get back. I'll need a few beers or I won't be able to sleep."

"Sounds good to me," I said.

"The new medic is already here working and I'm really free to go at any time.

Craig introduced me to his replacement. He seemed to be the affable kind of guy that would fit in well with Doc Q's demeanor. His name was John Adams, just like the president, and he had a tendency to smile with each comment he made or in response to your comments. I liked that in a person, once I knew the smile was sincere and indeed not a facade used to conceal other feelings or emotions. But he would not be the gregarious person that Craig was. I sensed he was rather straight-laced and tended to be more disciplined with his lifestyle. He might not, I thought, have the same receptivity as Craig did to the kind of perverse issues that commonly arose. Something told me I wouldn't find him in the little PX trading stories and engaging in the kind of mental gymnastics that we had grown accustomed to with Craig.

Craig and I decided to walk to the gate rather than search for a ride. The walk gave Craig time to reminisce about his tour there and the things he would miss. We ambled to the gate, showed our identification and passes to lethargic MPs and made our way to the Hope Bar.

Big Mama looked shocked when I walked through the door and waved at her. She turned and walked quickly to the back room. Craig and I went to the bar and ordered two Bamouibas. I noticed that the girls who would usually be circulating around the tables were huddled together in the corner engaged in rapid conversation, occasionally glancing in my direction. I was surprised that no one had acknowledged my return from the states. Everybody knew, especially Big Mama, that I had been gone for ten days. I thought they would be surprised at my quick return.

"Do you sense that there's something wrong?" I asked Craig. "You'd think we had never been here before."

"Yep, definitely something wrong. You didn't leave on a bad note, did you?"

"No, not at all."

"You didn't change deodorants or anything like that?"

"Hardly. Whatever it is, everybody knows but us."

"Roger that."

I saw Fifi looking in my direction and waved for her to come over. Much to my surprise, she turned away and went into the back room where Big Mama had earlier disappeared. Papasan walked by the bar directly in front of me and said nothing.

"Papasan," I said. "Where is Hoa?"

Papasan shook his head and said nothing. He continued to walk away from me.

I repeated my question, this time making it sound a little more demanding. "Where is Hoa?"

"You go talk to Big Mama," he replied.

I left the bar and made my way to the back room that served as a storage room for the food and alcohol they served. Big Mama and Fifi were in the room quietly talking. Big Mama motioned for Fifi to leave the room and she did promptly.

When we were alone, Big Mama began to cry softly and sat in the lone chair between cases of beer. Without hesitation she said "Hoa die last week."

I was startled with the abruptness with which this news was delivered. My first thoughts were that this was inconceivable and perhaps she didn't really know for sure. In a country where there is little good news and so much skewed and inaccurate bad news, the information she had could be wrong.

"How do you know this?" I asked.

"Her brother and mother come to Bien Hoa to get her clothes. They say the VC kill her."

"Why?" I asked.

"She go home to take money to her family when you go to states. The VC stop her on road and search her. Everybody here have to get card that say they are prostitutes. Hoa got one to be with you. They find Doctor's card that say she is prostitute. They cut her up and kill her and her father."

I stood there for a while. I didn't know what to say or what to do. Big Mama continued to cry. I succumbed to the feelings of helplessness which slowly gave way to anger. There is an infinite feeling of confusion associated with having no way to avenge such an ugly act against someone you care about deeply. I knew that the VC would not have killed her quickly. I imagined that she had been raped and brutally beaten while her father was forced to watch. When they had satiated their sexual appetites, she would have been shot or bled out with long surgical slices to her abdomen. I had seen their female victims before and I knew they went to great ends to exact an extremely painful and horrifying death.

Big Mama and I remained in the room for some time saying nothing, as if it was a way to memorialize Hoa and pay homage to someone who had meant so much to both of us. Eventually she rose from the chair and reached into a bag that lay near her feet. From it she produced a small folded piece of paper. She unfolded it to reveal the ring that I had given Hoa to hold in my absence.

"Hoa say you give her this ring," she said. "She no want to take it home. People ask too many questions. This is your ring and Hoa's ring. You take ring so you never forget she love you too much."

She placed the ring in my palm and slowly closed my hand. "I sorry, Bo. So sorry."

"I am too," I replied.

Big Mama left and I remained in the room for another minute or so. Eventually I joined Craig at the bar and told him what had happened. He was the perfect second for an occasion like this. He listened to my harangues of anger and confusion, adding words of support when they were needed and looks of concern when words were not needed. We left the bar and went to the compound where she had resided. The guard at the gate denied me entry so it was apparent that the ARVN military that operated the compound was aware of what had happened.

We walked back from the compound on the road where all the bars were located. I looked in each, subconsciously hoping to get a glimpse of someone I knew would not be there. Craig understood what was going on in my mind and said "You're not going to find her, Bo."

I knew he was right and I knew that I had entered a phase of mental quagmire and intellectual fidgeting that would drive me batty if I didn't find a way to control it. I was still trying to understand how I could remain so calm in the throes of such horrible news. My inside was jelly around my heart and stomach but the exterior didn't, and couldn't for some reason, display the prodigious magnitude of my feelings. I wondered what a normal human being would do when presented with such a catastrophe. Was I normal? I hadn't had time to think about Hoa's last days on earth and it annoyed me that I couldn't gain some sensibilities for what she might want to say to me. I knew that everyone in Vietnam was susceptible to the worst of calamities, including torture and death, so why would I believe that she could be universally excluded. Obviously, she had volunteered to get an examination and a medical card. Did the goddamn I-fuck-Americans card I virtually forced her to get to maintain our relationship cause her death? Was I responsible?

There were just too many unanswered questions. I knew I couldn't reach out in the dark and grab answers that weren't there. It would not be wise to reach the point where the body and soul have been mutually consumed by confusion and frustration and I knew I was getting close. I began to vociferate my thoughts and anger at what had occurred and my feelings of utter helplessness. Craig recognized my ramblings as tangible symptoms of one in dire straights and suggested that we return to post. We walked the rest of the way. Without warning, tears began to roll down my emotionless face, suggesting to a confused mind that it was alright to cry.

Craig and I returned to post. He had a bottle in the med station that he had saved for his last night in country. We spent the next two hours discussing Hoa and old times. He anxiously looked forward to returning to the states and now began to fantasize about air conditioning and great restaurants, and large round-eyed women. He wanted to stay in touch but I knew that life would take us in a myriad of directions and that might not happen. Perhaps it would be possible; perhaps not. I told him I would ride with him to the transfer point the next morning. We had a few more drinks and finally he felt that he had consumed enough alcohol to overcome the apprehension of the next day's activities and would be able to get some sleep. On my way out he said "Bo, Hoa will always be a jewel of your mind. Her epitaph should read that she was a woman of indomitable spirit who was loved and adored by all who knew her. Her grave is her final place of rest. She would not want it to imprison your mind. We will all miss her."

CHAPTER 8

The next morning Craig and I had coffee with Cookie before we loaded the quarter-ton Army jeep to take Craig to the airport. Craig's trip to the transfer point where the Pan Am was already sitting on the runway provided a final review of the landscape, and the last opportunity to commit to memory the events that would remain at the forefront of his mind for years to come. When we reached our final destination, I helped him collect his things and shook his hand.

"Damn, he said. "Now that I'm here, I'm not sure I should be leaving."

"Go home and have a good time," I said.

"Not that sure I've got a good reason to even go."

"Well maybe some of those wicked city women can change your mind."

He smiled. "Perhaps they can," he said.

"I'm going to miss you, you know," I said, a little embarrassed at my uncharacteristic show of affection. "Intelligent conversation and phase three thinking is unique here in Marlboro country."

"Thanks for putting up with me, Bo."

"Anytime," I said.

"Hey, I know you too well. About Hoa, don't go crazy trying to even the score, if you know what I mean. It could be dangerous."

"Yeah, I know what you mean," I said. "Thanks."

Craig shouldered his duffel bag and I watched him disappear into the tent where he would get his orders stamped and his name checked off the flight list for the last time on Vietnamese soil. He stopped once to wave before entering the tent and then he was gone.

In two days, I had lost the two people closest to me. In the process I had taken direct hits to my heart and soul. I knew that I would be my most ferocious enemy until I could resynchronize my emotions, reestablish an inner peace and slay the dragons that were spewing fire into the inner sanctums of my mind. The frustration related to finding yourself in an unexpected and anomalous situation can be overwhelming. It is hard to fight an enemy who has outposts in your head, and I knew the series of events for my immediate future would have to mirror those of Maslow's Hierarchy of Needs- the wartime edition. For the immediate future, I would be starting at the very bottom of the infamous pyramid.

I spent the rest of the day checking on aircraft in maintenance and doing the kinds of chores that can keep you busy. We just got a new shipment of ammunition and it was divided up between the platoons. The armorers usually kept tabs on the flow and availability of ammunition but we had been having problems with the cleanliness of the boxed machinegun ammunition. When the boxes were opened, the dust from all the helicopters settled in on top of the ammunition and we had experienced a few misfires from dirty belts as they were being fed into the machineguns from the door boxes.

There were always numerous little tasks involving ammunition and equipment that had to be resolved. I spent a couple of hours looking at maintenance records and found a few that were incomplete. During a periodic inspection, work had been done but had not been attested to on the maintenance forms. Some of the crews were complaining about hours that were not being logged toward air medals. Through an examination of flight records I discovered that the responsibility for maintaining logs for air medals had been switched to Battalion Headquarters. I knew the awards and decorations clerk and I wasn't surprised that we were experiencing problems. He was formerly a crew member who had managed to get a fortuitous injury in order to get off crewing duties and into something administrative that was more suited to his nominal level of courage. I advised Ops that we appeared to have problems with the hours being accurately tabulated and they typed up a request for a review of the accumulated hours of all crew members. I knew the request would not resolve the issue but it was the first step in many that would inevitably result in me going to battalion headquarters with the data I had gleaned from flight records and comparing it with theirs.

I couldn't get my mind off of Hoa. My mind was clouded with the mental pictures of her being savagely beaten, tortured and raped by the Viet Cong. I could envision her crying out for mercy that would not come from these ruthless men who cloaked and justified these heinous crimes as justifiable acts of war. She would have been strong but she must have known that the end was inevitable. My own experience told me that they would not have killed her quickly. Her death came slowly in a way that would strike a note of abject fear in the very souls of those who would consort with the enemy. Charley was an inexorable foe when he was killing his own people. He could be blatantly brazen and horrendously cruel with those who could not protect themselves, but when he was faced with a real threat, he had to hide, be a lot less conspicuous, and use the disgraceful tactics of a coward to survive. He could not win the war by defeating the enemy, but he could humiliate, debase, and slaughter his own people into submission. He would rape, plunder, pillage and mutilate his people until they capitulated to his every demand. Hoa was just one of many souls that would fall prey to his evil desires; serving only as a temporary fix for his unimpeded, unbridled lust that would not end until this war was over.

While these chaotic thoughts of Charley's anarchistic ways occupied my mind, I remembered meeting a man in a little bar in Bien Hoa near the Universal Restaurant. It was not a popular spot, rather an out of the way place near the end of the red-light district where you might find a half dozen people at any given time. If you blinked your eyes, you would miss it. I had dropped by there several times to meet with Vietnamese friends who preferred not to go to the more active bars where they would be forced to view their women acting like whores and the raucous Americans spending more money in one night than they made in a month. The man was dressed in camouflaged fatigues sitting next to me at the bar. He was in his mid-thirties, about six feet and four inches tall with premature salt and pepper hair, and I guessed from his peak physical condition that he was either a field soldier or someone who had been a field soldier. I didn't know if he was a mercenary or a civilian who just happened to dress in a uniform typically worn by military or paramilitary forces. In the course of light conversation, he asked me how the war was going. I gave him my pat answer, "Good, but it could be better." "We all have our wars to fight; you have yours and I have mine," he replied. We talked on for a while and I gathered that he was connected to the Provincial Reconnaissance Unit (PRU) forces, the Phoenix Group, or was a CIA type, commonly referred to as a "Spook." If my suspicions were accurate, I thought he might have a way to determine who was responsible for Hoa's death. If he was connected to field operatives in the Di An region where Hoa was killed, which wasn't that far away from Bien Hoa, it might be possible to identify those responsible as well as have them eliminated. I knew it was a long shot but I thought it was worth the effort.

Later on in the evening I went to the small bar where I had previously seen him. As luck would have it, he was there and I found a seat vacant next to his at the bar.

"Let me buy you a drink," I said.

He laughed. "Uh oh," he said. "Anytime someone offers to buy me a drink, it generally means they want something that I usually can't deliver."

"Well, I'll be honest," I said. "I guess I do have ulterior motives. Let me spit this out then you can tell me to go to hell."

"Go for it," he said.

"I don't know if you remember me."

"I remember you," he interrupted.

"We were talking about a variety of things which made me believe you might have some influence with local non-US forces."

He waved his hand to stop me from talking. "Let's not talk about what influence I may or may not have. We should not discuss anything like that here or anywhere else." He motioned toward a table in the corner as he slid off the stool. I followed him and we sat down in an area that was the darkest spot in the bar and away from anyone who could possibly hear us.

"Let's forgo all the talk about who I am or what I do and identify the nature of whatever the problem is you wish to discuss," he said. "I doubt I'll be able to do anything for you but you've managed to gain my interest, so please continue."

"I had a girlfriend that was recently killed by Viet Cong in or around Di An," I said. She was going home to take some money to her family when the Viet Cong stopped her at a checkpoint and found a US issued medical card that proclaimed she had been examined and was free of venereal disease. In essence, the card attests to her right to work as a prostitute, which by the way she was not, but that would be the perception made by anyone who read it. She was brutally killed by the Viet Cong. The rationale that one supposes was that she was killed because she was a whore for the Americans. She may have been killed for the little money that she took with her, if she had it in her possession, or for a variety of reasons."

"Yes, I'm familiar with that; it happened about a week ago," he said. "That's not unusual. Things like that happen all the time. Hey these VC bastards are ruthless; you know that. There are as many rapes and murders that go unreported as there are reported. I don't know if you noticed but we have this little war going on here, and things like that seem to happen in just about every war that I'm familiar with."

"Is there anything that can be done?" I asked.

He laughed softly. "Surely, you're pulling my leg. You're looking for revenge because your girlfriend was killed by Viet Cong who feel that sexed-crazed Americans are raping half their women and the other half are scandalous whores who are laying down for them? It's a fallacious argument and a pointless cause you've undertaken."

"I guess you had to know her," I said. "She was a kind and selfless person who was always giving. She just didn't deserve this."

"Well, she's not alone," he said. "There are countless scores of people who died at the hands of these evil bastards who kill and maim and rape with impunity. Charley has no check and balance system for his soldiers. They have but one mission and that is to create as much havoc and chaos as they can. They do a good job of it, too. A lot of these little splinter groups of killers aren't even affiliated with a VC unit. A bunch of idiots can wake up in the morning and say, "Hey, let's be VC today and go rape and kill a bunch of women in the name of war." The villages run rampant with these malevolent sons-a-bitches, which makes it hard to predict with any degree of certainty where they will strike next and what kind of physical or psychological warfare is needed to dispose of them."

"Isn't there a PRU element or some activity out there that would be interested in stopping events like this, or punishing those responsible for committing such heinous acts," I asked. "It seems like making people feel safe would have some benefits."

"Sure," he said. "There are units out there but they aren't active to the extent you would expect. Much of the data that is gleaned from the villages and outlying areas come from operatives that are there to look, listen and report. A lot of the information is weak. We pay these people for their information. They are not organized and just about everything we get is information that is passed by word of mouth. There's a good chance that we could find out who's responsible, but then what? No one is going to create a task force to go to Di An and chop up three or four people who killed someone who they thought was a prostitute. There are bigger fish to fry. That would have a low and meaningless priority and could blow some operative covers. Honestly, if I could help you, I wouldn't. It just doesn't pass the smell test for us and could never be justified. Sorry, my friend. I know she may have meant something to you but you're going to have to learn how to deal with this ugly turn of events. My own experience is that one day you wake up and realize you will never be able to put a lid on it, and you just learn to deal with it."

"Do you have a name I can use?" I asked.

"Sure," he chuckled. "Any name you want. I haven't used my real name for so long, I'm not sure what it is anymore. Tell you what. You can call me Andi. That's Di An spelled backwards. You probably won't have a hard time remembering that, I would imagine."

"Thanks Andi," I replied. "Hey the offer of the free drink still stands."

"No need," he said. "I carry my own cups and booze. I'll buy you one."

Andi pulled a flask and a couple of paper cups from a pouch on his gun belt and poured us both a drink of scotch.

"Two thumbs and a half," he said. "The perfect drink, especially if you have large thumbs."

We talked for about an hour and had another five or so thumbs of scotch. I was surprised to learn that he had been in a lot of countries where "protection of American interests was necessary." Evidently, he had been a soldier once upon a time. He was obviously familiar with military jargon and had a commanding knowledge of a breadth of acronyms that only military people would know. He was intelligent but not in a pretentious way. He told me a story about his wife who he had met in Thailand and brought to the states. He described her as "the last great love of his life." They had been happily married for ten years when an enemy he had made in some obscure little country evened a long-standing and bitter score by killing her. It was made to look like a car accident but he was convinced she had been killed with malice and forethought. He was never able to identify his old enemy as her killer nor did the obscure country from which the killer managed to disappear pursue an investigation into the facts surrounding the crime. "Much like your situation, there were other fish to fry and bigger fish to catch," he said.

He was a compelling speaker and was well versed in the political aspects of the war and its potential eventualities. I was literally spellbound with his extensive knowledge of combat operations and his interpretation of who could be trusted to persevere in what would inevitably become a psychological war embedded in the ugliness of world opinion and social unrest in America. "Regardless of who is deemed the victor, the south Vietnamese will certainly be the big losers," he said. His rationale for feeling this way was his knowledge of Vietnam and their protracted history of war. He outlined the wars they had been fighting for over 5000 years and the millions of lives lost to conflicts. "Drawing lines in the sand and establishing parallels will not end the war," he said. "History will show that it didn't work in Berlin or Korea. It's that Asian thing," he concluded. "You may force them to stop, but they'll never quit."

Before I left him, I told him my name and a little about me; where I came from, how long I had been in Vietnam, my unit, and general information that seemed to be self-evident for people meeting each other for the first time. He appeared unusually interested in my short conversational biography. He asked questions about the number of siblings in my family, what my father did for a living and my education. I had the feeling when I left him that he was a genuine person with great people skills. I doubted I would hear from him again, but I would make sure to drop by the bar whenever I was in Bien Hoa to keep tabs on him and see how he was doing. I liked him. He was an interesting person that I wanted to keep as a friend, if that was possible.

The next several days were spent putting the helicopters back together again. There was a lot of work to be done which included patching holes, obtaining new parts and getting them ready to go back on line. Battalion headquarters had managed to get the 1st Aviation Brigade to give us a week of down time. We would use it all, but it might be a month before we could get back to full strength.

A unit from IV Corp was picking up the slack for us. They were probably thrilled with the opportunity. IV Corp was a hot, flat desolate place, devoid of local villages, where troops were confined to posts when they weren't flying. Being in this neck of the woods meant they'd get into Bien Hoa and be able to sample the wares, and act like young men typically act in unsupervised convivial situations. That isn't always the best thing to do, but I was convinced that an occasional brushstroke of frivolity would do much for their morale.

I dropped by the orderly room late one afternoon on my way back to the barracks area. Smith was collecting papers and running to and fro as he usually did. I often wondered what kept him moving the way he did. Perhaps he was from the south and had a penchant for fidgeting. It must drive the first sergeant crazy watching Smith do a hundred laps inside this little room every day, I thought. I couldn't remember when he was ever seated when I entered.

"Well, well, well, if it isn't Sergeant Legend," he said, as he turned to pick up another piece of paper from a nearby desk.

"Sergeant tired legend," I responded. "Be a legendary secretary and tell me if there is anything I need to know."

"Nope, not that I can think of," he said. "You know, there is one thing. You obviously got a message from somebody. It showed up on the first sergeant's desk. Don't know how it got here either. It just appeared. Top didn't see anyone deliver it and I didn't either. Maybe it's from the ghost of Christmas."

He rummaged through a stack of papers and said, "Here it is."

I took the message which came in a small brown envelop that I immediately recognized to be different from any I had ever seen before. It was made from a thick paper stock, probably about four millimeters thick, and there were flaps at each end which came with a heavy coat of glue. Once sealed, it could not be opened without making a mess of the envelope. It wasn't tamper-proof but the receiving party would certainly know if anyone had tried to open it. My name was written in small bold letters on both sides of the envelope.

I tried to open the letter on the way back to my room, but couldn't. Once I was in my room, I found a pen knife and cut through one end of the envelope. The note inside read "New developments in- AnDi. Come see me." I took for granted that AnDi meant Di An, and was excited at the prospect that something had developed there that would pinpoint or identify Hoa's killers. It was getting late but it was not yet dark. I gathered that AnDi preferred the shroud of darkness and might not be there until later so I delayed a while before getting transportation to the bar.

When I arrived at the bar AnDi was seated at the corner table. I walked over and sat down across from him.

"Been here long?" I asked.

"About 15 minutes," he said. "But it doesn't make any difference. I usually stay until about 2200 hours then leave before the curfew."

"So, you have some information for me?" I asked a little too eagerly.

"Well, you got lucky," he replied. "As luck would have it, and I do mean luck, some of our operatives were making their rounds to meet field operatives, and one of the meeting sites is near Di An. Some low-grade, apprentice Charleys felt they had made our operative and followed him to the meeting site. Our operatives aren't stupid and have a habit of finding an observation post to watch the field operative walking the last hundred meters or so to the site to ensure he isn't followed. They saw him being followed and managed to get the drop on these four yahoos before they could cause any problems. They found some documents when they searched them that proved conclusively that they were Viet Cong. I had told the operatives to be on the hunt for any information about Hoa. They made the usual inquiries while pulling off fingernails and making a series of threats. In the process of the interrogation, the VC admitted to killing and raping Hoa as well as killing her father. The operatives knew they would have to kill these guys to make sure the field operative's cover wasn't blown, if it wasn't already. Evidently, it wasn't."

"Got any money?" he asked.

I looked in my billfold and found about forty dollars in piaster.

"Not much," I said.

"That's enough," he said as he took it from my hand.

"Wait here," he said, as he strode away from the table toward the door.

I saw him beckon to someone at the door. When a man arrived, AnDi exchanged the money for a bag the man held then brought it to the table.

"There's a couple of interesting developments," he said as he took his seat. "My friend there at the door is a Cambodian headhunter who works with my operatives. He has no allegiance except to money and the people who pay him. He gets paid for what he does and you just paid him. There are three sets of ears in this bag to attest to the deaths of those who raped and murdered your friend. There is another VC tied up and gagged in the back of the cargo truck sitting in the alleyway. What's particularly interesting is that the other VC who also took part in the rape and murder, according to the people whose ears are in this bag, is Hoa's brother. Evidently, he believed Hoa was a pig for sleeping with Americans and that she was guilty of treason or some other form of sedition, and his father had some degree of culpability for tolerating it. According to the earless ones, her brother was the cruelest of the lot, and tortured her mercilessly before finally killing her. Given the situation, my Cambodian friend thought you might want the honor of sending him to meet Buddha. You see, for him this is a storybook ending. He, like many warriors, looks at this as an event where pure justice comes to pass as a result of his doing, and it is something that he will be able to tell his children and grandchildren in years to come. You must understand that Hoa's brother has to die. We can't turn him loose. It wouldn't be too kosher to let him meander back to Di An and let the cat out of the bag about our operative."

Rather than try to rationalize the merits of this judgment handed down by AnDi's court of circumstance, I listened to the voice in my head that said "It is only befitting that this evil confused man who would commit such heinous crimes against his own family should die." AnDi rose from his chair and begin to walk toward the door that led to the alley. I walked behind him, suddenly very aware that I was walking to an execution. I had never done that before, at least one where I was the executioner, and it felt awkward. I was quite aware that my legs were a little heavier than usual and my mouth was a little drier. For someone who was soon to be an executioner, why did I feel like a person soon to be executed? I couldn't show mercy to this savage, yet I couldn't help but think that killing him in the act of his transgressions was much preferred to slaughtering him when he is defenseless and hog tied. That genus of death is more renowned to people like the Nazis in places like Auschwitz.

We approached the truck and the Cambodian lifted the tarp at the rear of the truck. A small figure lay gagged and bound in the floor of the vehicle. His neck and feet were tied tightly to a tree branch that prevented any movement of his legs or torso. The Cambodian lit his face with a flashlight and I could see is eyes. They were not the eyes of fear; they were the eyes of an animal yearning for the chance to attack. They were the unrepentant eyes of a cornered rat that would fight savagely even after sustaining ghastly life ending injuries. He struggled against his bonds as he looked at me. I could not believe that this man could be related to Hoa. His eyes told a different story than hers. Her eyes and face radiated a gentle and kind deportment that manifested itself in every word and expression. This was a beast with cruel and cold eyes. If this man was Hoa's brother, he had relinquished his right to ever say her name again or relive in his mind the shameless, sickening things he had done to her. He was a despicable and unconscionable man whose unspeakable acts against his sister and father were dishonorable and immoral. They must be avenged. Hoa would not forgive me for this, I thought. Her magnanimous personality would lend itself to forgiveness of her brother, even when his eyes emanated a hate that even she could not deny. But this was my call, and he had made it easy for me.

I found an Army issue water-proof bag near the tail gate and removed the pair of boots I found inside. I pulled it down over his head and tightened the attached drawstrings around his neck, cutting off any air from the outside. As I tied knots in the strings, he began to shake. The loss of air ignited his body's alarm signals, and he was fighting each dying moment with a renewed effort to break the bonds that held him. The bag's vanishing air caused it to adhere to his face, providing an outline of his nose and forehead, and a mouth agape that gasped for air.

I walked away before he died and returned to the bar through the alleyway door. AnDi followed me in and produced his oversized flask. We had more than five thumbs each of scotch, and talked about the weather. In due time, the conversation took new directions. We talked about cars and the worthlessness of Joan Baez and other anti-war activists. We never mentioned the dead man in the cargo truck. He belonged to an era that ended with his demise. He had killed those who were helpless to defend themselves and had died the same way. There is a battlefield code of ethics that remains in place much longer than the proverbial line in the sand that can be washed away in time with rising and falling tides. There may be incidents of confusion for some aspects of war but never for those that don't play by the rules. From tonight's events I had gained appreciation for yet another perspective on the unpredictable aspects of war; soldiers shouldn't play God, and God shouldn't make them.

CHAPTER 9

I spent much of the next day remembering the events from the night before while I stayed busy on the flight line. AnDi had gone out of his way to assist in finding an end to a dilemma that would have haunted me for a long time. I was in no position to return the favor, if that's what it was. I felt as if I had achieved some satisfaction that there had been a denouement to the injustices and ignoble circumstances that had taken Hoa's life. I had to admire AnDi's brashness. He appeared to conduct his affairs with impunity and had a confident and compelling personality that suggested he had no fear of anything or anyone. I knew there was more to him than I could ever expect to know, but I was satisfied that whoever he was and whatever he did, it had worked to Hoa's advantage and for that I was grateful.

We were making all the last-minute repairs as part of the stand-down. It was always smart to conduct cause and effect studies of every mission, particularly when contact was made with the enemy, to determine what could be done better and more efficiently in future missions.

All the bullet holes had been covered over with new metal squares and rivets. One helicopter had as many as 30 exit and entry holes in the tail boom and behind the doors near the engine cowling. Some of the squares were larger than others, depending on the size of the hole and the supporting structure behind it. The crew chief had drawn little stickmen on the side of the helicopter, indicating the number of kills with which he had been credited. There were almost as many stickmen as there were bullet holes.

At the end of the day there was a short formation conducted outside of the orderly room. A few awards were passed out and the first sergeant had more things to say about the latrine being dirty and the need to supervise and chide those who were observed being disorderly and not keeping it clean. Eyes rolled as he reiterated the need to think of cleanliness for the latrine in the same way you did the mess hall. By now we had gotten the point. Top had an obsession for clean latrines. Regardless, none of us could picture anyone eating off the floors. I heard someone behind me say "You know sometimes when I shake it, a drop or two kinda misses the urinal. Now I'm felling this horrible sense of guilt for not cleaning them up."

Several of us went to the little PX. I went along, primarily out of boredom. The usual crowd was there and I could tell that several got an early start. The company was in the "in between" mode. We weren't committed to a mission and we weren't gearing up for the next one. We were in a zone of listlessness that induces too little caution and not enough adrenalin to keep you on the edge.

Adrenalin is a part of the combat process. In a war zone there are different levels of anxiety: one level is reserved for the battlefield and a lesser level is for when you are somewhere that could become a battlefield. We had been put through the ringer lately and the down time we had was indeed appreciated. Historically, we were inclined to experience rapid peaks and valleys in the types and frequencies of assigned missions. It just wasn't smart to go too long between either. You needed the time to repair and re-arm but too much down time meant you could become lazy and careless.

I was talking to James and Steve when John Adams appeared.

"You need a beer," I said. "I'll buy the FNG a beer. It's the least I can do for someone that has a lifetime ahead of him in Vietnam."

Adams laughed. "What can I say," he replied. "If I wasn't here, I'd be somewhere else. The weather suits me, the camaraderie is too good to be true, and the potential for injuries is high enough to keep me busy. What more could a medic who's looking for a vast array of experiences ask for?"

"Well, it would be nice to think that we're going to make your life boring but history doesn't show that," I said. "Aside from the guys with sniffles, VD, rotten crotch and jungle rot, you do have to pull a few bodies from aircraft with some through and through gunshot wounds and other freaky things, but hopefully we can keep that to a minimum. All the big stuff goes down the street to the hospital. Why don't you go flying with us like Craig did? Actually, he became rather proficient as a gunner and even got a few kills along the way."

"I just might do that," he said. "It would be nice to go home with a few war stories. It might help remove the wussy label I got as a kid."

James laughed. "You don't want to fly with the famous Sergeant Hardin. He's also known as "magnet ass." If there's a bullet flying around, he can find it. Hell, there are some people that won't fly with him."

"You mean LTC Matson?" Steve asked.

"Precisely," replied James.

"Yeah, he was a trip," continued Steve. "The first three times he flew with us, we got hit. Every round seemed to be directed at Hardin. He took one through the visor on his helmet, one that came up through the floor and hit him in the billfold, and one went over his head and into the roof. Matson's eyes were as big as coffee saucers. The next time he was scheduled to fly, Matson said it'd be a cold day in hell before he flew Hardin's ship again."

"Maybe it's the bull's eye I wear," I said jokingly. "The truth was that each mission was an insertion and every time we went into an LZ, the bad guys were on the left side of the helicopter. Personally, I don't see his point. If I was a pilot, I'd be happy they were missing me and hitting closer to someone else."

"He was new in country then," said James. "He turned into a pretty good pilot after a couple of months."

"Didn't he go to Battalion?" I asked.

"He sure did," said Steve. "I think he was just here long enough to get some combat experience then they moved him to Battalion S-2 or S-3."

"I am interested in seeing the ville," said John. "I've heard quite a lot about it and I think it's time to see what all the hubbub is about."

"Are you after the wicked city women?" asked Steve.

"Not particularly," said John. "I'm in no way opposed to the fairer sex. Everything has its place, I guess. I am interested in the people and the culture and I would like to taste some authentic Vietnamese food."

"Everything has its price and limitations in Vietnam," said James. If you're going to eat on the economy, you have to worry about hepatitis; if you're going to partake of the wicked city women, you'll have to make sure you are well protected.

But I guess I'm preaching to the choir. You're the guy with all the penicillin."

Steve laughed. "According to the great and recently departed Craig, you should take a beer into the brothel with you, suit up, splash it good before you dive in, and then wash it with beer when it is clear of the sheath."

"Surely there's a need for sterilized tongs in there somewhere," I said.

"What about you, Sarge"" asked John? "Do you have a honey in the ville?"

"Nope," I said quickly. "Not anymore."

"Did you ever?"

"Not really," I replied.

"What happened to Hoa?" asked James.

"She left town," I replied. "It's a long story and I think it is better left untold."

I didn't want to get into the particulars of the last week. What had happened could not be told. There would be mixed reviews and in reality, this was the kind of event that what would inevitably become a war crime. There are certain events that were supposed to be reported. Although I could rationalize the merits of what occurred, any other person, particularly one who was supposed to uphold the law as a result of his position of responsibility, would probably report it. It was clearly a situation that required more than the usual level of discretion and I can say that in more somber moments there were fleeting regrets. Regardless, as an old friend from Baltimore used to say about the senseless blunders he would often make, "It is what it is and it was what it was. What's done is done and you might as well move on."

I wasn't going to worry about it. The war evinced the need for unconventional reactions to unusual circumstances and I wasn't going to try to discern that which was more right than wrong or more wrong than right for every situation that found its way to my doorstep. Somewhat related to my situation was a standing rule or aphorism involving the identification of casualties following a firefight, specifically; if he is dead, he must have been a VC. That was good enough for me and I wasn't going to teeter needlessly between emotions of guilt and regret while I had things to do that seemed to be a lot more important.

There were times that I felt I had capitulated horribly from my new-guy-in-country position, that one should always be magnanimous and humanly subservient to every living soul that deserved compassion and understanding, regardless of who he fought for or what uniform he wore. The ever-increasing intensity of the war and my growing callousness had changed many of my original convictions. I felt compelled to resist the temptation to feel sorrow for the pain I saw inflicted almost daily and to be a lot less tolerant of self-pity, mine included.

I was becoming emotionless, unwavering in my need for maximizing efficiency, and intolerant of youth and its pre-packaged ignorance. I regretted Hoa and the whole town affair. I could have done better things with my time and the proof is surely in the pudding, I thought. It would be better to keep my distance from Bien Hoa and concentrate on the daunting job that lay ahead of us. Invariably, I knew these fleeting moments of responsibility would be just that, fleeting moments. However, I could not stop myself from going to the ville. It was my own special therapy, my escape from the regimen of military life, a change in environment that would make the mean green machine and the long days I spent in a very hot country tolerable. But I was prepared to admit to myself that it could be dangerous, or at the very least result in some awkward moments that would have to be explained.

John persisted in his inquiries about the city and all of its little peculiarities. We gave him a pretty good visual image of the town and where to go and where it was inadvisable to go. His interest was piqued on the history of the area and the French influence. Unlike Craig, he didn't speak French but had an interest that seemed to be more than casual about the French. In reality he would see the dead rats and the small animals running to and fro and would have flaring nostrils from the smell of nuoc mam and the raw sewage that was deposited along the roadside. If you looked beyond these obvious drawbacks, you could see the history of the town in the age of its architecture and the beauty of its culture in the way people conducted themselves. It seemed there were two kinds of Vietnamese people; those that were kind and graceful in every detail and those that killed and maimed ruthlessly with little remorse. Americans often took advantage of the kinder lot, which might well have made many of them join forces with those of the other persuasion.

You could see the transition in newcomer's behaviors. When they first arrived, they were sensitive to the needs and desires of the townsfolk. Initially, there were always kind words and the usual American manners, albeit they are somewhat questionable. After experiencing the rawness and primitive ways of the Viet Cong in the field, their character changed. Townsfolk became somehow related to the actions of the Viet Cong and one could easily surmise that they supported them or were a part of their efforts. Stories abounded that prostitutes imbedded razor blades in their vaginas to wound and disable American soldiers, that the food was laced with undetectable, slow acting poisons that could cause a horrible death, and that the Bamouiba Beer was a form of formaldehyde that would slowly erode or atrophy your organs. None of these stories were true but many believed they were when they first arrived. Part of the in-processing regimen was to dispel, to the greatest extent possible, the rumors that had preceded their arrival. I would imagine that more than a few still decided to make close inspections of the women they slept with before indulging in any kind of horizontal recreation, and preferred to have someone take a bite of their food and a drink of their beer before indulging themselves.

Steve is looking at me now with a curious look on his face, analyzing what I had said about Hoa, all the while knowing that there is more to the story. He shoots me a familiar grimace as if to indicate he wasn't buying that but knew that I would prefer not to speak of it. I looked back with one of those deadpan not-up-for-discussion looks. He looked away in a sign of agreement and I turned my attention back to John Adams. "Where are you from?" I asked.

"A little town in Kansas near Topeka," he replied. "I say Topeka when anyone asks because they never heard of Alma. Actually, Alma is a pretty good distance away but it's small and in the middle of nowhere."

"Do you know Toto?" quipped James.

"No, I don't, but I had a dog named Bobo," John replied.

"Pay no attention to him," I said, pointing to James. "It's that kind of funny that makes his day."

John laughed. "It's terrible to think that the one thing that comes to mind when people know you're from Kansas is a little wooly dog. I think everyone in Kansas is tired of the Toto jokes."

"Like I said, consider the source. Did you go to school there?"

"No, actually I went to Ohio State. I didn't finish. Thought I would visit Vietnam before this was over and done with so I could tell my grandkids about it in years to come."

"Now there's an original thought that never crossed my mind," I said. "I'm not sure I ever thought I would have grandkids. I guess this means you have a girl back home?"

"Nope. A couple of near misses but I'm not sure I want to find the perfect woman just yet."

Steve laughed. "James knows several perfect women that he could introduce you to. Let's se there's Miss Kim, Miss Phuong, Miss Phan, Miss Truong, and a whole bunch of others Misses that are hard to miss on any given day."

"They're all alike," I said, pointing to James and Steve. "They are twins born of different families thousands of miles apart. Does that ever happen in Kansas?"

"Routinely," chuckled John, "especially in Alma."

"So, what did you study?" I asked.

"Well, I wanted to go to medical school but that didn't work out. The competition is keen since everyone is staying in school to avoid the draft. I took two years of Biology then changed my major to Political Science when I saw I wasn't going to be able to go to medical school. I got a little confused about what I really wanted to do and ran out of money at about the same time. It seemed like the ideal time to enter the service and then go back to school on the GI Bill after I finished my service commitment. In the meantime, I would get to endure the kind of life my father endured in WWII. That seemed to make him happy since he had spent his life savings trying to get me through college."

"Don't let the first sergeant know you've been to college," I said. "He'll try to wrangle you into the orderly room."

"I'm in a different unit," he said.

"Doesn't make any difference," I replied. "They're all accomplices in an underworld crime wave aimed at working the balls off of those they outrank. He comes up with something new for me every week and I have to continuously invent ways to get around him. I've fended off more jobs than you can imagine. Most don't mean much. He's just got to have a name on every line for every task. Last week it was the Re-enlistment NCO job he wanted me to take. I told him I didn't think anyone had any interest in getting re-enlisted in Vietnam."

"Thanks for the warning," he said.

"No problem, now" I said, "but as soon as you make staff sergeant, I'm going to put a bug in your ear to have you take the re-up NCO job."

"You're all heart," he laughed.

"It's the least I can do; it's all about upward mobility."

"Yours or mine," he replied.

"Both, of course," I said.

I eventually left the PX and went back to my room. Steve and James took John Adams to the ville to get him baptized in the sins of the city. I thought he would be a little more reserved than most on his very first trip there. He seemed to have more sense than most of us and I pictured him having a little more maturity than the average GI. He was a medic and they are traditionally a few points ahead of most on the Armed Forces Qualification Test which dictates some degree of intelligence and what kind of job you're going to have in the military. I felt he would help in keeping Steve and James out of trouble. Not that they were prone to finding problems but it is always nice to have someone with good judgment around when things get out of hand. And things could get out of hand in Bien Hoa. You had to rely more on good sense and less on the local police and scarce MPs when a situation got out of control. The problems encountered there were mostly fights and thefts. The young Vietnamese cowboys struck like sharks so in the span of a few seconds you were hit in the head, relieved of your money and just that quickly, the deed was done. The trick was to stay out of harm's way and avoid alleys and backstreets. To that end, Steve and James were the experienced ones and they would take John where he needed to go and keep him out of the high-risk areas.

When I got to my room, I poured a couple of thumbs of scotch from the bottle of Johnny Walker I had in my wall locker. The bottle came from pen pals who were farmers in Pennsylvania. Every month I received two bottles in the mail hidden carefully in two loves of hollowed out French bread. I don't think the bread was used to conceal the bottles. It was intended to protect them during their 25,000-mile journey. I had connected with the pen pals as a result of writing a letter to the Philadelphia inquirer. In the letter I introduced myself and described the members of the platoon as many young men who did not get a lot of mail from the states. Within a few weeks we were deluged with letters, all of which were addressed to me. Letters that were perfumed or felt like they contained pictures were the first to be seized, followed by letters that had return addresses that caught the interest of platoon members. Initially, everyone was kind enough to wait until I handed them out. I distributed them evenly, 20 or so per individual, then passed a few around to other platoons. After a week or so, if I wasn't there to supervise their distribution, the letter bags were torn into and the distribution method became something more like a lion pride feeding frenzy. I had come in from a late, night mission a year or so ago and found three letters on the floor that were either overlooked or held no interest because of their return addresses. Each of the letters resulted in new friends and an exchange of information that provided a lifeline to the states and what was going on there. I received pictures of new car models rolling off Detroit's showroom floors and news articles about the war. In many instances I became knowledgeable of family members and their dreams and successes. I would hear about how children were doing in school and the trials and tribulations of farm life. The Pennsylvania family was a free-spirited bunch and the family matriarch sent me photographs of her floating naked in her swimming pool. The grand prize was an eight by ten color photograph which highlighted the mother and wife's magnificent breasts and flat stomach while leaving everything else below the waterline to the imagination. Of course, the picture went on the wall of my room and for a month or so people would file in to view it as if I had a picture of a naked Marilyn Monroe, but interests soon dwindled and other than an occasional re-look by hard core perverts, the picture that had once aroused and tortured the sexual sensibilities of young soldiers was rarely scathed by lecherous eyes.

My eyes lingered on the lady in the picture as I drank the scotch. I knew from the tenor of her letters that the photograph was never meant to convey a sexual interest in me. Indeed, it was her way of providing support for the war effort in a tantalizing and provocative way. It was quid pro quo for what I gave her- a look into what it was like to be here and a view of the lives and struggles of men in this war that you just couldn't see on television.

I read a chapter from one of Henry Miller's books while occasionally glancing up at the photograph. In many ways I thought that he could understand better than most the convoluted issues of war. He had a unique and complicated way of describing some of the most daunting situations in a way that either sat them to music or horrifically detailed them with visual images that were as gripping as they were ghastly.

The next morning, I met up with Steve and James in the mess hall. According to the way they described it, they had an interesting night that included trips to a number of bars and eating establishments. John Adams, according to Steve, was a natural and seemed to take easily to the new environment. He was, as Steve further described, well at home and greatly at ease. James said that John met a man with whom he spoke another language. James thought that it was French, but wasn't absolutely sure. I found that strange remembering the conversation we had in the PX where I had indicated that Craig spoke French. He would have had the opportunity to relate that he too spoke French but didn't. I asked what the man looked like and James said that he looked military but was in civilian clothes. I was beginning to give John a lot more credence as an FNG. He might well be an apt replacement for Craig but there was this lingering doubt I had about him. Sometimes things just seem a little too perfect and I was yet to find a crack in John Adam's armor.

When you live, sleep and fight together, there are no secrets. Sooner or later, regardless of who you are, the character foibles and idiosyncrasies become apparent. If they are minor indiscretions, you are characterized as human as everyone else. If they are out of the norm, you get ostracized or relegated in status. Either way you are accepted because you are in Vietnam and no one can make you leave, but being ostracized means you aren't going to be welcomed by any group anywhere you go. Being relegated in status means you're tolerated but your presence is flippantly marginalized. In time we would find out where John Adams fell in the equation.

Adams entered the mess hall just as James and Steve were leaving. He got a cup of coffee and sat at my table wearing a sheepish grin as if he had some boyish secret to hide.

"Did you have a good time?" I asked.

"Quite," he replied.

"Did you see everything you wanted to see?"

"Hardly," he smiled. "I will have to go back a few times to get the full effect."

"Bien Hoa is a mystery wrapped in a riddle buried in an enigma, or something like that, to quote Winston Churchill."

"Being there was a mild form of euphoria. You have these almost childlike feelings as if you were in a playground of sorts. The bars were filled with gaiety and a carefree ambiance and the streets were like block parties. I felt as if I could stay there forever."

"You have been smitten," I said. "Don't get too addicted. It is better that you take these trips to fantasy land in small steps."

"I've heard that my medical attachment may be moving to the military villa in town right near the steam bath and massage parlor behind the temple. What a bonanza!"

"You may be beyond help," I laughed. "Don't forget you've got a year to do here and lots of time to sample the wares and become a full-fledged denizen of the land. Keep copious notes and record the events of your life well, my friend. Make sure what you record will be the good times and not a dossier attesting to your demise."

"That was rather poetic," he chuckled.

"But I speak the unvarnished truth. I have a breadth of experience that goes back for almost two and a half years. The Grand Puba of bad experiences has spoken. One thing I've learned; experience is what you get right after you make a mistake, and I have made many mistakes, therefore I am very experienced."

"Want to talk about them?" he asked.

"No," I said. I want to keep them to myself so I can wallow in self-pity for being stupid."

"Now I see," he laughed. "Craig said you had a flair for the flair and he was right on the money. I shall defer to the Grand Puba and will heed your advice."

"Are you interested in flying?" I asked. "Craig flew from time to time, usually milk runs or non-combat designated flights. They didn't always turn out that way, non-combat that is, but it breaks the monotony and makes the time go faster."

"I'll give it some thought," he replied. "Gotta go. I'll catch you later."

John was an affable sort I thought. He wasn't a Craig but he was congenial and fun to talk with. There was something missing though. He was well spoken and obviously smart. He could have stayed in college and done a lot of other things with his life rather than be running a medical clinic in Bien Hoa. Perhaps everything he said was true about his father and school yet there were some doubts in my mind.

Over the next few days, I discovered my yen to visit the city was dissipating. I was content to stay on post, which was completely out of character. I liked being with people and having a good time. It seemed as if there was no need to go there now that Hoa was dead. The luster of the city had vanished.

I rode the first chopper out of the compound that morning. We were headed for the horse shoe, a river area south of Duc Hoa and the pineapple plantation. It was a cloudy overcast day which by design left you lingering for something better and brighter. Days like this were almost saddening and created an aura of complacency in the entire crew. We picked up about three sorties of Vietnamese from the 25th Tiger Division and placed them in harms way. There were some casualties but no one seemed to care. It was a day designed for confusion and anarchy and the tenor of things would stay about the same until the sun came out. Then the brightness would spark feelings of life and a future filled with children and dreams of an environment that was bright with sunlight and laughter and hope. At the end of the last insertion Charley was now faced with the advancing line of ARVN soldiers and small arms fire was flying in every direction. Friendly casualties were being produced in large numbers from the indiscriminate firing and bodies were beginning to dot the fields in a grotesque and ugly way. The fog rolled in on them as if to pick them up and carry them away in the dank and gloomy hands of the devil. Behind the advancing ARVNs came a more disciplined line of combatants that moved stealthily and strategically, carrying with them a wave of death. Some 100 feet behind the wave was a striking figure who stood head and shoulders above his Asian counterparts that moved in a hauntingly familiar way. As we flew up and away from the last insertion point away from the maneuvering force, I could see the muscled jaw line and sinewy arms of someone who was either a dead ringer for AnDi, or his twin brother. As the moving angle of the helicopter slowly turned him away from my line of sight, I saw him walking casually from one dying Viet Cong body to the next directing well placed rounds into their heads. It was something he did methodically and without passion- a virtual walk in the park.

Some things make sense after they happen. I remembered that we had been given a negative suppressive fire order meaning that we couldn't fire even if we had been fired upon. No one ever liked that. It gave you the chills much like a horror movie or a black widow spider crawling up your leg that you were afraid to smack for fear of getting bitten in the process. The negative fire order was ostensibly the result of a written operations plan that programmed AnDi's squad of well-trained killers into the equation. Dang, I thought. This guy gets around.

If anyone saw what I saw they didn't say anything. Certainly, I wasn't going to say anything. My obvious culpability, related to the incident in Bien Hoa following Hoa's death, left me in no position to reel off explanations of the nature of my connection to AnDi. For the first time since the Bien Hoa incident, I was beginning to think that this whole issue was becoming increasingly onerous and could eventually become not only a source of extreme embarrassment, but a menacing matter of grave consequences.

I wanted to find a way to put a cap on this issue but wasn't absolutely sure of how to do it. I didn't really know who AnDi was and thought it better not to make inquiries. Perhaps this whole affair would take a natural death and perhaps it wouldn't. I felt as if I was being somewhat paranoid but wasn't really sure. It was not a good feeling. It's called regret, and I was angry that I felt anything other than fulfilled revenge. There had been a reckoning for Hoa's death and I should be happy about that.

We had to stop and refuel at a remote location near Minh Thanh. I watched the helicopters begin to land on both sides of the PSP airstrip near the fuel bladders that had been prepositioned for that purpose. Just as our skids touched down, I heard the sound of gunfire all around us. The pilot tried to pull pitch but was hit and slumped forward on the controls. I looked over at the new gunner that had made his first flight today and saw him frantically trying to undo his safety belt to depart the helicopter. On the other side of the airstrip a helicopter was trying to land. Evidently it had taken fire and the pilot had lost control of it as well. It landed atop another helicopter that had already landed and the big Lycoming jet engine was still turning its blades at full speed. The result was predictable. Little pieces of metal and flesh were flying everywhere. When our blades stopped turning, I ran across the airstrip to assist in extracting people from the wreckage. Enemy rounds were whizzing by with that distinctive sound that made you know you were in somebody's crosshairs. When I got to the intertwined helicopters, I could see a body beneath the wreckage. I fell to my stomach and tried to reach the crewmember who appeared lifeless. I don't remember much after that except someone trying to pull me out. He was a large fellow and I remember the pain in my legs as he pulled me from beneath the helicopter that had given way to the force of gravity and rolled atop me.

The voice I heard was a familiar one. "What is your name?" it said. "Do you know your name?" I struggled to open my eyes and when my vision cleared, I could see John Adams sitting next to my bed.

"Where in the hell am I," I asked.

"You're in the Bien Hoa hospital," he said. "You're lucky to be alive."

"You're not the first person to tell me that," I replied.

"And obviously I won't be the last," he retorted. "But don't you think you're running out of your nine lives?"

"I don't want nine lives. I want one very long one. An occasional interruption along the way is okay. What's the verdict, doc?"

"Well, we're really not sure. We know you have a messed-up leg, possibly two. We haven't found anything broken yet but we're still looking. Right now, it would be fair to say that you've been squashed, if you like that as a very technical prognosis."

"Do I have any bullet holes? I always wanted them, you know, just so I could say that at least one didn't miss. When you repeatedly say that you were almost hit but weren't, it gets a little trite and boring."

"Alas my Grand Puba friend, you're still minus a great war story that encompasses a silver bullet or poisoned tipped crossbow arrow. You do have a lot of messed up muscles and ligaments and whatever other stringy things you've go holding you together. I overheard the doc saying it would be best to just wrap your right side in a cast so you couldn't move anything until you heal. I do believe you're going home."

"That's bunk," I said. "This is my home. I've no intentions of going back to the states. I've still got a few months left on this tour and I planned to extend again for another six months."

"It's going to be a couple of months in a cast and then you'll probably need a month or so of physical therapy. Any injury that takes over forty-five days requires that you leave the country. I would imagine you know that."

"Well let's see if they'll send me to Japan for a couple of months then I'll return as good as new. These injuries can't be that serious."

"The nurse says they're not taking any more patients in Japan. I don't see how you're going to get around this one."

I spent the next two weeks convincing the hospital staff that I could get around on crutches. They were kind enough to cut the cast down a bit so I could move my leg and ambulate on crutches. I returned to my unit with orders to be on bed rest for thirty days. The hospital said they would take my request under consideration but they didn't. The next day they advised the unit that I should be placed on medical hold until I could leave the country. I needed a Godfather to extricate me from this mess and I didn't have one. The unit commander had his own trepidations about me being in country for so long. He used to joke about my tenure there, often saying that I had taken up permanent residence. On one occasion he said that if anything happened to me, he would feel personally responsible. The implication was that he should not allow me to continue to stay in country when it was apparent that I could be killed and someone at some level might question why I had been there so long. In the commander's mind, the risk factor rose exponentially when someone had been in country as long as I had, and part of his innate responsibilities included looking at the human side of issues and not just at filling a slot on the company roster. I couldn't blame him for that. Indeed, congress had appointed him both an officer and a gentleman, and this fell clearly within his responsibilities as a gentleman. It was more about caring and less about the perfunctory side of his unit or executive responsibilities.

    I finally reconciled myself to the idea of returning to the states. I had no idea what I was going to do there. I had no aspirations for a future in the states. I couldn't imagine what I would do there. I had grown accustomed to a different Army life. There were no inspections here on Saturday morning. Hell, we didn't know when Saturday came and went. Every day was about putting Charley in the crosshairs, keeping the helicopters airborne, drinking and getting laid. Life couldn't really be better than this. We were a young fighting force, and youth is a wondrous commodity that comes without the usual forms of rationalization for life threatening inevitabilities. The stateside Army was different. Army life in the "real world" was about starched uniforms, highly shined boots and formations and inspections, and there was this god-awful competition to get one more point on an efficiency report than your peers so you would win a faster promotion. I was content right where I was. The transition would be painful and I wasn't ready to put this simple uncomplicated life behind me and fly off to a new environment that would be more hostile to me than the one I was leaving.

I did manage to get a three-week reprieve. Although the hospital was essentially out of the equation and the unit was scheduling my return, I managed to get a note from the them saying that I should remain immobile, essentially lying on my ass, until some of the swelling subsided. That was a gift and I knew it. The logic in getting a reluctant doctor to write the note was that in three weeks I would be mobile enough to get around more easily on crutches and would not have to be medevaced in the classic sense, which amounts to being placed on a medivac aircraft and flown to a hospital in the states.

The first week went by rather quickly. I slept a lot. I was black and blue and as much as I didn't want to admit it, everything hurt. John Adams provided daily visits to my humble abode to check the cast and see if there was any unusual oozing or the rancid odor of pus. There never was, and I could tell the swelling was subsiding because I had more room in the cast. I was scratching the spots that itched with some heavy-duty safety wire that I begged from a guy in the maintenance hangar. The problem was perspiration. The cast did not come with air conditioning and my leg was probably losing a pound a day of fluids that trickled down my thigh and between my toes. I noticed that Adams was all business when he came around. There wasn't much small talk and he rarely stayed longer than was necessary. It was not that I needed his company but it was out of character for him not to kibitz a while or provide a little Kansas charm.

Smitty, the company clerk, dropped my mail off and asked how I was doing.

We spoke for a while and he gave me the rundown of the latest unit gossip. On a hunch I asked him if he could look into Adam's records at the medical detachment, he was reluctant but agreed to do it. He had a friend in the med detachment orderly room that owed him a favor. I went to sleep and began dreaming. I was drifting away in a surreal polychromatic world of hallucination that involved naked people in an air-conditioned room in Rome when Smitty woke me up.

"I got what I think you're looking for, Sarge," he said as he placed some notes on my chest.

"What is this?" I asked.

"Those are notes I made from his Personnel Data Card and 201 file that I copied down."

"Like what?"

Smitty grabbed the notes. "He is 25 years old; he went through basic training at Fort Dix, New Jersey, his home of record is San Mateo, California, his father is deceased, he is a medic who took training at Fort Holabird, Maryland, his last duty station was Fort Meade, Maryland and he is single."

"Was there anything else you could glean from the review?" I asked.

"Only that the clerk said that he showed up with orders rather unexpectedly. There was another medic who was supposed to be here to fill the position that Sergeant Hitechew vacated but he got diverted to another place."

"Thanks, Smitty," I said. "Please keep this under your hat. I wouldn't want anyone to know that it was me that made the inquiries."

"Not a problem. Mum's the word. As a matter of fact, the company clerk was leaving today to return to the states so the only people who know anything about this are you and me."

"Thank you," I said. "You are much appreciated."

"No problem, Sarge," he replied. "Do you need anything else?"

"No thanks," I said.

After Smitty left I looked at the notes. I knew from Smitty's brief review that there were some things that just didn't make any sense. He was 25 years old but according to him he dropped out of college and came in the Army, which would make him between 20 and 23 I would imagine. His father is deceased but he never mentioned that when we spoke. He went through basic training at Fort Dix, New Jersey. That was odd for someone who came in the Army from Kansas. Typically, they would have gone through basic at Fort Riley. His home of record was San Mateo, California, a long way from Kansas. He took his medic training at Fort Holabird, Maryland. Fort Holabird doesn't have a medical training school. The medical training school is at Fort Sam Houston in Texas. His last duty station was Fort Meade, Maryland, which is the home of the Military Intelligence, or spooks as they are called.

A lot of these anomalies could be explained, but I didn't think all of them could. From looking at the notes, one could conclude that this was a dossier that had been hurriedly constructed by someone who threw logic to the wind or gave little consideration to facts that would have given it an authentic appearance. What I found interesting was that if the spooks had anything to do with this, somebody had really screwed up. I did not anticipate this kind of discovery and it concerned me. Still, it was possible that I was reading too much between the lines and all of this may have a reasonable explanation. I put the notes in the ruck that sat next to my bed and went back to sleep.

The next time I awoke Adams was sitting next to my bed.

"Just came by to check on you," he said. "How's your body?"

"You tell me," I said groggily. You're the doc."

"You'll probably live," said Adams rather jadedly. "You need any more aspirin?"

"Yeah, you might leave a few with me. Sometimes it hurts at night and aspirin seems to help. What's the line- take two aspirin and call me in the morning? Say, on another subject, have you heard from your parents?"

"Yes," said John. "My mother is pretty upset over this whole Vietnam issue but my father seems to be taking it in stride."

"That's good," I said. "My father died not too long ago so I guess I'm sensitive to the needs and concerns of parents. You should write them often."

"Oh, I do," he said. "Are you ready to go back to the states?"

"Yes. I believe I'll probably go to Fort Dix from what they told me at the hospital. I have some friends who live adjacent to the post in Garnersvllle so I will have something to do until they make up their minds about where I'll be assigned."

"That's good," he said.

"Hey, thanks for all your help," I added. "You are greatly appreciated."

"Anytime," he replied. "I must go now. I'll check on you tomorrow."

"Fine," I said. "Thanks again."

After Adams left I pulled the notes from my ruck and reread them. He had taken the bait, hook, line and sinker. The fact that his father was listed as deceased could have been a mistake of sorts but my conversation about Fort Dix did not elicit any response from him which was odd for someone who had purportedly been stationed there, especially for basic training. To the best of my knowledge there was no place called Garnersville anywhere around Fort Dix. Anyone that's ever been there knows that Wrightstown is the adjacent city commonly referred to as a GI town. It is flooded with soldiers undergoing basic training. It is well renowned for its wicked city women and shiny trinkets. That couldn't be overlooked. For some inexplicable reason, Adams was not who he said he was. At least his records didn't align with what he was saying about his past, or more importantly what he wasn't saying about his past.

Mother Nature called and I had grown tired of using the honey bucket next to my bed. I decided I was going to the latrine like normal people. I discovered I could sit up in the full leg cast and after several attempts I was able to get my legs off the bed and my body upright. I grabbed the crutches and stood erect. All the blood that had been casually circulating around my torso started flowing south and I felt a little faint until everything stabilized. Finally, I was able to begin crutching my way to the latrine. It was a trip of about fifty yards from the latrine to the mess hall and I began the journey, propelling myself by swinging my injured leg forward while balancing my body behind it with the crutches. This repetitive motion kept me moving in very short steps and I knew it would take me a while to get there. When I was half way across the open area in front of the mess hall I heard a small explosion from the runway which was a mere 200 yards from our compound. I looked in the direction of the explosion and saw an Air Force

F105 fighter jet in smoke and flames turning upside down 100 feet above the runway. The pilot ejected from the aircraft while it was upside down and was virtually fired like a rifle bullet into the runway below. The aircraft began coming apart in two pieces. The body and right wing went forward and the flaming left wing and part of the fuselage was coming in my direction. This didn't look good for the home team, I thought. Based upon my experiences with other dilemmas of similar angst and awe, I knew that immediate action is paramount to remaining a living breathing organism. With that in mind I threw myself forward with the intention of falling face forward, but I didn't. My cast bearing leg intertwined with my right crutch and I found myself flat on my back looking skyward. In a split second a large fiery object violated the airspace directly in front of my nose and I felt the heat from the wing tip as passed over me. I watched the several thousand pounds of flying wreckage make a slow eerie bounce off the ground a mere 30 feet away from me and continue on its way in the direction of the VNAF hospital. I had a rush of adrenalin and found myself moving rather quickly on two hands and one leg as I dragged the leg with the cast toward the mess hall door. I didn't hear another explosion for about five or six seconds but when it came, I knew that somebody got hurt and probably badly. Cookie had come to the door when he heard people yelling and running around frantically and helped me to a standing position. There was no need to run now that the danger had passed but I was still in a hurry and wanted to get inside the building. Cookie was chattering something about me dying before I got out of country but I really wasn't paying any attention. Once inside, I stumbled to a chair and asked Cookie for a cup of coffee.

"What happened out there?" he asked.

"I almost got clipped," I laughed, "clipped by a wing of a jet aircraft. The damn thing just passed in front of my nose.

It blew up coming in for a landing, I'm guessing. The pilot jettisoned when it was upside down and blew himself straight down into the runway. I bet that hurt. The left wing bounced off the ground and went airborne again. It hit something down range, probably a building. I could feel the heat as it crossed over me. I got lucky this time. Hey, you could get hurt around here. Did you know that?"

Cookie didn't see the humor in my comments and acted like it was a legitimate question.

"Damn right you could," he said emphatically. You better speed up your DEROS. I'd be checking your hooch for spiders and two-steps if I were you. You're going to mess around and get yourself killed, you know that?

"Please don't hit me with that nine lives stuff again. Everybody seems to connect me with that old adage that has little to do with me. Damn, I wish I could get comfortable with this thing on my leg. I wonder if it would feel better if I put some ice down it to cool it off. Maybe if I wrapped in ice on the outside. Would that make it feel better?"

"I wouldn't fuck with it if I were you," said Cookie. "If any of that were possible, the hospital would have told you it was possible."

"Yeah, but just talking about it makes me feel better. My crotch is on fire from the rubbing of the cast against my balls. It sets right next to them and its driving me crazy. As soon as I can get my hands on a jock strap..."

"There you go bragging again," Cookie laughed. "Say, did you ever hear the joke about the sergeant that was offered retirement pay in the amount of $100.00 for every inch from the head of his dick to his balls? He agreed and got millions because his balls were still on Omaha Beach."

"No, I didn't hear that one, but I feel for the guy regardless of where his balls are. Wonder if he could still get it up?"

"Hey, it's a joke," said Cookie.

"Yeah, but people did lose their balls on Omaha Beach," I said.

By now the activity outside was at its height. Soldiers and airmen were jumping on vehicles and speeding to the scene of the crash. Emergency sirens were going off everywhere. It seemed that every unit on post had its own alert system. I would have been there myself but the cast made that impossible and Cookie never left his post.

Two years before Charley bombarded Bien Hoa with rockets and mortars and several of them struck armed and fueled aircraft on the airstrip near the 118th Thunderbird's James Honor Compound. The explosions had a domino effect. One exploding aircraft caused another to explode thereby causing a series of explosions. Before long, between twenty and thirty aircraft were exploding, throwing engines to and fro, and one of those engines struck the cook's tent. For the next few weeks, the troops did their best to fill the shoes of the lost cooks but to no avail. Some dishes, even though they looked like they were palatable, were totally tasteless from a lack of condiments. Conversely, some dishes were so salty you couldn't eat them. For several weeks breakfasts were served three times a day. It's hard to mess up eggs and toast but even those fell prey to several novices who thought they could cook for the multitudes as easily as they prepared breakfast for themselves back in the real world. I guess the institutional memory of the unit never forgot this dilemma and cooks were never called upon to man a post outside of the mess hall or respond to an emergency that would put them in harm's way.

James had returned from a flight and had been able to view the exploding jet from an altitude of 100 feet. He had jumped on an ammo mule and rushed to the area where the remnants of the aircraft had struck. He said that the catapulting wing had struck a VNAF hospital quenchant hut where 30 beds and almost as many patients were located.

"It didn't look good," he said. "The wing went from one end of the building to the other. There were people running all over the place trying to get inside. The biggest problem was water. The runway fire engines that were rigged to put out fuel fires had a difficult time getting through the throngs of people that were trying to help. When they arrived, it was just about over. There were a lot of crispy critters. I don't know if anybody got out of there alive."

"Sometimes where you're sitting, standing, or laying in this case, is a crap shoot," I said. "This seems to fall in that "collateral damage of war" category. So many unexpected deaths are anticipated and you have to program them into the expected fatality rate because some politician somewhere who has never had a weapon in his hand except to go bird hunting is inevitably going to ask the Steverals "how come you didn't expect this and prepare for it.""

James laughed. "Well, when I make Steveral, if this war is still going strong, I will tell the politicians to pound sand."

"You do that," I said. "Although the people who died were not American, the press will have a field day with this. By tomorrow morning this will be on television all over the USA and soon we'll be getting letters asking if we're still alive."

James and Cookie continued their conversation as I left. Cookie was explaining to James how close I came to death and the certainty that I was reaching the end of my nine lives. It took me a good ten minutes to negotiate the short trip back to my room. I was exhausted when I got there and the sweat was rolling down my leg again with a fervor I hadn't seen before. Maybe my leg is going to sweat off or atrophy, I thought.

I slept for a while and was awoken by the sound of Adam's voice. "Well, how's the fallen soldier?" he asked.

Still groggy, I found some basis for humor. "Well, if airplanes and helicopters don't get me, I'll be fine. I'm keeping my eyes peeled for trains now. You haven't seen one out of control lately, have you?"

"Hardly. They seem to be in short supply in this country."

"Oh, they're here alright. You just have to look for them."

"You read people rather well, don't you sarge?

"Oh, I try. Sometimes I'm wrong, sometimes I'm right, and it never really makes any difference."

"But sometimes it can lead to incorrect conclusions, can't it?"

"Yes, it can, particularly when the conclusions have little impact on the good order and discipline of things. But when they do have an impact on the good order and discipline of things, it's an entirely different issue."

"What brought this on?" I asked. Was this confession time, I wondered. If this guy was CIA or Military Intelligence or some other form of clandestine emissary, was he prepared to bare his soul or was he just going to play this indirect, skirt the real issue game to try to quell or placate someone who had in some way called his hand.

"You just seem to be the center of the game. The ball always comes to you before it goes to the forward. You know the players better than anyone. You know their weaknesses, their strong points, and their vices. And I get the feeling that you know when to pass off the ball and when to go for the basket."

"We are just loaded with euphemisms, aphorisms and metaphors today, aren't we?"

"I just find you interesting," Adams smiled. "This whole place is like a small theater production. The cast of players is small but the play's denouement is huge in terms of world history. As in every play, there must be somebody that plays the catalyst to keep the play moving in the right direction. Things can never be too obvious, too certain, or too predictable."

"But when you leave the theater, you step back into reality. A protagonist in a play is different than a protagonist outside of the theater. One is a provider of entertainment; the other is someone who is expected to be humanely or inhumanely committed to another cause."

"Regardless of the forum, there are scriptwriters for both," said Adams. "Somebody always has to write the rules. No one should really lose sight of that. We all have our little sins and one should not suffocate himself with self-righteousness."

Adams left on that note but the message was clear. There was some connection between him and AnDi, or at the very least he was aware of what had transpired in the village to revenge Hoa. I surmised it was time to get out of this country. It was time to get far, far away and escape the twisted plots of forces I had no control over. This was over my head, it was out of my league, and suddenly I felt that the actions in which I had become involved, though well intended, were as repugnant as they would be difficult to explain to a military tribunal.

The next day I hastened to the orderly room and was able to move up my departure. I could catch an early morning flight a mere three days away. There would be no long goodbyes. With the help of Smitty, I was able to turn in my gear and get my clearance papers stamped the next day. Technically, I had left the unit. My travel orders were signed and returned from Battalion Headquarters and the first sergeant was kind enough to let me sign out on a post-dated sign out sheet. The following day I moved into the transient quarters at the personnel transport facility. I made arrangements to have my duffel bag inspected and placed in the security area so all I had to do was wake up and crutch my way to the airplane for the famous "freedom ride" I had heard so much about but had never taken. I would be flying to Philadelphia where transportation personnel would pick us up and take us to Fort Dix. I would be assigned to the Fort Dix Medical Holding detachment until I was able to return to duty.

My last night in country was hectic and unnerving. I didn't know how I wanted to leave Vietnam but I was sure this wasn't it. It seemed so anticlimactic. I wanted to take one last trip to town but I couldn't; I wanted to take one last flight over the post to see the familiar sites I had welcomed so many times when coming back with a bloody floor and bullet holes in the aircraft; I wanted to say goodbye to all the people I had known for so long and had done so many favors for me; and I wanted to take that leisurely stroll around the perimeter to give the one-finger wave to Charley who I knew would be out there watching. None of those things were possible now and it saddened me. Since I didn't want to broadcast my departure, I hadn't said anything to James or Steve and the platoon leader agreed to forgo announcing my replacement until I was in the sky and headed for America. I was leaving my family behind and that bothered me. I was a loner again as I had been many times before. It was never a good feeling and there was always a mad rush to make new acquaintances and find new places to frequent. Life for me included friends and people with whom I could converse. I should be feeling a sense of relief, not a sense of anguish.

CHAPTER 10

The day I departed Vietnam was much like the day I arrived. It was rainy and hazy and I had just as much trepidation about leaving as I did when I arrived. The flight back had its highlights. Since I had a leg that couldn't fit easily under the seat ahead of me, I was assigned the seat just inside the front door where I was lauded with the attention of the stewardesses, all of which were gorgeous. Sitting next to me was a colonel who had previously been assigned to Tokyo before is tour in Vietnam. He had arranged to be picked up in a staff car when we landed at Tokyo and took me along with him to a steam bath where we were treated royally before returning for the next leg of the flight. I was very appreciative of his thoughtfulness and he proved to be a very interesting and intelligent person that I really enjoyed speaking with.

The lights of San Francisco were somber reminders that I had returned to America. Regardless of how long you've been gone, the size and commerciality of America re-registers quickly. I had a two-hour layover and I spent the entire time just looking around and smelling aromas that were faintly familiar. The clothing fashion had changed and bellbottom pants were in vogue. I noticed two men standing in line to board another aircraft. One was pointing at me and whispering to the other man. I guessed that they were probably making small talk about soldiers and I imagined that they were discussing my rank or unit insignia. Possibly one of the men might have been in the same unit once upon a time or was familiar with the decorations I wore. I really didn't know nor did I care. I was walking directly toward them and expected one of them to say something to me because they continued to stare as if they were prepared to speak. Surprisingly they did not, but when I had moved about six feet beyond them, one of them said in a hardly audible voice, "I wonder how many children he killed." I hesitated momentarily wondering if I should ask the spokesman to repeat what he said. The comment was not made with the kind of authority that you would expect from someone who really wanted a confrontation. I knew that I didn't want one and neither of these men looked like they were the type to purposely cause problems. They were dressed well and were not of the build or demeanor that made you think they were looking for trouble. I just couldn't leave it there though and turned where I stood keeping my distance and not moving toward them in a way they could mistake as menacing.

"I'm sorry," I said. "I couldn't hear you."

I saw the man who had made the comment searching for the courage to repeat what he had said. The head bowed somewhat and his eyes darted. I felt that he had backed himself into a corner of sorts. He had been so bold as to make a comment that evidently represented his feelings or take on the war but had done so sheepishly, probably to impress his friend. Now he was going to have to find a way to save face when confronted with someone who took exception to what he had said. To abate the risk of argumentative or physical confrontation, he decided to restate it a way that wasn't quite so pejorative.

"The news keeps reporting that GIs in Vietnam are killing children. Has that been your experience?"

I moved closer to them merely for the sake of not having to speak so loudly that other people could easily hear us. Both inched backward as if they thought I was going to do something.

"When you say news, exactly what do you mean?" I asked.

The shorter of the two, who was also the one who made the comment, spoke. "Well like the television and the newspaper."

"Precisely what did they say?"

"That it was commonplace for soldiers to kill children. Of course, I would imagine that some of the deaths could have been related to accidents that occurred when you were overrunning a village or something like that."

I got the point. We were being made out as savages and the doves were exploiting us as baby-killers. I could treat this as a serious matter and engage in an argument I wouldn't win or I could take a light-hearted ludicrous approach and give it the ridiculous response it warranted.

"That's not true," I said. "Nothing could be farther from the truth. You see there are all kinds of regulations that address that sort of thing. Once upon a time we had that problem and the brass in Saigon sent out all kinds of edicts addressing the indiscriminate killing of children. It was decided after much consternation that only women could be killed with impunity. The new regulation was very definitive. You got two points for a girl child over 10, four points for a young mother and 6 points for a grandmother. Only officers who observed the killings could award points so it wasn't always easy to collect regardless of how many you killed. I was fortunate because there always seemed to be one hanging around when I shot one. After you collected 500 points, you could leave Vietnam early and celebrate for a weekend in San Francisco at expense of the taxpayer. And that is the gospel truth and explains in a nutshell what I'm doing here today."

Both men looked at me, never cracking a smile, while I delivered my ridiculous dissertation. When I had finished, the larger man began to laugh and began goading the smaller man about the comment he had made. When I started walking away the larger man caught up with me.

"I've got to hand it to you, Sarge. You handled that well. No one could have refuted that accusation in a better way. That was impressive."

"I'm glad you liked it," I said.

"I want you to have a couple of drinks on me," he said, while sticking some money in my pocket. He turned away and began walking back toward his friend.

"That's not necessary," I said trying to return the money.

"I insist," he said, now twenty feet away. He joined his friend. Their line began moving and I could see their aircraft was loading. I wasn't going to worry about returning the money, which I discovered was a fifty-dollar bill. I was amazed. That was a lot of money. I wasn't getting combat pay anymore and this would replace the thirty dollars a month I would lose as a result of being back in the USA. It would be nice to think I could replace it by walking around airports and defending the military, I thought.

I got on the flight to McGuire Air Force Base a little wealthier than I was when I landed. I imagined that the money would come in handy. I had a month's advance pay and $140.00 I had kept in the company safe. The first sergeant laughed when he handed it to me and said, "Don't spend it all in one place." I assured him that I wouldn't.

I was not accustomed to worrying about money because I rarely needed any. The C-rations we got in the field or raided to avoid having to go to the mess hall, came with small packets of cigarettes. There were about four per pack and everybody traded with each other to get their brand. Salems, Camels, Lucky Strikes, Chesterfields and Pall Malls were popular. I wasn't picky and would smoke anything. Cigarettes were $1.05 per carton in the PX and a bottle of cheap scotch was $1.10. I needed about two of each, monthly, to get me by. Everything else was provided free of charge. The hooch maids washed clothes and took care of the incidentals. Mine would bring me Chao Gai, which was something like egg-rolls. You had to eat them within 24 hours unless you had some kind of refrigeration, which I didn't.

Life in the USA was going to be very different. I would need money and lots of it. There had to be some discipline and there would have to be some decisions made regarding the wife I still had. She had taken the lion's share of my money while I was in Vietnam and although she had indicated she wanted a divorce, she had done nothing to initiate an end to our legal union. I had changed my pay options to receive all the money except that which she was entitled to according to Army regulations. I knew when she got a smaller monthly check, I would get a response and it would be ugly. Getting this settled would take a trip to Fort Bragg or wherever the divorce would be awarded and that would also take money that I didn't have. Oh well, I thought. Welcome to America. Maybe the vacation was over.

The Pan Am aircraft lumbered onto the runway at the Philadelphia airport. I followed the "military personnel-this way" signs to the desk where you would expect to find transportation specialists. No one was there and I waited for about an hour before deciding that I was going to have to do something else. Obviously there had been some miscommunications about the need for transportation for this flight. It was a big Army and perhaps no one had checked the flight manifest to determine there was a need to have someone picked up. I was the only person needing transportation so it was possible I had been overlooked.

I was struggling with the crutches and cast on my leg. I finally managed to stand erect and thought I might attempt to go to the baggage pick up point and retrieve my duffel bag. It would be difficult but this wouldn't be the first thing in my life that had been difficult. I would get a shuttle bus to a point near the post then make my way to Fort Dix tomorrow.

I heard a voice behind me. "Soldier boy, you look like you could use a hand."

I turned in the direction of the voice. She was tall and dark haired, wearing a red curvaceous dress that looked somewhat large for her frame. She was muscular and had an air of confidence about her that came with the rather formidable stature.

"Now there's an original opening line," I said.

"It's not a line at all," she laughed. "Seriously, you look like you could use some help."

"Well, you're probably right. I can get around okay though."

"Skip the heroics, Sarge. The way I see it, you're in a pickle of sorts. Do you have any baggage?"

"One duffel bag at the baggage pick up point, I hope."

"I'll help you get to your car or wherever you're going," she said, moving forward to assist me.

"Really, I think I'll be okay. I expected there would be military transportation here but evidently there was some mix up."

"Where are you going?

"Fort Dix or anywhere nearby."

"This is your lucky day," she smiled. "I'm going to Vincentown, so I can take you the rest of the way. It's really no trouble. Besides, in your condition, I don't think you're much of a threat."

"And how do you know this isn't a fake cast?"

She laughed a hearty laugh. "Because I'm a nurse and I've seen enough of those things to know a real cast when I see one," she said.

We walked together to the baggage pick up point. I didn't set any land speed records in the process and she was patient. I apologized and told her again that if she wanted to go ahead it would be quite alright. She was insistent and was particularly helpful going down the stairs to the baggage pick up area. I took one step at a time laboring with the extended leg for what seemed a lifetime.

"Did you break your leg?" she asked.

"No, as a matter of fact I didn't. The doctor was insistent on putting the entire leg in a cast because he thought I was going back to the states in a medivac aircraft. I had what could classically be referred to as a severe crush injury. I think they did something with my knee but beyond that the doctor said it would just take time to heal and he would prefer to have it in the cast. I had a lot of swelling but I believe most of that went down."

"I can't imagine making it as high as he did," she said. Immobilizing the knee is one thing but bringing it almost to your crotch seems a little cumbersome."

"It is. Trust me," I laughed. "It makes for some awkward moments, not to mention the rash it creates."

"Poor baby," she said, not venturing into anatomical discussions regarding the exact location of the rash. I assumed her profession would give her an insight into the problem that others wouldn't have.

We found my duffel bag. It was an odd-looking luggage in the row of Samsonites that lined the middle of the room and was easy to spot. When we got to it, she lifted it easily and started toward the door. I was impressed with her physical prowess and felt almost dwarfed by her apparent capabilities. In my condition I appeared little more than helpless and that was not to my liking. She left me standing on the curb and went to get her car. She returned in a sleek and dynamic looking automobile that I couldn't identify. It looked expensive. It would take me some time to figure out the difference between a Chevrolet and a Ford. I had been gone a while and I had a lot of catching up to do.

When we were seated inside the car, she extended her hand and said, "Hi, my name is Ada Udahl."

"Oh, I'm sorry. I should have introduced myself before. Where are my manners? My name is Bo Hardin."

"Nice to meet you, Bo."

"And it's very nice to meet you," I said. Again, I can't thank you enough for the ride and your hospitality."

"It's funny," she said. "Before this war started the local townsfolk went out of the way to avoid men in uniform. You guys had a bad reputation and every father wanted to make sure his daughter steered clear of unscrupulous men who had but one thing on their mind. Now we pride ourselves as claiming you as one of our own. There's some ownership that came out of all of this Vietnam stuff. We worry about you and take it personally when you fellows get hurt or worse."

"Well, I guess that's a good thing," I responded. "You'll have to excuse me. I may sound a little goofy. I have been out of country for a long time, almost two and a half years to be precise, except for one short trip back when my father died. I am in absolute awe of everything I see and hear. I can't believe that I'm back and I can't imagine meeting someone as kind as you. I thought I was going to spend the rest of the night dragging my bag around looking for a motel."

"I have a suggestion," she said. "What say we drop by my apartment and I'll cut that cast away from your groin to free up your family jewels, as you fellows like to call them? That should help with the rash and make you a little more comfortable. This is strictly professional, of course."

"I couldn't say no if I wanted to, which I don't. Anything to get this thing out of my crotch."

"Afterwards you can get a good night's sleep and I'll take you the rest of the way tomorrow morning."

"Lord, it's getting better all the time. But there's no guarantee that I'll sleep without some degree of difficulty. This scenery is all new to me. I'm not used to nice bathrooms, televisions, a choice of radio stations and air conditioning. I haven't had a hamburger in months, not to mention spicy foods, deserts, milk shakes, sheets that aren't starched like a board and the list goes on ad infinitum."

"Well, you deserve a break today," she said. "There's a diner up the road at the traffic circle and we'll just stop long enough for you to get your belly full."

"I must warn you. I may eat like a pig."

"I'm sure it's authorized every few years. I'd say you're a little overdue."

"You're really an angel, aren't you? I couldn't imagine this happening...I mean meeting someone so kind...when I was sitting at the airport."

"Au contraire," she laughed. "I get to do something nice for someone and made a friend in the process. I was bored to tears when I saw you. I dropped a friend off at the airport. She's off to have a good time somewhere in Florida and I seem to have this rut of a lifestyle that consists of little more than work and sleep. I really needed a little company and something about you said you were it."

We parked at the diner. It was a little after eleven which didn't mean a lot. The neon sign over the door read open all night. There were plenty of seats available and we found one well away from the cash register and front door.

"I can't imagine all night food," I said. There aren't a lot of people in here," I remarked. How do they stay open?"

"The bars close at two in the morning. When that happens, they'll be pouring in here."

"Let me guess. The crowd might consist of wooers who failed on the dance floor and feel a meal might be an alternative woo, or those that struck out altogether and come here with friends to discuss the failed salacious events of the night."

She laughed. "Of course, there is the other category consisting of people who just happen to be hungry early in the morning, GIs who haven't eaten civilian fun food in a long time, and good Samaritans like me who bring them here."

"I suppose I'm being too judgmental."

"Obviously, you've been gone too long," she remarked. It may take a while to reacquaint you with civilization. Getting over a primitive lifestyle is something you will certainly do but perhaps there are certain imperceptible benefits to remaining primal for a little while longer. You keep your senses keen that way, don't you? I think Americans are perhaps a little too aristocratic and certainly too complacent with everything that goes on around them. We are without conscience sometimes. We send our good men to war while we indulge those that do nothing for this country but tear it down."

"I haven't been a part of that great philosophical upheaval. I have only been a part of the sword set into motion by this country to resolve issues that couldn't be resolved at the negotiation table. Are objectors and protesters really positioned so well that they could change direction of the government?"

"It would appear so," she replied. "Opinion seems to be winning out over fact these days. Those that oppose the war are holding the politicians hostage. If they don't speak out and vote against it, they will be without jobs. The question is what does that mean? Does it mean more people than not are opposed to the war? I don't think so. Most of the resistance comes from industrialized areas and California. Since the politicians of those states carry more electoral votes than the other larger land masses, they will inevitably control the government if they are successful. It's a bit of a mess."

"Dang," I said. "Don't tell me I've spent the last two and a half years for nothing."

Ada smiled and used her best Bettye Davis accent to reply. "No darling, it's never a waste unless you do nothing with it."

"Oh dear, the ambiguities are killing me."

"Where did you learn to speak like that? You have excellent command of the language dear boy," she said, this time sounding more like Betty Grabel.

"My father had a thing about English. When I was a child, we learned a new word every day and had to use it in a sentence five times. Au contraire, I was amazed at the many ways you could articulate things. I'll just remain a little primitive if it's okay and leave the stage to you," I said, badly mimicking W.C. Fields. "By the way, you really do those imitations very well."

"Any woman should," she said. "We spend our lives acting. We smile when we are sad, cry when we are happy, say everything is fine when we know it's not and do award winning performances when we fake orgasms. Acting just comes with the territory, excuse the cliché. It's an intuitive ability that comes with the chromosomes."

"And you do it so well," I said. "Conversely, men are theatrically childish and immature. They're inclined to transcend reality with grandiose notions about what could be, where women do not. I think men are dreamers because they don't have enough sense of direction to be anything else. I must admit that women are the beacons for men in terms of pointing out the direction they need to move, and men understand that women usually are right on common sense issues, especially when it comes to morality or anything related to doing the right thing. Women's intuition is really not something surreal. I think it would be better described as well directed karma."

"And what about you, Bo Hardin? Who are you and what is your life all about?"

"I don't know," I said honestly. I'm in the throes of divorce. I haven't seen my wife in years. We're both predisposed, or should I say in total agreement, to setting the union asunder. She went her way, I went mine, and it's a chapter out of both our lives we'd both just as soon forget. I went to Vietnam in 1965 and I've been there ever since. I had no reason to come back nor was I inclined, but that's a very long story. Two weeks ago I thought I was going to stay in Vietnam forever or until the end of the war, whichever came first. Now I'm in a diner in New Jersey wondering how I'm going to survive life in a very alien country. Who woulda thunk?"

"So where is home?"

"Knoxville, Tennessee, originally. My father was a doctor who adopted my brother and I at an early age, not that it makes any difference…being adopted, I mean. It just seems to help put a little sense into a life that seems dysfunctional to everyone but me. Actually, I'm in complete control. Can't you tell?" I asked facetiously?

"Never a doubt in my mind," she replied.

"I'd like to redress that if I may. I'm not a psycho. I'm currently snuggled between remarkable events in my life and it throws me out of kilter, if you know what I mean."

"Oh, I understand fully," she said. It's not like the rest of the world has ever been out of sync before. We all go through that sooner or later. Some people dwell or rely upon it as a way of life and some don't. Some tend to lead such a dull existence that they would welcome a little disharmony or even uncontrolled pandemonium into their life. No man, or woman, is an island."

"What about you, Ada Udahl?"

"What do you think? Please indulge me with your best guess."

"Honestly,' I said?

"Yes, of course."

"You stay on the leading edge and well in control of most relationships. At five foot 8 with a probable six-pack, you command respect and are pleased with those who are in awe of your physique. You are loaded with wit and charm and are characterized by your peers as someone who is reliable and more than just a little intelligent. You care about people and are sometimes disappointed because you expect more from them than what you get. You are in a relationship or have had a relationship that meant a great deal to you. You have an easy gait with men, which tells me you are comfortable with them and are either married or have been married. You are a physical specimen and the fact that you exercise to excess is clearly evident from your legs and rather noble stature. You are flawless by design. Anyone who exercises the way you do does so with a purpose. It is either because he or she is a professional athlete or because there is a need to use physical exhaustion to eject a recalcitrant devil from the mind. But you are a mystery. You are breathtaking in every detail and I have no idea what you are doing here with me in a diner at midnight."

The waitress arrived with our orders; a full-blown hamburger and fries with extra grease for me and a salad for her with no dressing.

"Are you really with the CIA?" She asked.

"You know better," I laughed.

"Have you read my dossier?"

I laughed. "Didn't know you had one."

"Bo, you are so remarkably right. Ugly right, but right."

"I didn't mean to be ugly."

"I asked you to give me your best guess and you did. I was

going to lie to you and tell you that you were wrong about everything." She laughed even harder.

"That's not your style," I said.

"I may turn your cast around backwards."

"Better to have your cast turned backward than never to have it turned at all."

"Nice quip, bad metaphor."

"It's what came to mind. Touche," I said.

"Too much comes to your mind."

"I work off prompts."

"Your wit is too facile." She winced and pointed at me with her finger.

"I'm working hard to simplify it."

"You're failing miserably."

"I'll try harder."

"You should."

"Should I kill myself?"

"Not without my help."

Ada was fun. She had an unmistakable zeal and playfulness that you had to like. I continued to wolf down my hamburger and thought about getting another one to go. She picked at the salad with her fork as if she were checking it for bugs.

I realized that Ada had told me nothing. She let me ponder what the truth might be, but she had not revealed any facts about herself. I could only conclude that she had a reason or need to protect vital details but I didn't know what they were. I decided not to probe for answers because I wasn't sure of what her reaction would be. Some things are better left alone. Certainly, she was entitled to her privacy. I had met this remarkable woman a mere two hours before and I felt very comfortable with her. She was being more than kind to me and I felt as though I shouldn't intrude into her personal life or violate a sanctum of information that she ostensibly chose to protect.

We left the diner and arrived at her apartment. Fortunately, hers was on the ground floor which eased transporting the leg that didn't seem to care for stairs. The apartment was squeaky clean and perfectly arranged and decorated. I hadn't been around civilized living arrangements for some time but I knew it took painstaking steps to keep everything so meticulously organized.

"Oh my," I said, "the perfect little household. I am really impressed."

"Well, I'm glad you like it," she said, expressing a tinge of embarrassment that I knew was genuine. "Now if you'll sit right there at the kitchen table, I'll get my handy dandy kitchen surgical equipment and we'll cut that cast down to size."

I took a seat in the hardback chair at the end of the table and turned my leg so she could get to it. My pants were draped over the cast at a length a one legged pirate would expect to wear. Ada stared at me with a puzzled look. "The only way we're going to get this done is if I get access to the area where I must work. These are crude tools," she said, holding up a large bread knife and a small grating rasp. "One minor slip and one could lose a very important appendage, if you know what I mean."

"Aye my lady," I said, doing my best pirate accent. "Shiver me timbers, give me thy appendage or give me death."

"A little Captain Hook and a little Patrick Henry, all in the same sentence. Very, very good."

"I thought they were homosexual lovers."

"Your history book must have been revised and edited by drug addicts."

I laughed. "Promise me you'll keep this clinical."

"You have nothing to worry about," she said. "I am a professional."

"Uh oh," now I'm worried."

Ada took a kneeling position on the floor directly ahead of me. I had lowered my pants down around my ankles and she gently pushed my legs further apart. My boxer shorts were under the cast and she pulled them up and pushed them to the side. She moved her hand inside the cast to protect my leg from the serrated bread knife. Of course, when she did, the back of her hand rested against my testicles. Of course, when that happened, I found myself getting aroused. And of course, it became evident to both of us that blood was being displaced disproportionately."

"My apologies," I said.

"There's no reason to apologize for involuntary body functions," she said almost smiling."

But things got worse. My left knee was raised to give Ada room to use the knife and my body was leaning at a right angle to provide Ada the best possible access to the area. Gravity pulled the flailing appendage at the most direct route to Mother Earth which happened to be the back of Ada's hand. She pushed it gently away and I held it to the left where it was out of the way. Ada continued sawing through the cast with the bread knife until she had removed the upper three inches.

It was instant relief. The removal of the cast from the groin revealed a rash where the cast had rubbed the tissue beneath. She retrieved a topical ointment from the bathroom and applied it to the rash.

"There," she said, "that should do it." "And by the way, you should leave those pants off so the area can air out. Those khaki pants don't breathe very well. Now how about a drink?"

"Sure, that would be fine."

"I have vodka, scotch and bourbon."

"Scotch neat."

"I should have guessed."

"You don't have American Eagle, do you?"

"What the hell is American Eagle?"

"It's probably the worst scotch in the world."

"Then why would you want it?"

"I don't. I just wanted to make sure you didn't have any. In Vietnam the Air Force ran the liquor stores. All the zoomies got their booze first. All that was left by the time the Army got there was a few bottles of cheap vodka, which goes great with Kool Aid, and American Eagle scotch. According to a lot of people, you have to develop a taste for scotch. Drinking American Eagle scotch requires a second level of development. If I ever bought another bottle of American Eagle, it would be to remind me of the years I had to drink cheap lousy scotch."

"How about Chevas Regal?" she asked.

"It sounds deliciously regal. I forgot there was such a thing."

She brought me a glass that was shaped like a chalice and sat it before me on the table.

"I don't think I can ever remember being this comfortable in my entire life," I said.

"Are you glad to be back?" she asked.

"Two hours ago, I would have said no, but now I am feeling a lot more at ease, thanks to you. I have a few butterflies about what the future holds, but I'm sure I'll get over them."

"After an hour of talking about world issues and Ada's job as a nurse, I had finished a second drink and was getting weary. Ada could tell, and said it would be a good idea if we got some rest. She objected when I said I could sleep on the couch. "Don't be silly," she said. "I have a large bed and it's the only one since this is a one bedroom. We'll be fine. You can wash up in the bathroom."

I sat on the edge of the tub and washed with the wash cloth Ada had laid out for me. The hot water and soap created an unusual sensation for my skin. The pores seemed to open wide in acceptance of something strange but sensual. I lingered there for a while, unsure of what was going to happen next. Eventually I went down the hall to the bedroom in nothing but my underwear. Ada scurried by me to the bath without speaking. The covers were drawn down carefully and I got into bed. The sweet smell of perfume in the room intoxicated me and the softness of the silk sheets seemed to touch me everywhere I had skin. If this wasn't heaven, it was just around the corner.

Several anxious minutes later Ada arrived in a silk nightie that protected nothing from the imagination. She pulled it over her head and let it fall to the floor and I lost my breath the second after. That couldn't be a body, I thought. It was a hand carved ivory sculpture of undeniable and indescribable perfection. There was muscle where there needed to be muscle and soft curves in locations that would make the masters of art like Michelangelo and Rembrandt drool in anticipation of capturing them.

Ada turned off the lights and got into bed while rockets were exploding in my mind. Instantly she was by my side. I felt her hands cupping my face as she said "I am so glad you're home." "I am too," I said.

"Reckless abandon" would not describe the endless and relentless sex for the duration of the night. It was rough, hard, fast, slow and soft. Ada cried, screamed and moaned. When I thought I could do no more, I did. When I thought she would rest, she didn't. Her needs were insatiable and the heights of her orgasms were only equaled by the depths of her efforts to have the next one. Bathed in each other's sweat and saliva, we finally went to sleep but not before doing everything, and I do mean everything, two people of the opposite sex can do to each other while one has his leg in a cast.

Ada awoke me the next morning with a cup of coffee. She had already been out for her morning run. I had problems raising myself to a sitting position. I had used muscles I hadn't used in a while and my body was sending strong signals to my brain that it had been screwed really well and that repairs were necessary. I looked at Ada in disbelief.

"Did you do your usual ten miles today?" I asked.

"No, only five," she replied. "I was a little tired."

"Dang, I need two medics and a gurney to get out of bed and you're a little tired?"

"Who's the pussy here?" she laughed. "I'm going to take a bath and get you to post."

"I'm going to search my duffel bag for clean underwear and socks."

"Don't bother. Look in the upper left-hand drawer of that dresser and you'll find both."

Ada went to the bathroom and I went to the drawer she pointed out to find underwear. Lifting the socks and briefs I found there revealed a picture of a military man and a newspaper article. I imagined that the picture, from the type of frame that contained it, had set atop the dresser and had been recently placed in the drawer. The picture was that of Lieutenant James Udahl and the news article was an announcement of his death. Also in the drawer were a few letters she had written to him. Each letter started with "My Dearest Soldier Boy." From reading the article, I learned he had died in Vietnam in 1966. He left behind a wife, Ada, and no children. The article spelled out some other interesting details. Unaware of his death the day before he was supposed to leave the country, Ada had gone to the airport to pick him up. She waited there for sixteen hours before returning home to find an Army chaplain standing at her front door. I finished reading the article while Ada was in the bath and returned it and the picture to the drawer.

Suddenly the comments I had dismissed as confusing but credible took on a new light. She had called me "soldier boy" at the airport, the same name she used in the letters to her husband. I told her I was married and she accepted without question my explanation that it was soon to end. She had cupped my face in her hands and said "I'm so glad you're home." She had made reckless and unbridled love to me with an abandonment you would expect reserved for a spouse or someone with which you shared a longstanding intimate relationship. She had tenderly cared for me and welcomed me to her bed as if I were a loving soul for which there was an irrefutable connection of the heart and mind. In her mind, I was indeed James Udahl. It was clear that a sad set of extraordinary circumstances had put me in her bed, and I had inadvertently become the surrogate lover for someone that would never return.

The victims of this war are many, I thought. A shot gets fired on the other side of the world and hits two people; one is the intended victim and the other is the victim's survivor who tries in whatever way she can to hang on to life as she once knew it. When the mind cannot accept or acknowledge the truth, it must compensate in a circuitous way with alter truths that become the fanatical origins of erratic and bizarre behavior.

I didn't know whether I should broach the illegitimacy of the events of the night before. To let it go seemed to be the wisest selection of alternatives. It was Ada's business, and she was the one that had to call her own shots. Any judgments I made aloud would be met with some resistance, I imagined. Besides, it may be that she was comfortable with what she was doing. It was improbable that she happened to be at the airport and was indeed a Good Samaritan and ultimately liked my looks.

Ada exited the bathroom in bra and underwear and proceeded to don the rest of her clothing in front of the bedroom mirror. She looked remarkable and I was tempted to try to restart the engine that had run perpetually the night before but thought better of it. This was her apartment and she brought me here. It was her call, not mine. There are rules of engagement that had to be followed both on and off the battle field and I could tell from Ada's demeanor that further engagement was out of the question.

"You are very beautiful," I said, watching her intently as she applied her makeup.

"Well, that's a very nice thing to say."

"I mean it."

"I believe you do."

"How do you stay in that kind of shape?"

"I have to. I just don't feel comfortable any other way. Any weight gain goes right to my butt. It takes a week to put it on and three to take it off."

"It wouldn't bother me."

"Yes, I imagine you're like most men. They don't care how big a woman's butt is until it gets too big or obscenely disproportionate. The problem is that once it's hanging behind you in ample supply, it's there forever. I don't want to chance it."

"Well let me congratulate you for keeping it under control."

"Thank you. I hope you're not going to be late."

"I doubt that seriously. They never seem to have stopwatches for cripples. I believe I'll be assigned to the Medical Holding Detachment after I process through the personnel detachment. I'll probably have little to do thereafter."

"Lucky you. I'm starting a long shift today, 24 hours, and will be dog tired for 12 hours thereafter then another long shift then I'll be off for 4 days. Maybe we can get together afterwards."

"That would be nice," I said, sensing that she wasn't really chewing at the bit to see me again. Maybe in my current state I was bad in bed, I thought, but quickly dismissed the idea.

The conversation was becoming trite and uncomfortably jaded. I believed it would remain that way until she dropped me off at Fort Dix. I detested this cloud of confusion and ambiguities that enveloped us now. I opined it would be much easier for her to say what she felt. Direct and honest comments such as "I've had second thoughts; the reason I brought you here was to relive a relationship that is gone forever; I have a problem accepting the truth about my husband; and no, I don't want to continue this relationship," would suffice. Any of those comments could chase away the miasma of uncertainties and clarify the events of the night before, but it wasn't going to happen and I knew it.

We didn't waste any time getting to the car or arriving at the post. The small talk was boring and guarded and I was polite and courteous. By the time we got to the post it was clear that there wasn't going to be anything else as far as we were concerned, and I didn't belabor my departure. I said "thanks for everything" and she helped me remove the duffel bag from the back seat. I watched her drive away, noting that she didn't seem to peer into the rear-view mirror or make any attempt to get that last look, or wave as if to indicate there was any further interest.

The rest of the day went as expected. I processed through personnel which could not seem to marry up my records with the travel orders I carried with me from Vietnam. I wound up at the hospital eventually where I was assigned to the Medical Holding Detachment. The next few days were spent making appointments for X-rays and blood work. I had some torn ligaments and other extraneous bailing-wire abnormalities but the doctors concluded that "watching" was the best medicine, rather than operating. The old battle-hardened doc who examined me sized it up rather well. "Hell, man," he said, "You came out smelling like a rose."

"I want to go back," I said, spontaneously and somewhat involuntarily.

"Are you crazy?" the doctor asked.

"No sir," I replied. "I could handle another assignment, possibly in I Corp."

"You're talking to the wrong guy," he laughed. "You need to see the head doctor."

By the time I left the hospital I had arranged for lodging and meals. A kind medic cut the cast to just below my knee which made it far easier to move. The Medical Holding Detachment offered me a bed and wall locker. I accepted the wall locker where I could ditch my duffel bag and opted to sleep elsewhere. The Medical Holding Detachment had some loose rules regarding those assigned to it. I could sign out on convalescent leave as long as I had a telephone number where I could be reached. There were no formations or roll calls; I only needed to be contactable. The hospital had made it clear. My next appointment was in 60 days at the medical clinic. At that time, they would determine whether I could be returned to duty or remain on convalescent leave.

CHAPTER 11

I spent the night in a Wrightstown motel. It's clearly a GI town and the aspect of seeing the glittering neon lights of the city was more appealing than the olive drab of an Army post. Payday was more than a week away so I knew my finances wouldn't hold up much beyond that. It dawned on me that I had the number and address of a pen pal that I had written infrequently from Vietnam. This came about as a result of a letter I had sent to the Philadelphia Inquirer at least a year before proclaiming the loneliness of soldiers whom had little to look forward to or very little contact from those back home, many of which were receiving Dear John letters from girlfriends that had decided not to wait. I had written love letters for a few of them which amounted to desperate pleas for them to just hang on a little longer. Oh, what the heck, I thought. It can't hurt to call them even if it is just to say hello.

I dialed the number and spoke with Joan Randall, the pen pal and mother of seven children and a dog. She was more than cordial, speaking as if she had known me forever and was very excited. She asked me where I was, and when I told her she said "That just won't do. We're picking you up."

One hour later I was sitting in their house in Willingboro New Jersey with a beer in my hand. Joan was a work of art. She was funny, intelligent, inquiring and friendly. Her husband Bill was a little reticent to speak and I could tell, metaphorically, that he was along for the ride on Joan's coat tails. They insisted that I stay there for a few days and as hard as I tried to say no, after three beers I just couldn't do it.

The Randalls were perfect hosts but after three or four days I thought it was time to say my goodbyes. They were insistent that I attend a PTA meeting with them that evening and the children were adamant that I go with them. When we arrived, there was the usual classroom visits then a general meeting of parents and teachers. As the meeting was ending, the speaker said to the audience that he would like to recognize a "True hero who had returned from Vietnam" and pointed in my direction. Joan goaded me to stand up, which I did, to a round of applause. Needless to say, it caught me by surprise, and beyond a little embarrassment, I felt no other emotions. Hero wasn't a word I was accustomed to nor were any other words of praise that could be labels for men or women who had donned the military uniform. There were those assigned to a combat zone who would not see combat, some would be in harm's way and others would put it all on the line, finding themselves in do or die situations. Regardless, all should be recognized for whatever is deemed a sacrifice or actions taken in the service of their country.

The Randall children were clapping and laughing. It was nice to see the genuine glee that only children can impart. I got a lot of hugs from them and we walked along the school corridors to see where their classrooms were. I spoke with several of the teachers, mostly small talk. One very attractive teacher made it a point to keep the conversation alive, inquiring about where I was from and family. My military service didn't come into play and I was pleased to avoid any discussions of anything that would take me away from the moment. At some point I concluded that she wanted something more than conversation. I asked her if she wanted to talk more over dinner, which was insane given the absence of a car and any knowledge of the area. But this wasn't the first time my mouth was in direct contradiction with my capabilities and it certainly wouldn't be the last. Surprisingly, she closed the loop on that suggestion by telling me that she would love to but was getting married that weekend. Any thoughts I had about giving myself an award for reading signals just went out the window. She added that she had a friend, Carol Duvinski, who was also a teacher that I might find interesting. She quickly wrote down a name and number and handed it to me.

I told the Randalls about what had transpired and they insisted that I stay another day or two. At Joan's insistence I called the number and made a date of sorts. Joan would take me to this teacher's apartment and drop me off. The teacher had a car and she would provide transportation to a movie and restaurant then drop me off. I wasn't too keen on this kind of arrangement. I felt like a high school student getting parental escorts to see a girlfriend. Nevertheless, given my current situation, it was necessary to gulp down pride to meet the tenets of my predicament.

I knocked on Carol's apartment door. Suddenly she was there, dressed to the nines, as the expression goes, with a blonde bombshell appearance, every hair in place, sporting a confident smile. Was I outclassed, I thought. Was this just too good to be true?

"I must apologize for the circumstances of today," I said, not wanting to call it a date.

She laughed. "It is a bit unusual but not to worry," she said.

Carol had the day planned. At her recommendation we were going to The Pub, a restaurant in Philadelphia, and then a movie. I felt impotent in an embarrassing way. Typically, I should be making the arrangements for an evening but could not. I felt underdressed, having bought cheap clothing on the spur of the moment thinking it would suffice. I could only hope that my masculine appearance could serve to undermine some of these obvious shortcomings.

My first impression of The Pub was that it would be the kind of enormous mess hall that Cookie would love. It was one gigantic room with a 60-foot ceiling and a side bar. We had a drink or two and ordered food that was way beyond Cookie's capabilities.

"Do you come here often," I asked.

"It's one of my family's favorite places," she replied.

"So, it's not a place you often bring wayward soldiers who are without cars, great wardrobes and no immediate sense of direction."

She laughed. "There was another soldier."

Now where this is traditionally the ideal time to change the subject to cars or sports, no one ever does. Does she have a penchant for soldiers, is it something kinky, or is it just happenstance.

"Something recent," I asked.

"Yes and no, but I'm certain it's over."

She continued to explain her long relationship and engagement to another GI that started in her college years and ended when he found someone new. He had made Captain and was still on active duty.

Well, there you go, I thought to myself. Once again, I have been outclassed multiple times in a period of a few hours. The aura of respect and self-admiration I had enjoyed suddenly slipped away. Hardly inexplicable, I deserved it. What was I thinking? Had I become something to do in the absence of something better?

The problem I had was that I wasn't sure I wanted this to end. Regardless of my abject inferiority, I found this woman delightful, not to mention that she met all of my physical criteria. Finding a woman with blonde hair, long legs and a butt that was 13.25% overweight was highlighted in my rolodex as a major goal and objective.

We left the restaurant and went to the movies. A crowd had assembled outside the theater awaiting the doors to be opened. I stood next to Carol at the back of the crowd. When the doors opened, there was a mad rush to get inside. Suddenly she was gone, making her way through the crowd toward the entry door. It was a maze of flesh, moving as if someone would die if they got left behind. I could see Carol about 15 sardines away and she slowed her movement to let me catch up with her.

"Whoa," I exclaimed. "Is every movie like this?"

She laughed. "This is New Jersey, not Tennessee. This is typical for New York and New Jersey."

Apparently, I am in the land of hurry, I thought. These are yankees. In my home state of Tennessee, I had been told about yankees and how they differ from good southern folk. I knew they spoke at a record-breaking pace but I didn't know there could be such a display of impetuous behavior. Conversely, the almost tyrannical mentality of the military prevents

mob creation and insures civility in most venues. People are informed that some things are nice and some
things ain't.

The night ended without a good night kiss. We agreed to see each other again and we did. In July of that year, we
got married.

Life over the next year served to shape the years beyond. I healed quickly and managed to get my legs back under me. I went to Drill Sergeant School and did a stint as a drill sergeant in a Fort Dix Basic Training Company. I went to Officer Candidate School (OCS), where I was commissioned as an Infantry officer, followed by a few months in Vietnamese language school, Airborne training and Jungle School. The next assignment was in Germany where our first daughter Kim was born, then I had orders back to Vietnam.

CHAPTER 12

The trip back to Vietnam was a rerun of what I had experienced before. A good friend, Lieutenant Bobby McNaught, had left Europe ahead of me and had greased the skids in personnel channels for me to be assigned to his unit, the 173rd Airborne Brigade in LZ English. I was anxious to see him and get his review of mission activities in the area and his feelings for what the future held in that region.

I was dropped off in front of the Battalion Tactical Operations Center (TOC) or S-3 tent with little fanfare. There was no welcoming committee and few people turned their heads when I entered.

"Can I help you?" a soldier said from the corner of the tent.

"Yes," I said. "I'm Bo Hardin. I just arrived from the states. I've got orders in my duffel bag."

"No need," the man said, advancing forward to shake my hand. "I'm Lieutenant Martin. We've been expecting you. Had you arrived yesterday, you would have been in the field today. We were short one platoon leader but we were able to move folks around to fill the slot."

"There have been personnel shortages?" I asked.

"Well, we've lost a few men, including one platoon leader in the last month."

"Speaking of platoon leaders, I'm looking for Bobby McNaught. We served together in the 3rd Armored Division in Germany."

My comment got the attention of the other two men who turned their heads to look at me with a look of concern.

"Oh, man, I'm sorry," said Martin. "McNaught hit a trip wire on a booby trap last month. He died instantly."

This was not good news. I was floored. Bobby was not the first friend I lost in Vietnam but Bobby and I had a history that included my family. In Germany, he would escort my wife, and others, to the commissary and Post exchange when everyone else was in the field. He had an amicable, outgoing personality that made him a friend of everyone.

"Damn," I whispered. "Damn, damn."

Martin told me where I could find the Admin Officer and after a few minutes with him, discussing Bobby and the basic sign in needs, I dropped my duffel bag in my assigned tent. It's a very austere environment, I thought. The bed was a step up from a cot. There was a metal frame with a 3-inch mattress cloaked in heavy layered mosquito netting. No pictures adorned the walls and no carpets covered the floors. I wasn't expecting the likes of a Holiday Inn but the rooms lack of life reminded me that I had, indeed, returned to Vietnam.

My introduction to the Battalion Commander, LTC Rogers, was brief. He was a very busy man with a lot on his plate. He had to plan for major operations involving the entire battalion, he was running both security and operational patrols around the clock, and he was monitoring staff operations, all while tending to the needs of each individual within the unit. From what I understood, he did it well.

"I see you've spent two and a half years in country already," he said.

"Yes Sir," I replied. "Primarily in III Corp, around Bien Hoa."

"You're a glutton for punishment. You have to know that you're pushing the envelope and upping the odds."

"Yes Sir," but I feel like I'm needed here."

"Got a family?"

"Yes Sir."

"What did you come back to Vietnam for?"

"A better resume," I said. "This is my first officer combat assignment and I want to be competitive in the future."

"I guess everything comes at a price in this business," he said.

"Yes Sir," I replied. I wanted to ask him for a field assignment but thought better of the idea. He didn't need some lieutenant dictating assignments. I knew he had a sixth sense about people and their potential. He didn't climb the ladder to LTC without learning the basics of sizing up capabilities of those under his tutelage. Body language meant a lot; penetrating or inquiring eyes, strong speech patterns, a strong posture and a host of other things that interpret nonverbal actions. Officers had to be forthright in manner and speech. Orders stated in a direct manner had to be followed and they had to be accompanied by an understanding of what it took to follow them.

"We need an S-2 Intelligence Officer so I'm going to assign you to that position. It's important so you'll need to get educated rather quickly. Field operations are highly reliant on the movements of enemy elements. You need to get with Brigade Intel so you can start daily briefs. The S-3 will fill you in on that end."

"Yes Sir," I replied.

"Good to have you on board."

"Yes Sir," I said, knowing that was my cue to leave. I saluted, did an about face and left the office.

Oh boy, I thought. This was not what I was expecting, but then again, what was I expecting. I had been an S-2 in Europe because the unit I was in didn't have enough officers to fill all the positions. Typically, an S-2 slot was filled by an Intelligence Officer. My first battalion briefing consisted of explaining the requirements for sending, reading and interpreting radio messages in code, and I bombed it. Somehow, I stammered my way to what I had concluded was the end, peering out at 50 or 60 confused people who were wondering just how long I had lived on earth. An understanding Battalion Executive Officer suggested that I give this briefing again to all individual units to ensure "a comprehensive understanding" of the radio requirements. At that moment I was willing to put him in my will.

When I got back to the S-3 I ran into Brookes. He was an Officer Candidate in my class at Fort Benning and we discussed old times for a few minutes before I started plying him with questions about how things worked in the TOC. The picture he painted was rather gloomy.

"Well, last night at O'Dark 30 we had an Ops patrol that couldn't find a safe location to bivouac and literally crouched down in place while a hundred or so Charleys walked by within yards. They went radio silent because even the slightest squelch break would have given way their location. We sat here for several hours wondering what was going on, thinking the worst. When they did come back up on the net, they said they were missing one man. Evidently the tail guy in the squad was the first guy privy to the enemy movement so he dropped further away from the group. They eventually found him. We couldn't get helos in there to pick them up but we pummeled the areas where we believe Charley was located with artillery. The squad is holding in place. We don't know at this point whether Charley is using that area as a corridor to funnel troops to the south so everything is touch and go at this point. Brigade is looking at putting in a blocking force further to the south and given the terrain, we might be able to eliminate a bunch of Charleys between the blocking force and positioning flanking elements on nearby high ground areas. We'll have to get that squad out because they need resupply of just about everything. That board over there on the wall shows what we think is the on-ground situation for friendly and enemy forces. Needless to say, it is subject to change in a moment's notice."

"Dang, you stay busy," I said.

"Well yes and no. Sometimes you can go three or four days and everything is ominously quiet. I don't like that. It makes me edgy. We've got a couple of outposts that are manned primarily with Vietnamese. You never know when they are going to call. Their tactical situation is different from our battalion or brigade units so they kind of march to the beat of their own drums. They do the best they can. There's nothing to keep you awake here at night except the sound of radio squelches and conversations with whoever is here with you. We rely on perimeter units to check in periodically to stay awake and on top of things."

"I'm beginning to get the picture," I commented. "My job is going to be taking enemy reports from the field and feeding them to brigade, and brigade sends me data from reports sent in from other field units."

Brookes smiled. "Something like that. But you will see that nothing follows a perfect script around here. We are all reactionaries so to speak. There's no such thing as simplicity in any endeavor. You'll get the hang of things in due time."

Brookes continued. "The saving grace, in one respect, is that brigade calls the shots when it comes to major operations. Of course, they are getting their direction from III Corp command and control elements. The system works as it should. In the 6 months I've been here, no one has played the blame game or done any finger pointing."

Well hell, I thought. Everything is clicking along in accordance with prescribed military manuals and then I arrive to fill a position in which I have little training. What rapidly came to mind was my blundering attempt to brief radio security codes as a young lieutenant in Europe. Does my past define the future?

In days gone by I had nagging insecurities about my capabilities. In conversations with other officers about where they went to school, I was embarrassed. I was envious of the likes of UCLA, MIT and Notre Dame graduates. The West Point group tended to avoid me after giving them my educational history, which consisted of dropping out of Holston High in my sophomore year, getting a GED then cramming in as many night college courses as I could. Their comments like "that's nice" or "you're kidding" tended to undermine confidence in my abilities. My life's resume was a mess. I was adopted at 4 years old, ran away from a great home when I was 14, married when I was 15 and later divorced, spent a year and a half in juvenile detention and found myself in the Army at the direction of a judge who didn't think stealing a neighbor's tires, though done in jest, was funny.

But the army had given me a chance to put the past in the rear-view mirror and imbed in my future a little poise, esteem and self-respect. To camouflage my ineptitudes, I would often acclaim in a boisterous and obnoxious way that I was the erudite officer that could be matched by no other, scrupulous in every undertaking, and able to leap tall buildings in a single bound. I did everything I could do to get a leg up on the competition. I got to work early and left late, I read every manual that addressed my duties, I listened intently to those who were acknowledged as the best in their field, and I volunteered for everything, even when I despised the task. As time went by, the self-aggrandizement or boasting lessened, my confidence rose, and I was recognized as a competent and reliable officer.

Now this new job meant that I would have to apprise myself anew of the infinite details needed to accomplish all related tasks. I picked up all the manuals I could find and planned to visit the brigade S-2 to pick his brain. I sat in the corner of the TOC for the next three hours reading everything I could about field communications and tactical operations. With Brookes assistance I collected the last dozen or so intel Situation Reports (sitreps) regarding current operations.

Brookes advised me that the Battalion Commander would introduce me tomorrow at the evening briefing and I could, to the greatest extent possible, brief on the current intel situation.

When that time came, I felt I was as prepared as possible. I had spent some time with the brigade S-2 and he had given me a map overlay, showing the details of movements, contacts and sightings of all enemy forces. According to the S-2, map overlays had not been provided in the past and he would continue to do that as long as he wasn't engaged in other tactical matters that would prevent him from doing so.

The briefing went well. LTC Rogers liked the overlays, and defining sizes, locations and types of elements was easy. That was the first hurdle, I thought, and it went well.

The next several days were without incident. There was no such thing as morning Physical Training (PT) and the mess hall provided a breakfast that was as good as it could be. Shit on a shingle (SOS), eggs, toast and bacon. What more could you ask for.

I spent most of the days in the TOC. There was little else to do given the absence of bars, movies, bowling alleys and dance halls. From 0600 in the morning to 2200 hours at night wasn't unusual. On several occasions there were flights out to field locations which gave me an opportunity to see the terrain and get a better feel for how units could maneuver or how they might be restricted.

It was 2200 hours and I was getting ready to leave the TOC. Brooke got a message from a field unit and snapped his fingers as I was standing up to leave. He motioned for me to come closer. I could hear some whispering coming in from a field telephone.

"Can you hear me," the voice asked.

Brooke whispered back "Yes."

"We're missing a man. He was out at an early detection post. No contact."

"I have your location at 31456529."

"Roger TOC. We're hearing noises all around us."

Brooke turned to me. "Call brigade TOC and tell them what we've got."

I grabbed a radio that was already set to the right frequency and called the brigade TOC. They indicated the closest on-ground support was an hour away and they couldn't get a gunship in there for another 30-45 minutes but could get artillery in close if that would work.

As I was informing Brookes, all hell broke out on the ground. The platoon leader had pushed the talk button for us to hear. The sounds of rifle fire and machine guns filled the night. Brookes was yelling now. "I'm sending in artillery." "Do it," the platoon leader responded.

Typically, the platoon leader would request the artillery but given the circumstances, he could not. Brooke called the brigade Artillery Liaison Officer (ALO), and gave them adjusted coordinates to fire. The first round should land about two hundred meters to the north of the unit. Within 3 minutes the first round was on its way. The platoon leader spoke with heightened emergency in his voice. "Good round, fire for effect." Three rounds followed then there was silence.

We waited in silence for another 10 minutes then the platoon leader came back on the radio. "It looks like they're gone," he said. "I'll give you a sitrep as soon as possible."

"Roger that," replied Brookes. "But I'm sure that's not the end of it," said Brookes as he sat the handset down.

We both knew that Charley would be laying booby traps along his escape route. Booby traps represented about 30% of his combat operations plan. They caused casualties and their explosions served to notified them of ground force activities and locations in the area. When he was exposed from a firefight or incidental sighting, he knew that a combination of flight Ops and ground intel could lead to other contacts with ground or air forces. The size of his unit was the determining factor in escape and evasion procedures. Anything, in terms of size, above a squad was unusual and finding company size units was rare. Any element that entailed a force of 60 plus men had the earmarks of North Vietnam assistance and seized the attention of Corp command levels. A lot of S-2 briefings touted "the potential for company size enemy units," but rarely did you hear that one was cited and confirmed. Charley might configure his units in smaller elements that he could merge if needed, but merging them into larger elements put him at great risk. Confirmed sightings of his small elements usually meant that artillery was on its way. Artillery was operational anathema for Charley. He couldn't outrun it, but keeping maneuvering units small meant that he could separate personnel by using different escape routes that would avoid concentrated artillery barrages, thereby cutting his losses.

I worked day and night at the TOC, and like others, learned to sleep and work in a piecemeal process. An occasional shower, taken outdoors under a barrel with a pull string that doused you with water, gave me temporary relief from the heat. I had lost weight, as everybody does in this heat. Somebody had made some 20 and 30-pound dumb bells and I started using them daily to commit myself to some kind of exercise regimen. I still wanted a field command but I wasn't going to rush it. I kept thinking that someone would rotate back to the states and I would be considered. Of course, there was Brookes and we had never discussed his desires to take a field command. Indeed, he was both confident and competent in the job at hand. I would get sent to field locations for a variety of reasons but Brookes never was. I had been involved with TOC operations and would often fill in for Brookes so I felt confident that I could handle all tasks associated with his duties and the demands of the job. A field command job opened up and it was quickly filled by a captain from a sister battalion. The captain had a field command in his battalion but was removed for unknown reasons and sent to our unit with brigade directions to fill our open command slot. Could have been a member of the West Point "Ring Knockers Society" I thought, or maybe a General

Officer's relative. Then again, it may be something entirely different. Who knows, who cares, I conceded. I told myself that my time would come, but I was beginning to have my doubts.

Almost 5 months had passed. Brookes and I got promoted to Captain since we had the same date of rank. We now had a full complement of TOC officers, which freed me up somewhat to linger at the mess hall and do some evening jogging. I concluded that I was a little out of shape and had managed to pick up a little weight. We had taken casualties from time to time and I felt fortunate that we hadn't lost more. I have to credit operational successes to the wisdom and effectiveness of leadership at all levels. This was what they trained for and they carried out the mission exceptionally well.

I was informed by the battalion executive officer that LTC Rogers wanted me to go to LZ Lindy, a small outpost manned by two of our troops and a company of Vietnamese. There had been some indications of enemy movement north of the area but Vietnamese patrols had not found or reported any evidence of movement in the area around Lindy. He was concerned that patrols were not being run far enough away from Lindy to properly report enemy activity in the area. We knew that no US personnel accompanied them on these patrols, primarily because of language difficulties. There were no Vietnamese interpreters there and regardless of the requests we had submitted, none had been provided.

I arrived there the following day. The site was about 300 meters wide with a typical barbed wire zig-zag perimeter backed up by sandbagged machine gun positions. There were also mortars in the center of the site. There was one ALO, Captain Jones, assigned to coordinate all artillery operations, and an infantry officer, Lieutenant Swanson who coordinated patrols and perimeter security.

Jones was a big man with rusty-colored hair from Arkansas. There was little hint of an accent when he spoke. He was an avid reader. A box of books in the corner of the TOC attested to that.

"Do you get much of an opportunity to read," I asked.

"Unfortunately," he replied. "This place has really been boring for the last month or two. I'm looking forward to rotating back to brigade headquarters within the week."

"Will they send a replacement?"

"I'm going to recommend that they don't, if given the chance. I can't see a need for an artillery officer here. Swanson knows how to call it in. Vietnamese artillery is out of range so I'm thinking that's why brigade opted to have me here. Still, there's no need."

"How about the security patrols," I asked.

"That's Swanson's responsibility. Evidently, his Vietnamese counterpart prefers that he stay behind. Other than drawing routes of recon on the map they're supposed to use, Swanson has no input. There's always the language barrier. We still don't have an interpreter. Usually that would be a Vietnamese Lieutenant that could both speak English and provide direction to his troops based on our input. We're doing everything now using hand and arm signals."

"What kind of security defense is out there?" I inquired.

"The usual stuff," he said. "We've got Foo Gas all around to prevent penetration of the barbed wire, there's claymores, of course Machine guns, and I've got preregistered locations for artillery."

Foo Gas was a great invention for perimeter security. If Charley inadvertently tripped a wire while trying to crawl his way through the barbed wire that was the last line of defense for a fighting position, it would trigger a heavy gas that would catch fire and explode. The resulting feature was a gooey mixture that would stick to the body causing a very painful death. Charley had trained soldiers to sneak their way through the wire, avoiding trip wires and causing havoc thereafter. These brave souls were called sappers. I had seen the bodies of more than a few of these that had the appearance of crispy bacon. Sapper operations usually followed a barrage of mortar fire which made defense forces take cover and leave perimeter positions, giving the sappers time to make their way through the wire. Once through the barbed wire, they would toss gas grenades and canvas satchels loaded with explosives into TOCs and weapons locations. This kind of operation was more typical of the NVA but its successes were limited.

I talked to Swanson about the patrols and basic defense posture. He was an ROTC officer who graduated from a small school in Missouri. He was short and thin and looked more like the intellectual book-worm than the seasoned officer. Not that such an appearance would mean he wasn't capable. I had seen a lot of short wiry types whose bravery was unquestionable. Their size meant nothing when the chips were down.

I asked him about the patrols and the fact that he didn't accompany them.

"That's been a real bone of contention," he said. "We run intermittent patrols for obvious reasons; we don't want Charley to be expecting us if we made them routine at the same time or the same day. The squad that goes out knows how to conduct clover leaf patrols and the times I went with them, almost a month ago, they did well. We had an interpreter then which made preparation and execution easy enough, but when we lost the interpreter, the squad leader didn't want me to accompany them."

"I'll be going with them," I said. "Battalion is concerned about the lack of intel they are getting. Really, I guess no news is good news but it depends on the way you look at it."

I didn't waste any time getting to the squad leader who was conducting the patrols. In my limited Vietnamese, I told him that we would be going on a patrol tomorrow at 0800. He nodded indicating that he understood. I thought that I would get some resistance but it didn't happen. I guess he understood that if battalion sent somebody out to this location, they were here for a reason and this was it.

We departed the next morning with ten men. There's a lot to be said about patrols. People have to be trained to observe, maintain silence, take evasive action, use hand communication, etc. I had to admit that each man knew his job and did it well. I extended the length of the patrol away from the site to almost a kilometer which seemed to make the squad leader a little uncomfortable. I never had that sixth sense that we were being watched nor did I see any physical evidence of enemy activity. We returned in several hours without incident.

I called the battalion TOC and gave them a report of my activities. The TOC now had a Major appointed as the S-3. We had been struggling along with senior captains in that position which is highly unusual. The Army was struggling to fill all positions in a timely manner. Promotions were coming faster, particularly from 1st Lieutenant to Captain, in order to fill numerous open command and staff positions.

I went to sleep in the site TOC that night after eating my coveted ham and lima beans with juices C-rations and smoking two of the Chesterfield cigarettes enclosed in the accessory pack. I awoke to the familiar sounds of incoming small mortar rounds. Swanson was already on the radio calling battalion. I didn't see Jones.

"Where did Jones go?"

"Down to the wire on the north side. They think they've got sappers coming in there and he took a grenade down there to make sure the Foo Gas is tripped. He should have been back by now."

"Jesus," I said, leaving the confines of the sandbagged TOC and running toward the north side of the site. There was some small arms fire coming at us but it seemed to be going overhead. I hid behind a sandbagged machine gun position to view the wire to the north. Then I saw Jones, twisting and turning in the rolled barbed wire, appearing to be unable to free himself. If the Foo Gas was tripped, he would most likely be severely burned or worse.

When I got to Jones, I could see that the barbed wire had wrapped three times around his right leg and two of the prongs were embedded in the hard sole. He couldn't get to it because there was too much wire between his arms and his foot. I was able to free him within seconds. We began to run toward the TOC after he had thrown the grenade he had gripped in his hand into the wire. Within 7 seconds the grenade exploded and the Foo Gas lit up the night.

When we got to the TOC Jones began calling in artillery. The explosions echoed all around us. Another Foo Gas exploded and there was the continuous rattle of machine guns and 50 Caliber weapons. Swanson had left the TOC before Jones and I arrived. He was running from gun position to gun position checking on ammo and trying to get a feel for the tactical situation. As best as we could tell, there were no Charlies inside the wire and we hadn't suffered any casualties other than Jones' cut up leg. Jones continued to call in artillery further and further away from the site thinking that he might be able to put something in Charley's back pocket as he was making his withdrawal. Eventually, everything quieted, and within an action-packed hour it was over.

I gained a lot of respect for Swanson. He had been everything you would hope for in a field officer, running between gun positions, directing fire and maintaining good order and discipline. He finally got back to the TOC and looked at Jones wiping blood from his leg.

"You Ok? he asked Jones.

"Yep, fine," he replied.

"Hardin, I guess I could put you in for an award," Jones laughed.

"Yeah, then you'd have to talk about getting caught up in the wire, not to mention with a grenade that you had pulled the pin on that could have killed both of us."

"Oh, you noticed that. I was hoping you hadn't seen that. You could have just left me there."

"Nah," I laughed. "There would have been way too much paperwork."

"I guess I owe you."

"Yeah, you do," I said, still laughing. "How about a steak dinner in DC when we're both stationed at the Pentagon."

"Deal."

A helicopter arrived the next day to pick up Jones and me. It brought two lieutenants; one to assist Swanson and another artillery officer. Jones and I got a chance to talk. I concluded that he was quite the intellectual, indeed something that would never register at first glance. He was reading one or two paperback books a day. There were no constraints about the types of books read. It could be Zane Gray or old classics or science fiction. I learned that he was well respected by senior officers and viewed as someone who would rise up in the ranks.

I met the new S-3, Major Jenkins, when I returned to the TOC. He had one previous tour under his belt and knew his way around. He fit in well and spent as much time in the field as was possible. I liked that. If you're going to commit people to battle, you should know something about how they operate on the ground and have a feel for their strong and weak points. For the most part, soldiers were 18-20 years old. They were well trained, both physically and in their individual skills, but they were young. They needed leadership of the highest quality and unvarnished integrity. They responded well to truth, honesty and wisdom.

Major Jenkins advised me that LTC Rogers wanted to see me the following morning. I thought he probably wanted to pick my brain to get first-hand knowledge of what had occurred at Lindy. I discovered that I was tired. I also discovered that Brookes had a bottle of Jack Daniels that he was prepared to share. So, after a shower under the barrel, a change of clothes and a couple of drinks, I slept hard and dreamed of a woman and a little blonde girl I loved very, very much back in New Jersey.

The morning came and LTC Rogers waived me into his office. He pointed toward the only chair in front of his desk. I took my seat, acknowledging to myself that I had not saluted first as was the custom. I assumed that he had not expected it.

"Good to see you in one piece," he chuckled. "It appears that you fulfilled your mission. After having no contact there for so long, we were beginning to wonder if it was necessary to keep Lindy staffed. The Intel guys think it was a squad sized element that made contact. We know there is the prospects of a company size element operating about 20 kilometers northeast that may have come off of the Ho Chi Minh Trail, but that hasn't been confirmed. What did you think of Lindy overall."

"It is situated well geographically and makes good use of the high ground, I replied." "There's good use of claymores and barbed wire, and potential kill zones are well cleared if grazing fire is called for. Patrol elements are well trained and performed well. I do see the need for an artillery officer, and I do believe the artillery sent Charley packing after that last contact."

"Thanks, he said. "I agree with your findings and appreciate what you did there. What I wanted to talk about was an assignment. We need a seasoned officer at the Brigade School. I know about your extensive time and training in this country and when the brigade commander asked for recommendations, your name was suggested by a brigade artillery office; a Captain Jones. Jones is admired by the brigade staff so the general said Ok, let's do that. I know that you really wanted a field command, and I can relate to your feelings. I didn't fight this decision for two reasons. One is that he is my boss and that was an order, and two is I have a son about your age. Bo, you have been here too long. I can't begin to imagine the near misses you've had, and in the last few days you've skirted disaster again. The school is not a cake walk. You'll be charged with running security patrols and maintaining a perimeter."

I knew that now was not the time to start begging and I wasn't going to test his patience. He had to approve my efficiency report that would be written by the S-3 and I had every reason to believe that this would be a good one.

I stood up to salute and be on my way. Rather than return my salute, he stuck out his hand for me to shake. I did so and with a smile I said "Thanks again Sir."

Jones, you son-of-a-bitch, I thought. I guess this was his idea of paying me back for pulling him out of the wire. Should I have left him there, I wondered. Nah!

CHAPTER 13

The helicopter landed at the school helo-pad and created a dust storm that sent people scurrying. I jerked my duffel bag and weapon off the seat. The helicopter lifted off and sent my hat bouncing across the dirt in the direction of the mess hall. I saw a huge tarp displaying the 173rd patch on a hill about 400 yards away. Well, there's little doubt who we are, I thought.

The unit First Sergeant, given the sobriquet of Top in the Army, approached me with my hat that he had picked up after exiting the mess hall. "Welcome," he said, as he saluted.

I pointed at the mess hall and asked if we could get something cold to drink. We found a seat in the mess hall.

"I wanted to talk to you before you got into the headquarters building," he said. "I didn't know if you knew but we still have a unit commander that you will replace. His name is Captain Sanchez. His claim to fame was the Bay of Pigs. Evidently, the Army was tasked to reward him with a rank and future for his efforts as a civilian cohort for what happened in Cuba. He speaks broken English. He doesn't want anyone saluting him outdoors. He thinks that will tell Charley that he's the guy in charge and they'll shoot him. We have a sniper out there somewhere that pops up every few months. He's a terrible shot. He hasn't hit anything but the mess hall roof and we usually fire a couple of mortars and he disappears. Sanchez has been here for about two months and is supposed to be leaving the day after tomorrow. We converted an ammunition shack into quarters for you until he leaves."

I laughed. "No problem," I said. I wondered just how much brigade knew that hadn't been passed down. I guess somebody did somebody a favor and no one was in a position to say no. It happens, I guess.

I met with Sanchez who didn't really want to talk about anything. He was of diminutive stature with a three-day growth of beard that gave the appearance and demeanor of a Che Guevera. I spent all of 10 minutes with him and he suddenly turned and walked away. Oh well, I thought. To each his own.

The unit First Sergeant, Sergeant Rainy, was a seasoned veteran. He was tall and lanky, sporting a small but discernable mustache. This was his second tour to Vietnam and he had spent all of his career in Airborne units. The training NCOs were equally qualified to train personnel whom were headed for field battalion assignments. Many were Ranger and Jungle School graduates and all of them had spent time in combat units. I knew that I could learn a lot from them and as time went by, I did.

Over the next few weeks, I led patrols across the mountain to the west to make sure there were no signs of enemy activity in our area. A Korean Battalion was positioned a couple of kilometers west of us so we had to coordinate patrol routes with them, which wasn't a problem. Two new lieutenants were assigned to the unit, which made training evaluations easier.

I received a call from brigade to inform me that a USO group from Australia was going to put on a show for us in out company area. I coordinated security concerns with our infantry element and got with TOP to arrange for an area where it could happen. There was a large open area in front of the mess hall so we decided that would be best. Several days later the show group arrived. They had their own stages and quickly had everything set up for the show that would start that afternoon at 1400 hours. The music was good and the 6 bikini-clad women who danced for the troops put on quite a show. The non-Airborne unit, or legs, as they were called by airborne personnel, requested to attend and I didn't object. The show ended at dusk and TOP and I made our way to the orderly room through the sizeable audience that lingered behind, smoking and drinking. The smell of marijuana filled the air which would ordinarily cause us to go looking for offenders. Given the mixture of airborne and non-airborne personnel, I elected to ignore it. The troops were having fun and I knew this was something they would tell their grandkids about one day.

Three hours passed and the crowds had thinned out. The stage was packed away and it looked like things were getting back to normal. Top and I were commemorating the events of the day and how attractive the girls were when Lieutenant Collier entered the orderly room.

"You're not going to believe this," he said, laughing with a rather sinister smile. "It appears that the girls that were shaking it on the stage are taking on all comers for twenty dollars each in the bomb shelter by Tower three."

"Jesus," I said. I looked at TOP and he looked back with that well-what-the-hell-do-we-do-now look on his face.

"Well, I guess brigade would expect us to do something. We can't really afford to get labeled as the brigade house of ill repute."

Top laughed. "Let me handle this," he said. "It probably wouldn't be a good idea for a captain to go down there and run people out of a whorehouse."

"I'm sure you're right," I said.

Top left and returned to in about 30 minutes.

"Got it under control, "he said. "There are three guys left who have already paid. The male band members are taking the money outside the shelter. They assured me that it would be shut down in 15 minutes."

"Dang, I've heard of sloppy seconds but this goes way beyond that."

Top laughed. "I'll go back in a few minutes to make sure that the shelter has been returned to its original use."

Top returned and acknowledged that the whorehouse was closed. Now the question was do we advise brigade of this activity? I thought we should because of the leg outfit that had also been in attendance. If their commander talked to my commander and he didn't know, that would be a problem. I could hear the conversation now. "Oh, you had a bunch of whores down there and you didn't think I needed to know?" Not good, I thought.

The next day I called the brigade S-1 and told him the story.

"So what?" he said after I revealed the details of what happened.

"So, I don't want any surprises."

"So, the brigade commander has bigger concerns."

"Roger that. Just note that I reported this."

"Will do."

I wasn't crazy about the S-1's response but I could understand his concerns about its importance in the scheme of things. My concern was that I wanted to show accountability with what had happened in such a way that no one could ever question my actions regarding this matter. I put this out of my mind and wrote a dated statement regarding my actions taken.

A couple of days later I got a call from the brigade S-3 office, specifically Captain Jones. "Guess what," he said. "I'm coming your way."

"What do you mean."

I'm being assigned as the S-3 Rep to handle the departure of the 173rd from Vietnam. We are going to be the 1st Airborne brigade of the 101st Airborne Division."

"You're kidding."

"No, I'm not."

"When will you be here?"

"Tomorrow," he said.

"What's the timetable for withdrawal?"

"Two, maybe three months."

"Dang, I'll see you then."

I was caught completely by surprise. I did not want my tour to end this way. In a way Vietnam was a conduit to the future for me in the military. I wanted everything I could get out of this tour and it didn't look like it was going to happen.

The next morning, I was able to contact friends that I had gone through OCS with who were former Special Forces and were in country on SF assignments. They contacted their personnel office and cleared a way for me to get accepted by the unit for the duration of my tour. I only needed to make myself available at their personnel office in Saigon to show that

I was a real person and get a paragraph and line number. This would secure a position within the unit until my departure date in January of 1971. I was able to accomplish this within two weeks. This meant that when the 173rd departed I would get on a plane and go to SF headquarters for an assignment to a unit in close proximity to the Ho Chi Minh Trail.

When I returned, Jones had arrived at the unit. He had settled himself in the one cushioned chair that I had and finally raised his eyes to acknowledge my arrival.

"Have fun in Saigon? he asked.

"No. I flew in one day and flew out the next morning."

"Well, I'll be leaving tomorrow on R&R for Australia. Since the unit is departing Vietnam early, I had to use it or lose it."

"I'm envious. Thought about going there myself but elected to go home instead. Do you know anyone there?"

"No, I've never been there but heard nothing but good things about it. Anyway, as I said, it's now or never. It seems that we have a schedule for getting units processed through here. It starts next month and ends with the last flight out sometime in mid-August. The S-4 is supposed to start dragging tents and supplies in here. The only large open area is the one near the mess hall. Fifteen GP Large tents and cots should handle each battalion as they pass through."

"I've got 80 replacements in training and I haven't been told to stop," I said. I guess there may still be a use for them if they are employed locally for security patrols. These guys are sure going to be happy when they hear they are going home. It's probably not a good idea to make any of this known until brigade makes it public. The cat will be out of the bag though when the S-4 pitches a bunch of tents and creates more latrines."

The next morning, I put the two pages of information, including a paragraph and line number for my SF assignment, in a delivery pouch that would be sent to the brigade S-1. This would end my assignment with the 173rd and cause them to complete an efficiency report attesting to my actions at the school and those taken to process the unit out of the country. I imagined that the report would have to be written by the brigade S-3, a person I had met only once. He would have to rely on reports I had rendered and observations of those who had visited the school to complete the report. Of course, a lot of the report would reflect what happened with the out-processing of the 173rd from Vietnam.

As time went by, The S-4 trucked the needed tents and supplies on to the site. In a couple of days, we were ready to start processing units. Jones had returned from Australia and had, in his words, found the woman of his dreams. She was drop-dead beautiful, had kept him in her apartment, bought him food and drinks and met his every need, particularly those for which he was trying to make up for lost time. Before leaving he bought her beautiful expensive clothes in an effort to repay her for her kindness. He wrote her a letter every day upon his return telling her about his plans to continue this new exciting relationship. Then that itchy thing happened with the accompanying drip that foretells the need for tetracycline. Not to worry about treatment though. We had a medic and he was sworn to secrecy. Of course, the 50 or so people he would share this secret with would probably not be those who would carry the story back to the brigade staff…if you were lucky. Needless to say, this short-lived romance became a bitter memory of the past. Was I compassionate? Yes, to some extent because I liked

Jones. Did I think it was funny? Oh Lord yes. Did I ever bring it up again? Absolutely not.

All of the field units processed through. Jones and I were busy taking care of administrative tasks. There were rules about what could be taken back to the states and what could not. Military Police were confiscating skulls, jars of teeth and strings of ears that were removed from enemy dead. The engineer units had the majority of those with drug problems. We processed them through a Detox center in Cam Ranh Bay. There was some success there but not what we had hoped for.

And suddenly it was over for the school. Vietnamese soldiers replaced American soldiers in perimeter tower positions. As we drove away, the "leg" unit started firing mortars at the big 173rd tarp that set on the hill overlooking the valley. Tacky, really tacky, I thought.

On the last night in Vietnam, I shared at tent with a LTC John Hampton. I surmised that he was the last leg of Brigade staff that had responsibility for bringing up the rear. He was very sociable and friendly and we talked late into the night. We had a few drinks and finally turned in for the night.

The next time I saw him was at the base of the stairs leading up to the cabin of the last flight home for the 173rd. I stood there with my duffel bag, prepared to watch the last of the troops get on the aircraft. I felt a nudge in my back and turned to see LTC Hampton standing there.

"Get on the aircraft," he said.

"I can't, Sir. I have orders taking me south and on to another assignment." Of course, he knew that from last night's conversations, I thought.

"I want to be the last 173rd soldier on Vietnam soil," he said. "Take your duffel bag with you because it is 173rd property as well."

"Yes Sir," I replied, and climbed the stairs into the aircraft. He followed me close behind.

I gave him room to pass through into the cabin. He put his hand on my shoulder and said "Sit down, Hardin."

A little confused I said "Sir, I have orders for an SF job."

"No, you don't. Your orders have been cancelled and you're going home. Listen to me, you've been here too long. You're going to have a long career, one that you'll be proud of, but you're pushing the envelope. It's time for you to go home. There's a family back there waiting for you. This war will soon be a thing of the past. This is not the time or the place or the war for you to try to enhance your career. Trust me."

There was a seat right up front that was vacant. Under ordinary conditions it would have been filled. I knew that LTC Hampton had ensured that it would be open for me. A little befuddled, and trying to process what had just happened, I sat down and began the process of reconceptualizing a future that for the moment was a mystery. In time I stuck my hand out to him where he sat on the aisle across from me. He shook it and smiled.

CHAPTER 14

I was disheartened as much as I was confused as I watched the contours of the Vietnam mountains slowly fade away as the jet rose into the clouds. And then they were gone. I knew the memories of this entire experience would come in due time when I had time to assemble them in my mind. I didn't know then that I would eventually detest and abhor some of them as much as I took pride in others.

A lot of brave young men had given their all in this war. For some, their last conscious thoughts were terrifying. They went home in flag draped coffins. Many others were maimed and crippled and would bear the scars of war in a country that rarely showed appreciation for those who served, often calling them baby killers and other disparaging names. It's good to see that the national mood has changed and that service men and women are now praised and glorified for their service. I often elect to leave my Vietnam Veteran cap behind to prevent being flooded with "thanks for your service" comments from strangers. There are many funds and programs that meet the needs of those who are severely wounded, unlike the period that followed the Vietnam war which, by the way, is still officially labeled as a conflict, not a war. Tunnels to Towers is a godsent and every American should be contributing to it.

Post Traumatic Stress Disorder (PTSD) is a real phenomenon that effects most people who were in Vietnam, even the straphangers or Rear Echelon Mother Fuckers (REMFs) as those in secure areas or serving in non-combat roles were called. You were never far away from a falling mortar or a well-placed booby trap. Fear, indeed, takes its toll and affects different people in different ways.

We knew that the deals that had been made via the Paris Peace Accords meant simply that we would leave the country and that North Vietnam, now supported by the Russians and the Chinese, would move south and crush South Vietnamese forces. South Vietnam never truly had their heart in this war, not just as a nation but as it pertained to the individual soldier as well. They relied on American support to conduct operations. When enemy contact occurred, they were inclined to be more evasive than tactically reactive. Soldiers would often walk away from posts where they were assigned and disappear until payday arrived. One unit, atop a mountain post where 6 or 8 Americans were assigned, often saw as much as 50 percent losses in South Vietnam personnel throughout the month.

The old adage "Armies fight to win; guerillas fight not to lose" comes to mind. Charley and the North Vietnamese got their butts kicked overwhelmingly, taking over 650,000 casualties. Overall, 1.3 million died. Nevertheless, the country is under one leadership now and is open for tourism. In reality, there was no winner.

In succeeding years there were no other conflicts for me, other than those you have with people about ideas and decisions that are a part of military life. The Army recognized my efforts and awarded me with a wealth of education and the opportunity to rise to the highest levels of military leadership.

Unfortunately, the injuries I had resulted in a medical retirement that I fought but could not overcome. Captain Jones and I would serve together at Fort Campbell and again in Korea. Eventually, marital discourse and the love of another woman would effectively end his career. He retired and resided in Korea until his eventual death. Craig, the medic and good friend that supported the 68th AHC I served with in Bien Hoa, is in my email contacts and we speak frequently.

My wife has often been my sounding board for those occasions when after a few drinks I find it necessary to reflect on times and events that can never be changed. She listens with empathy and respect, and I have to remember that she too has endured just as much as I have. She lived in a world of uncertainty that could just have easily ended with an official telephone call or uniformed men knocking at the front door. Indeed, some angels don't wear wings.

In due time, a Veterans Affairs psychologist would ask me about my time in Vietnam. I told him that in a way I grew up there, found out who I was there and who I wasn't. He said he didn't quite get it and I replied, you had to be there to both understand and appreciate it; you had to be there to see the best and worst of humanity; and you had to be there to experience the depth of emotions that are exclusive to those whom both hate and love combat.

It was the life I chose, the life I needed, and the life tailored specifically for me. In so many ways I am still there. Now aging in declining years, and having the time to look back upon it all, I shall always believe that I was just fine in Vietnam.

ABOUT THE AUTHOR

Bo Hardin was a United States Army Soldier. He spent over 22 years on active duty. He was initially enlisted before going to Officer Candidate School in 1969. He spent over three years in Vietnam in both infantry and combat aviation assignments. He was assigned to MACV, the 118th Assault Helicopter Company, the 68th Assault Helicopter Company, the 145th Aviation Battalion and the 173rd Airborne Brigade. He was medically retired in 1984.

www.ingramcontent.com/pod-product-compliance
Lightning Source LLC
Chambersburg PA
CBHW050536170426
43201CB00011B/1451